BEHIND THE WHEEL

the learner driver's handbook

4th edition

Graham Yuill, *ADI*

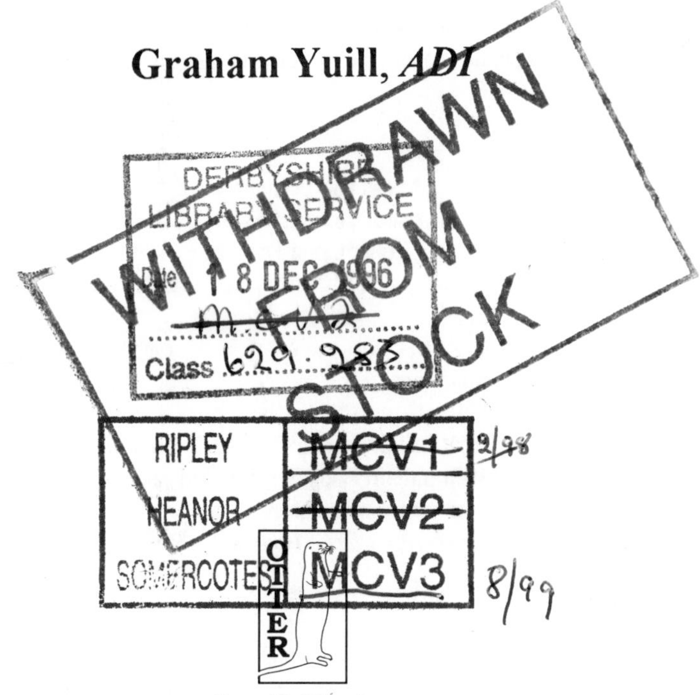

Otter Publications
Chichester, England

First and second editions published in 1990 and 1992 by The Glasgow Publishing Company. The third edition in 1995 by Otter Publications.

This fourth edition published in 1996 by **Otter Publications**, 5 Mosse Gardens, Fishbourne, Chichester, West Sussex, PO19 3PQ.

The male pronoun has been used throughout the book. This is simply to avoid ugly and cumbersome language, and no discrimination or bias is intended.

British Library Cataloging in Publication Data
A CIP record for this book is available from the British Library.
ISBN 1 899053 04 2

Acknowledgements
Crown copyright is reproduced with the permission of the Controller of HMSO.
The publisher would like to thank John E Ayland, Chief Examiner DIAmond Advanced Motorists, formerly Deputy Chief Driving Examiner, Driving Standards Agency, Department of Transport, for both his technical advice and proof reading skills.

Text design by Angela Hutchings.
Cover design by Jim Wilkie.
Printed and bound in Great Britain by Hartnolls Ltd., Bodmin.
Distributed in the UK by Grantham Book Services Ltd., Isaac Newton Way, Alma Park Industrial Estate, Grantham, Lincolnshire.
The Otter Publications logo is reproduced from original artwork by David Kitt.

Contents

Foreword

The subject of driving is perhaps important to you now with your learning to perfect the skill and obtain the knowledge to pass your test. However, driving is a skill for life and you must adopt the attitude that you have never stopped learning the subject. Listen to the advice of your professional driving instructor and take further training after you have passed your basic driving tests, for Post Test Training and even to coach you for your DIAmond Advanced Motorists Test.

Adopting the techniques as discussed in Behind the Wheel will make you a safe and competent driver for life.

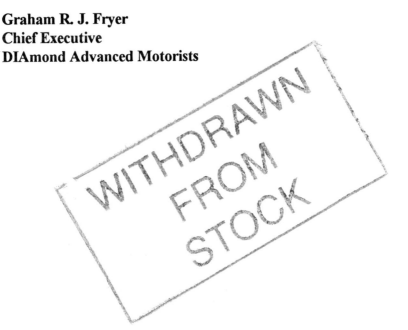

Graham R. J. Fryer
Chief Executive
DIAmond Advanced Motorists

Chapter 1

GETTING STARTED

The first thing you must do before learning to drive is to apply for a provisional driving licence. You can obtain an application form from any main post office. If you are 17 years old or over and have reached certain requirements, the Driver Vehicle Licensing Centre at the DVLC in Swansea will send you a provisional driving licence within 21 days. Persons receiving a mobility allowance may start driving a car when 16 years old. When you receive your driving licence, you must sign it and make a written note of your Driver Number in case you lose it.

You must ensure that your eyesight is up to the required standard. On the day of your driving test, the driving examiner will not permit you to enter your car until he has checked your eyesight. You will be asked to read a vehicle number plate at a distance well over the standard required. You should wear your glasses or contact lenses if you need them, and continue to wear them for driving. The exact distance will only be measured if your eyesight is borderline. The standard requirement is to be able to read in good daylight a motor vehicle number plate 20.5 metres away, with symbols 79.4 mm high. If you are unable to do this, you will fail your driving test. It is an offence to drive with incorrect vision, so if you are in any doubt, see an optician. You must be medically fit to drive. You are required to inform the Drivers Medical Branch at the DVLC in Swansea at once if you have any disability or mental condition that might (or may in future) affect your fitness as a driver. If you are at all unsure you must consult a doctor.

Choosing a good driving instructor can be very tricky. As with most professions, there are "cowboy" driving schools. Be careful, as I have come across some over the past few years. Drivers who have passed the Department Of Transport's Driving Instructors examination, have had to sit three very stringent exams. The first exam is a written theory, the second an advanced driving test, and the third an examination of "on road" teaching ability. By law, driving instructors must display a green card on the windscreen next to the tax disc. This licence has to be renewed every four years (a pink card indicates a trainee driving instructor).

When you select your driving instructor, do not choose the cheapest possible. Driving lessons cost money, so many people tend to look for the cheapest which may prove to be false economy. If the instruction is poor you may never reach test standard. On the other hand, if it is good you will learn how to drive well and pass the test. The best qualification is a personal recommendation. Ask your friends if they can suggest anyone. Do not pay for a course of lessons before you have the chance to meet your instructor. Ensure that the car is relatively new and clean and with no dents. It should have dual controls. Your instructor should turn up on time and make sure you receive a full hours lesson. If you enjoyed your lesson and felt that you had learned from it, then book more lessons. However, if you were not completely satisfied with the lesson then re-book with someone else.

Don't be lulled into a false sense of security by the fact that a driving instructor has a major school name behind him. Some driving schools offer to teach driving in one or two weeks in an intensive course. For many people this is not the ideal way to learn, unless they have had previous practical experience. You are paying for a professional service so make sure you choose the right one.

Lesson 1 - The safety checks and controls of the car

Most people feel nervous when they have their first driving lesson. A good driving instructor knows that you are nervous and inexperienced and so does not expect you to do everything perfectly. He will make you feel completely at ease when you enter the car.

Make sure you get a good nights sleep, and **do not** consume any alcohol prior to your lesson. Even a very small amount of alcohol could cause tiredness. If a doctor prescribes any drugs for you, ask how it will affect your driving. Always wear loose fitting clothing and comfortable shoes. If you wear glasses or contact lenses make sure you bring them with you.

When you enter the car for the first time, your instructor will teach you certain safety checks followed by the major, minor and auxiliary controls of the car. It is important that you know where all the controls are within your car. Your driving instructor will talk you through these controls step-by-step. The following safety checks must be carried out when you enter the car. They can easily be remembered by the following code:

- **DOORS**
- **SEAT**
- **STEERING WHEEL** **(D.S.S.S.M.- see figure 1)**
- **SEATBELT**
- **MIRRORS**

Doors
Check all doors by the "pull and push" method to ensure that they are all properly secure, preventing any rattle or noise which may distract you during your journey. Do not lock the doors as you may need help from the outside in the event of an emergency.

Seat
Adjust your seat so that you are in a comfortable position and have easy access to the foot pedals and the hand controls. To achieve this,

move the seat (you may have to use a lever), until you are able to push the left pedal right down to the floor with your left foot. You should have a slight bend at your left knee and you should be able to push down the clutch pedal to its fullest extent without having to stretch your left leg. This will be the furthest distance your left foot will travel throughout your journey.

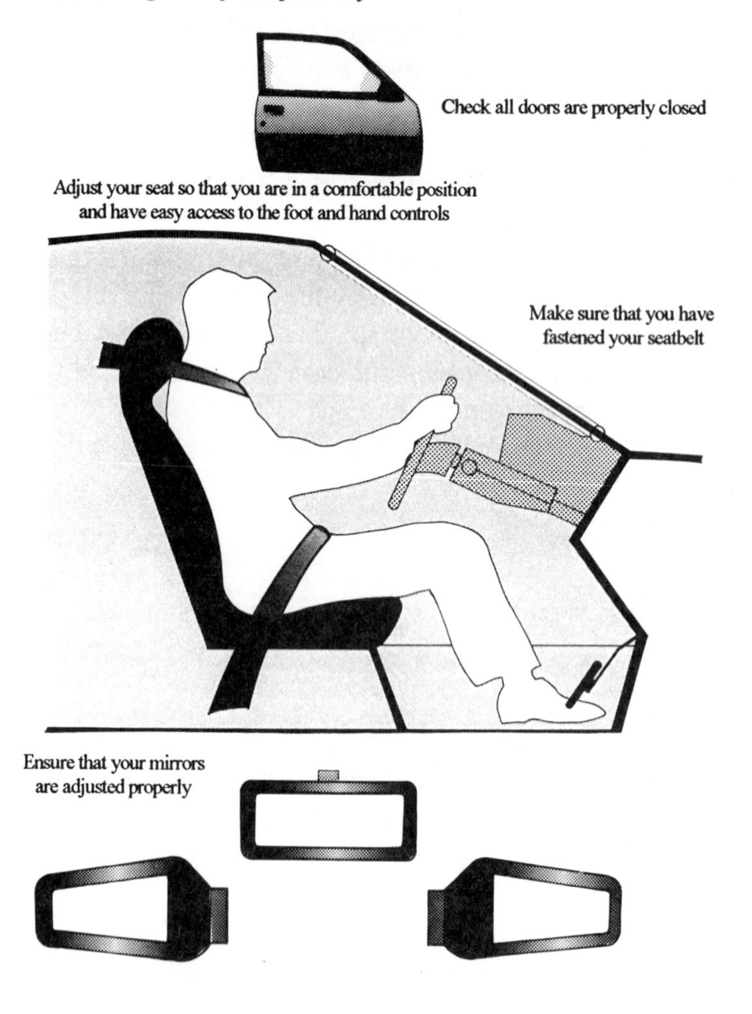

Check all doors are properly closed
Adjust your seat so that you are in a comfortable position and have easy access to the foot and hand controls
Make sure that you have fastened your seatbelt
Ensure that your mirrors are adjusted properly

Figure 1. The safety checks to be carried out before starting the engine.

Steering wheel

The back of the seat should be adjusted to enable you to reach the top of the steering wheel without stretching. A correctly adjusted seat will allow you easy access to the foot controls and you will be in a comfortable position, high enough to be able to see clearly ahead over the steering wheel whilst driving. Place both hands at the top of the steering wheel making sure that your arms are slightly bent. You should have freedom to move your hands round the wheel.

Head restraints

These should be correctly adjusted to give you maximum protection to your head and neck in the event of an accident. You must ensure that the top of the rigid part of the restraint is positioned at or above eye level and as close to the back of the head as possible.

Seatbelt

When you are in a comfortable sitting position you should put on your seatbelt. Look over your right shoulder and take hold of the silver buckle with your left hand. Slowly pull it towards the top of the steering wheel and place your right hand through the "V". Put the silver buckle into the anchor point, on the left-hand side of your seat. Make sure you hear an audible clicking sound and ensure that the seatbelt is not twisted. The lower belt should be running across the hips and the top belt on the right shoulder without touching the neck. Give the seatbelt a good hard pull to ensure it is secure. When you place the seatbelt back to its original position, make sure you do so with caution. If you do not, the silver buckle may strike and possibly damage the window. Wearing a seatbelt is not only a legal requirement, it makes good sense. Researchers worldwide say that a person not wearing a seatbelt can be seriously injured or killed in a crash when a vehicle is travelling at not more than 12 mph. Failing to wear a seatbelt may also affect your claim for compensation if you are involved in an accident.

Mirrors

It is important to have the mirrors correctly adjusted before moving off. Do **not** adjust the mirrors whilst driving because you will have only one hand on the steering wheel and you will be taking your eyes off the road longer than necessary. To adjust the mirrors always start with the interior mirror which shows what is behind you. Take hold of the frame of the interior mirror with your left thumb and index finger and line the top of the mirror up with the top of the rear window.

Avoid touching the glass because grease from your fingers will distort your vision. By adjusting the interior mirror in this way you will achieve the best possible view out of the back window. You should just be able to see the left side of your head or hair at the right edge of the mirror. When you have found the best possible view out of the interior mirror, adjust both exterior mirrors until you can get the best possible view along the off-side and near-side. The exterior mirrors help to reduce blind spots (see figure 2). They are used in conjunction with your interior mirror, and they must always be used before overtaking parked or moving vehicles. Remember that you must check your interior mirror before the exterior mirrors. There are 2 other safety checks which must be carried out which will be explained later. Adopt the habit of using the D.S.S.S.M. method every time you enter your car.

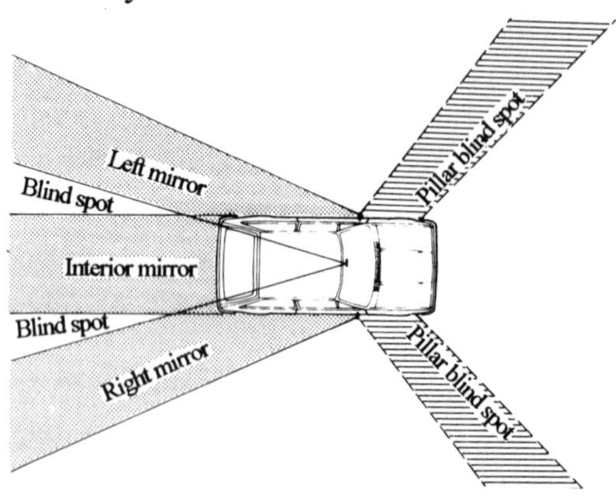

Figure 2. The mirrors, visual controls and blind spots.

THE SAFETY CHECKS

QUESTIONS (refer to figures 1 and 2) (See page 245 for answers).

Q1. What five safety checks should you carry out when you enter the car for the first time? Complete the following words.

1. **D**□□□□.
2. **S**□□□.
3. **S**□□□□□□□ **W**□□□□.
4. **S**□□□□□□□.
5. **M**□□□□□□.

Q2. Why must you **not** touch the interior mirror glass?
A. The mirror may fall off the windscreen.
B. If the glass breaks, it is irreplaceable.
C. You may break the glass.
D. Grease from your fingers will distort your vision.

Q3. What method would you use to ensure your doors are shut?
A. The "pull and push" method.
B. The elbow method.
C. The "push and pull" method.
D. The wrist method.

Q4. Why should you wear a seatbelt?
A. You do not have to wear a seatbelt.
B. It will not help save your life.
C. It is a legal requirement.
D. Because your driving instructor told you to.

Q5. What is the best way to learn the "push and pull" method?
A. Use your interior mirror.
B. Use an ashtray.
C. Use a circular disc.
D. Use a spare wheel.

Q6. Which mirror gives a true image of what is behind you?
A. The interior mirror.
B. The right-hand mirror.
C. The left-hand mirror.
D. None of these.

MAIN CONTROLS
After your instructor has explained the safety checks you should carry out when you first enter the car, he will then move on to the Main Controls. The Main Controls will be dealt with under 2 sections: the controls which are operated with the feet and the controls operated with the hands. The foot controls are the accelerator, brake and clutch (see figure 3). Think of ABC. The hand controls are the gear lever, parking/hand brake and steering wheel. We shall start with the foot controls.

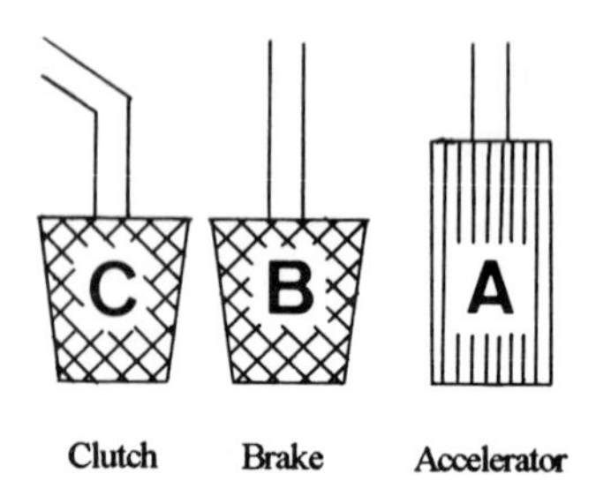

Figure 3. The foot controls.

Accelerator
If you look down at your feet you will see three pedals - the one on the right is the accelerator. Your instructor may refer to this as "the gas pedal" - it is used to control the speed of the car. The more gas you apply, the faster the car will travel. The gas pedal **must** be operated by the right foot only and should be used gently and progressively. When the engine has started, you can practice (without looking down at your feet) getting the correct pressure on the gas

pedal to avoid jerky starts, and making the engine roar. Imagine it is a wet sponge and you are gently squeezing out the water. Place your heel on the floor and use the ball (middle) of the foot. The reason for using the ball of the foot is to avoid your foot slipping off the pedal. Releasing the gas pedal will not stop your car altogether; the engine will tick over until you switch off your engine. Your instructor will use the following terminology when referring to this pedal:

- Set gas - gently apply pressure to the accelerator pedal.
- More gas - gently push the accelerator pedal down more.
- Less gas - gently ease your foot off the accelerator pedal.
- Off gas - remove your foot completely from the accelerator.

Footbrake

The middle pedal is the footbrake. When you depress the footbrake, pressure is applied to all four wheels of the car, and two red warning lights are illuminated at the rear of the car to warn traffic behind that you are slowing down. Again the footbrake **must** be operated by the right foot only and use smooth and progressive braking to slow your car down. Avoid using the footbrake like an on and off button, and never slam your foot down on the footbrake as this could make your car skid and you may lose control.

Using smooth and progressive braking will also help you save fuel. Place your heel on the floor, and use the ball of the foot just like the gas pedal. You can practice moving your foot from the footbrake to the gas pedal a few times, without looking down at your feet, keeping your heel on the floor if possible. This will allow you to judge the distance your foot must travel between the 2 pedals (see figure 4). The following terminology will be used when referring to this pedal:

- Cover brake - place your foot over the pedal but don't touch.
- Gently brake - apply firm pressure to the footbrake.
- Gently brake to a stop - apply firm pressure to the footbrake until all four wheels come to a complete stop.

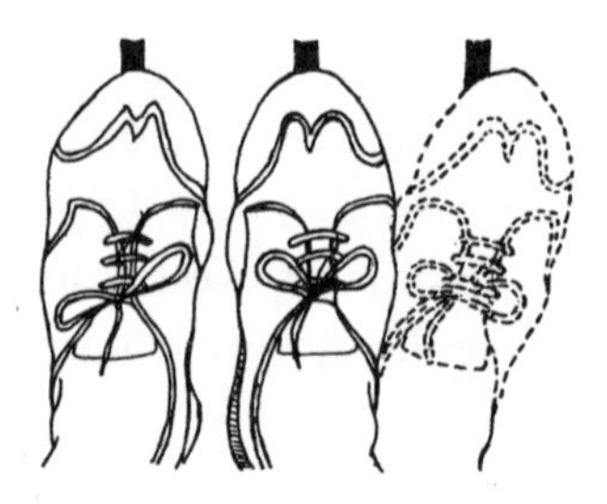

Figure 4. Practice moving your feet from the footbrake to the accelerator without looking down.

Clutch

The pedal on the left is the clutch. The purpose of the clutch is to connect smoothly the power from the engine to the driving wheels (see figure 5). The clutch will also let you change gear smoothly. This time the pedal must be operated by the left foot. You can push the clutch down as fast as you want in any gear but you cannot bring it up quickly if you are in a stationary position.

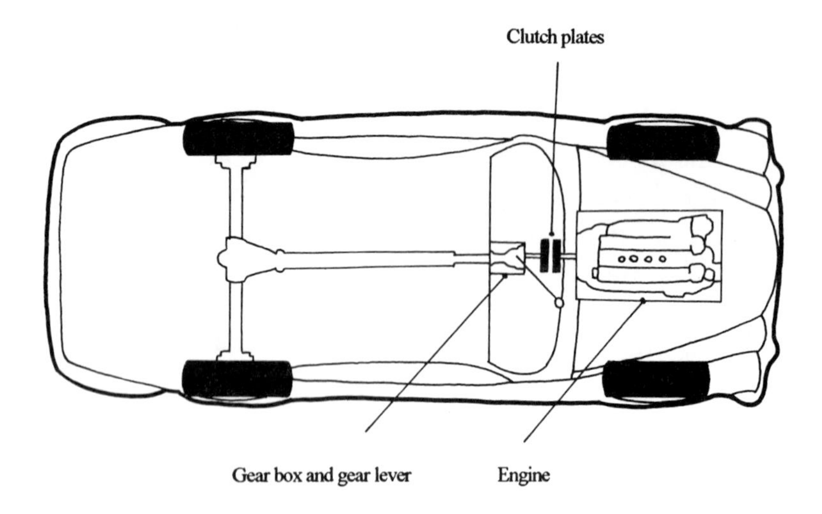

Figure 5. The workings of the clutch.

I will explain the mechanics which take place as you use the clutch when driving. Attached to the engine is a metal plate. If you set the gas the metal plate starts to spin. The more gas you apply the faster the plate will spin. Attached to the gear box is another metal plate. Push the clutch down and select first gear (see figure 6).

Set the gas by applying gentle pressure to the gas pedal. The metal plate attached to the engine will spin faster. Now ease the clutch up slowly. This will move the metal plate attached to the engine closer to the metal plate attached to the gear box. When the two plates touch the plate attached to the gearbox will start to spin. The power will then be transferred from the engine to the driving wheels and the car will start to move forward. If the two plates are brought together too quickly you will not get a smooth connection and the car will lurch forward and the engine may stall (cut out). Your instructor will use the following terminology when referring to this pedal:

- Cover clutch - place your foot over the pedal but don't touch.
- Clutch down - push the clutch right down to the floor.
- Slowly clutch up until the engine note changes, keep both feet still.

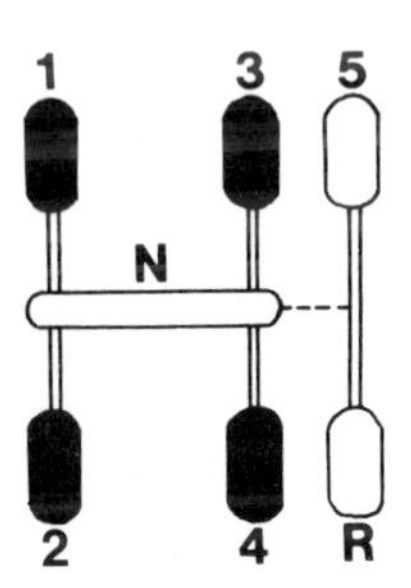

Figure 6. Position of the gears (reverse position may vary between cars).

When you are driving, never "ride" the clutch by resting your foot on it as this will wear it away and the clutch is very expensive to repair. If you are having problems reaching the foot controls you can place a large telephone directory or book under the floor mat to assist you so long as the floor mat does not obstruct the movement of the foot pedals. Remember, you must avoid looking down at the foot controls when driving as you will not be able to see where you are going and there is the possibility that you could endanger other road users.

THE FOOT CONTROLS

QUESTIONS (refer to figures 3 - 6) *(See page 245 for answers).*

Q1. What are the three types of foot controls? Complete the missing words.

1. The **A**□□□□□□□□□□.
2. The **F**□□□□□□□□.
3. The **C**□□□□□.

Q2. What is the purpose of the accelerator or gas pedal?

A. To slow the car down.
B. To control the speed of the car.
C. To stop the car.
D. To go as fast as you can.

Q3. How do you operate the accelerator pedal?

A. Use your big toe.
B. Use your heel.
C. Use the tip of your foot.
D. Use the ball of the foot.

Q4. What is the purpose of the footbrake?

A. For slowing down or stopping.
B. To stop the car stalling.
C. To speed up the car.
D. None of these.

Q5. How should you operate the footbrake?

A. With the right or left foot.

B. With the left foot only.
C. With the right foot only.
D. With both feet at the same time.

Q6. What is the purpose of the clutch?
A. To stop the car stalling.
B. To connect the power from the engine to the driving wheels smoothly.
C. To make the car travel faster.
D. To break the car's speed.

Q7. Which foot should you use for each of these controls. Fill in the missing words.
1. Accelerator use the □□□□□ foot.
2. Brake use the □□□□□ foot.
3. Clutch use the □□□□ foot.

Q8. Fill in the missing word.
The accelerator can also be called the □□□ pedal.

HAND CONTROLS

After your instructor has explained the foot controls, he will then move on to the 3 main types of hand controls. They are as follows:

- Gear lever and gears.
- Parking/hand brake.
- Steering wheel.

Gear lever and gears

A greater effort is required to increase the speed of your car than to maintain it, so to make things much easier we use the gears. It is important that you make smooth coordinated gear changes as this is essential for good driving. You must know how, when and why you should change gear. Normally you move off in first gear as this is the most powerful gear. The gear lever allows you to select the required gear. It is operated by the left hand only. Place your hand firmly but not too tightly on the gear lever and use the palm of your hand to push the gear lever in the correct direction. Think about the positions of the four wheels of your car. This will help to remind you where the gear positions are to be found.

Imagine first gear as the front left wheel, and second gear as the rear left wheel etc. Selecting the gears should always be done gently. There are four or sometimes five forward gears and one reverse. Most car gear lever positions form the letter H (see figure 6). The approximate speeds for changing up are:

- 1st gear - between 0-10 mph approximately (a power gear).
- 2nd gear - between 10-20 mph approx. (a working gear).
- 3rd gear - between 20-30 mph approx. (a working gear).
- 4th gear - above 30 mph (a cruising gear).

The approximate speeds for changing down are:

- From 4th - 3rd gear - 20 mph.
- From 3rd - 2nd gear - 10 mph.
- From 2nd - 1st gear - under 5 mph.

Fifth gear

Fifth gear should normally be selected when the car is travelling at approximately 50 mph. It is an economy gear (if used correctly), allowing you to save fuel and so gives the car 'longer legs'. Since the car is already moving at a fast speed the momentum of the car itself is enough to push it forward with very little help from the engine.

Reverse gear

Reverse gear will make the car go backwards. Only select this gear when the car is stationary. If you don't, you will damage the gear box.

The neutral position

Neutral means no gear has been selected and the car cannot be driven forwards or backwards.

Making proper use of gears

Gears are used to make the car go faster and they assist the car to slow down in conjunction with the footbrake. By changing up the gears at the correct time you will save petrol and avoid wear and tear on the engine. You should listen to the sound of the engine to determine when to make a gear change. The gears which should be used are dependent on your speed. In other words, ***the slower the speed, the lower the gear: the higher the speed, the higher the gear***.

How to change gear

After you have moved off in first gear and you wish to change into second gear (approximately 10 mph), push the clutch down and come off the gas simultaneously otherwise the engine will start to roar loudly. Take hold of the gear lever firmly and select second gear whilst tensing your right hand slightly to give you more control of your steering. Bring the clutch up and gently apply more gas. When changing gear, place your hand firmly round the side of the gear knob. The palm of your hand should be facing in the direction of the intended gear change i.e. palm towards your instructor for first and second, and palm towards you for third and fourth (see figure 7).

Don't look down

Don't be tempted to look at the speedometer or down at your feet whilst changing gear as this may cause your car to wander all over the road. Assess the relative speeds visually rather than by looking at the speedometer when a gear change is being made and try to get into the highest possible gear as soon as possible. Although the gears are numbered 1 to 4 it is not necessary to use them in that order. You can move off in second gear on a very steep hill if travelling downwards as there is less effort needed to move your car forward since the hill is doing most of the work for you. You may change from fourth to second gear or fourth to first gear and miss out third gear altogether.

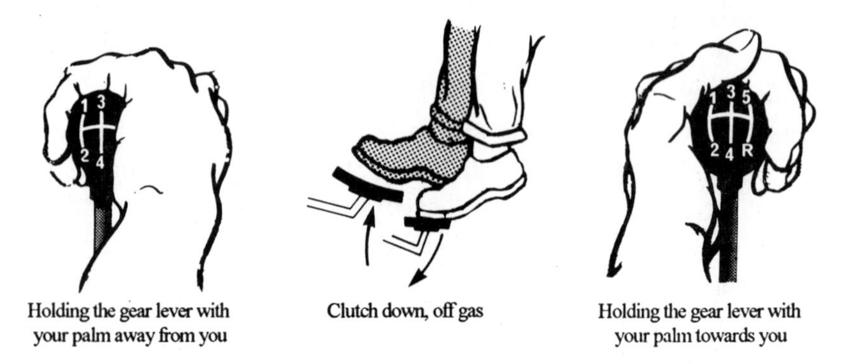

Holding the gear lever with your palm away from you

Clutch down, off gas

Holding the gear lever with your palm towards you

Figure 7. Holding the gear lever and changing gear.

Parking/hand brake

The parking brake, often referred to as the hand brake, is used to secure the car when it is stationary by locking the two rear wheels, is normally found on the left-hand side of the driver's seat and is operated by the left hand. The parking brake is also used for safety reasons - for instance, when the car has been parked on a gradient, when it has stopped at traffic lights, pedestrian crossings, or queuing behind other vehicles, unless you are likely to be waiting for a very short period of time (no set time is stipulated in the Highway Code). If you are bumped from behind, the parking brake will reduce the amount your car is pushed forward. The instructor will use the following terminology when referring to the parking brake:

- Prepare the parking brake - hand on the parking brake ready to release it.
- Release the parking brake - hand on the parking brake lift it slightly pressing the button in, then push it down and release the button.
- Apply the parking brake - hand on the parking brake pressing the button in, then pull it up and release the button.

Remember to keep the button pressed in when you apply the parking brake. If you fail to do this you may cause damage to the ratchet. Never apply the parking brake when your car is moving as this will lock the rear wheels and your car may skid. The parking brake can also be used in an emergency if the footbrake fails.

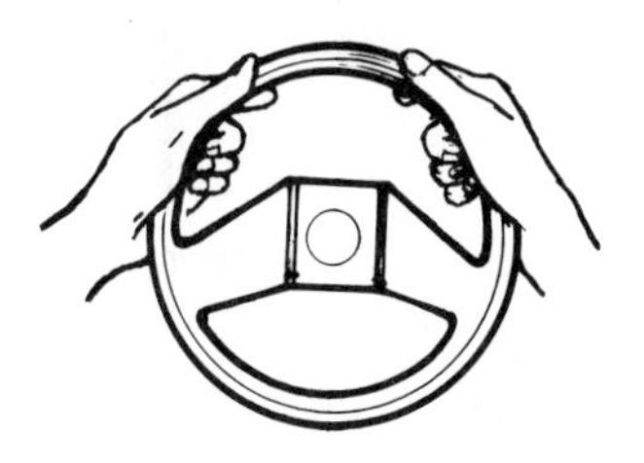

Hands at the ten to two position

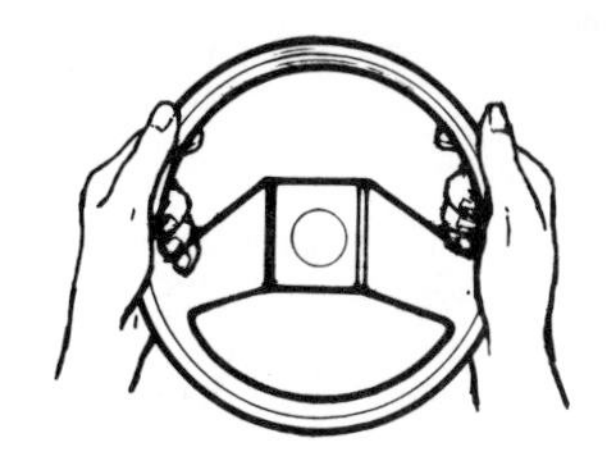

Hands at the quarter to three position

Figure 8. Holding the steering wheel.

Steering wheel

The steering wheel normally works directly on the front wheels and changes the direction of the car to the right or the left. Hold the steering wheel with both hands, lightly but firmly and avoid wrapping your thumbs around the rim. Imagine the steering wheel as a clock and place your hands in a position corresponding to the hands on a clock face, either quarter to three or at ten to two, whichever is most comfortable for you (see figure 8).

During normal driving the steering wheel should be fed through the hands by means of a push and pull method (see figure 9). Avoid turning the steering wheel when the car is stationary as this may damage the steering mechanism. Never take both hands off the steering wheel at the same time whilst driving and avoid resting your elbow on the door ledge. The steering wheel steers the front wheels of the car and if you turn to the left, you must remember to turn the wheel to the right to straighten up (or vice versa). The sharper the turn you make, the faster you will have to turn the wheel back in order to straighten your car.

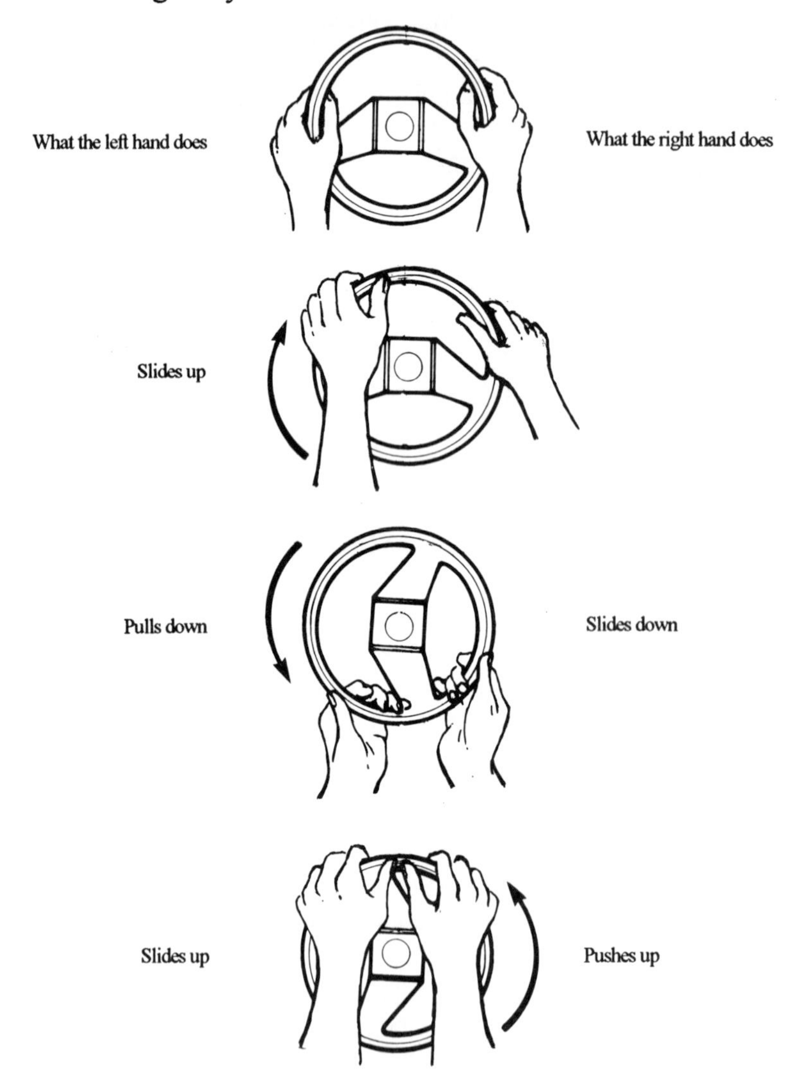

Figure 9. The "push and pull method".

THE HAND CONTROLS

QUESTIONS (refer to figures 7 - 9) (See page 245 for the answers).

Q1. Why does a car need gears?
A. To slow or stop the vehicle.
B. To control the speed so that you do not travel too fast.
C. To allow it to travel at different speeds.
D. So that the car can speed up quickly.

Q2. Which letter do most gear lever positions form?
A. The letter R.
B. The letter H.
C. The letter X.
D. The letter Y.

Q3. What is the advantage of changing through the gears at the correct time?
A. You will save fuel.
B. You will decrease wear on the tyres.
C. You will be able to drive out of any danger more quickly.
D. You will save time.

Q4. What does neutral mean?
A. Second gear has been selected.
B. First gear has been selected.
C. No gear has been selected.
D. Any gear has been selected.

Q5. Should you ever select reverse gear when the car is moving?
A. Only select reverse gear if you are driving under 5 mph.
B. Only select this gear when the car is stationary.
C. Only select reverse gear after applying the parking brake to stop.
D. None of these.

Q6. What are the approximate speeds for changing up the gears? Fill in the missing numbers.

GEARS	MPH
1st	0 - ?
2nd	10 - ?
3rd	20 - ?
4th	above ?
5th	about ?

Q7. What are the approximate speeds for changing down the gears? Fill in the missing numbers.

GEARS	MPH
4th - 3rd	?
3rd - 2nd	?
2nd - 1st	?

Q8. What is the purpose of the parking brake?
A. To stop someone stealing your car.
B. To slow or stop the vehicle.
C. To enable you to change gear.
D. To secure the vehicle when it is stationary.

Q9. Why should you keep the button pressed in when you are applying and releasing the parking brake?
A. To enable you to hold the steering wheel tighter.
B. In case your hand slips off the parking brake.
C. To avoid damaging the ratchet.
D. To make for a quicker manoeuvre.

Q10. Name four occasions when you should apply the parking brake? Fill in the missing words.
1. On a **g**□□□□□□□.
2. At **t**□□□□□□ **l**□□□□□.
3. At a **p**□□□□□□□□□ **c**□□□□□□□.

4. When **q□□□□□□** behind other **v□□□□□□□**.

Q11. Why should you avoid turning the steering wheel when the car is stationary?
A. You will cause unnecessary wear to the tyres.
B. The wheels may fall off.
C. The tyres may burst.
D. None of these.

Q12. Why should you use the "push and pull" method whilst turning?
A. It is safer because it is easier to see the road ahead.
B. It is safer because both your hands are always in contact with the steering wheel.
C. It is safer because both hands will never fly off the steering wheel.
D. It is safer because you can use your interior mirror simultaneously.

Q13. How do you hold and operate the steering wheel?
A. With both hands lightly but firmly at either quarter to three or at the ten to two position.
B. With both hands firmly at either the quarter to four or ten to one position.
C. None of these.
D. With both hands firmly on the steering wheel at any angle.

Q14. Can you take both your hands off the steering wheel whilst driving?
A. Only to protect your face before crashing.
B. Never.
C. To straighten up quickly after turning a very sharp corner.
D. Only under exceptional circumstances.

THE MINOR AND AUXILIARY CONTROLS OF THE CAR

After you have been taught the foot and hand controls of the car your instructor will teach you the Minor controls followed by the Auxiliary controls. Let us look in detail at what your instructor will teach you about the Minor and Auxiliary Controls (see figure 10). It is important that you familiarise yourself with the location and function of the car's minor and auxiliary controls, as you are very likely to make use of them on your driving test. Your instructor should explain the minor controls in a methodical manner, starting from the right-hand side of the dashboard and finishing on the left-hand side. On or near the dashboard of a typical modern saloon car, you may find the following instruments:

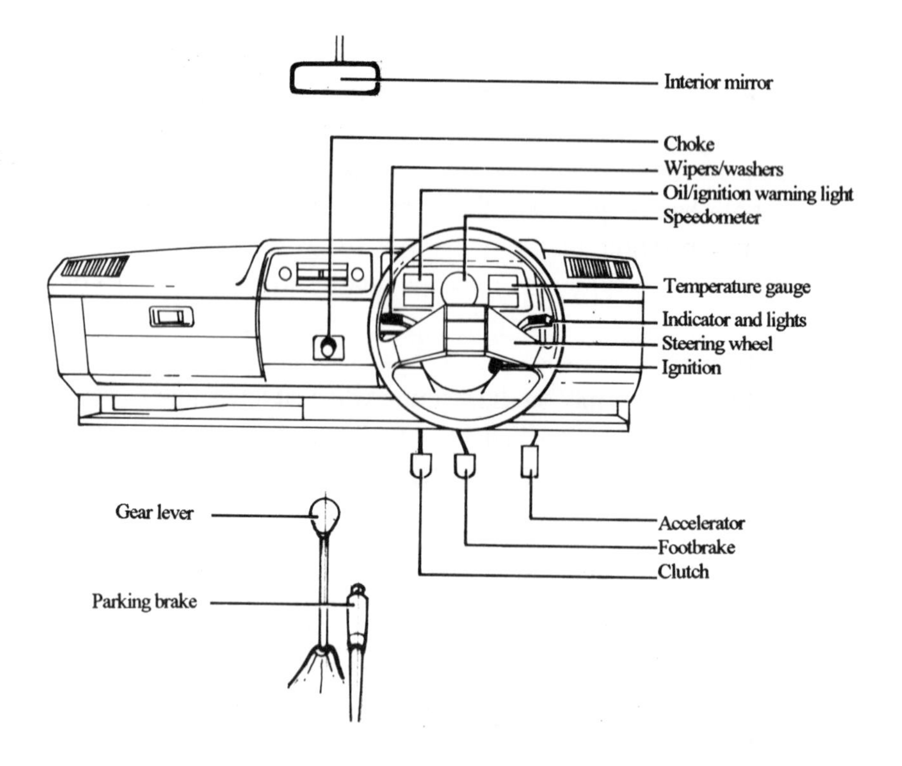

Figure 10. The minor and auxiliary controls.

METERS/GAUGES

The speedometer and odometer

The speedometer shows the speed of the car. Speedometers may be marked in regulated scales showing both kilometres and miles per hour. The odometer records the total distance the car has been driven.

The trip odometer

The trip odometer records the distance of individual trips.

The horn

This is an instrument which gives off a beeping sound in order to warn other road users of your presence and never used as a rebuke.

The windscreen wipers

The wipers are operated by a lever (normally found close to the steering wheel) which allows you to wipe the windscreen of the car at different speeds by means of rubber wiper blades. Water may be ejected onto the windscreen by pressing the water "scoosher" switch/lever which then enables the windscreen wipers to clear away dirt and dust.

The indicators

The indicators allow pedestrians and other road users to know of the driver's intention to turn. They are normally operated by a lever close to the steering wheel. You should try to operate the indicator with one finger without taking your hand off the steering wheel. Flashing lights will remind you that your indicator is on.

1. *Brake warning light*

This light lets the driver know that the parking brake is in the "on" position. However, if the light does not go out when the parking brake is released, this indicates that there is something wrong with the braking system and this should be checked immediately or that the parking brake has not been fully released.

2. ***Turn signal/hazard indicator light***
Flashing lights will remind you that your indicator or hazard switch is turned on.

3. ***High beam indicator light (normally blue)***
Powerful lamps are positioned at the front of the car. When this light comes on it indicates that the headlight beam is on and goes out when the low beam is selected. Headlights should be clean and working properly at all times.

WARNING/INDICATOR LIGHTS

1. Brake warning light
2. Turn signal/hazard indicator light
3. High beam indicator light (Blue)
4. Charge warning light
5. Door open reminder light
6. Oil pressure warning light
7. Rear window defogger indicator light
8. Low fuel warning light
9. Rear fog light indicator light
10. Hazard warning flasher indicator light

Figure 11. The warning and indicator lights.

4. ***Charge warning light***
If this light comes on whilst the engine is running, it indicates that there is something wrong with the charging system.

5. ***Door open reminder light***
This light comes on when any of the doors are not properly closed.

6. ***Oil pressure warning light***
This light warns of low engine oil pressure.

7. ***Rear window demister indicator light***
This light comes on when the rear window demister is activated.

8. ***Low fuel warning light***
This light comes on when the fuel tank is almost empty. You should always ensure that you have plenty of fuel before driving off and that the correct 'star' grading of fuel is used.

9. ***Rear fog light indicator light***
This light comes on when the rear fog lights are activated.

10. ***Hazard warning flasher indicator light***
This light will flash when the hazard switch is turned on.
Always remember that your speedometer, headlights, windscreen wipers, indicators and horn must be in proper working order at all times otherwise driving your car will be illegal.

THE STARTER CONTROLS

The ignition switch

This permits you to start the engine of a car. A key is normally inserted into the ignition switch to activate the electrical circuits necessary to start the engine.

VEHICLE HANDBOOK

I have only covered some of the controls normally found on a typical family saloon car. You should consult your vehicle's handbook to obtain further details about its minor and auxiliary controls.

BLIND SPOTS

If you refer to figure 2, you will see how your mirrors help to reduce "blind spots". There are many parts of your car which can cause a blind spot and will obstruct your view; in fact there are six major blind spots. Take this into consideration at all times when driving.

Lesson 2 - Moving off, gear changing and stopping

In the early stages of driving you may find moving off difficult to master. However, with plenty of practice you will soon find moving off an easy manoeuvre. Take your time and do not put yourself "under a stop watch". When you have completed all your safety checks, you must know the procedure for starting the engine. The first lesson referred to the following important safety checks that you must carry out every time you wish to start the engine:

- Check the parking brake is on.
- Check the gear lever is in neutral.

If you start the engine when the car is in a forward gear, your car will lurch forward (see figure 12).

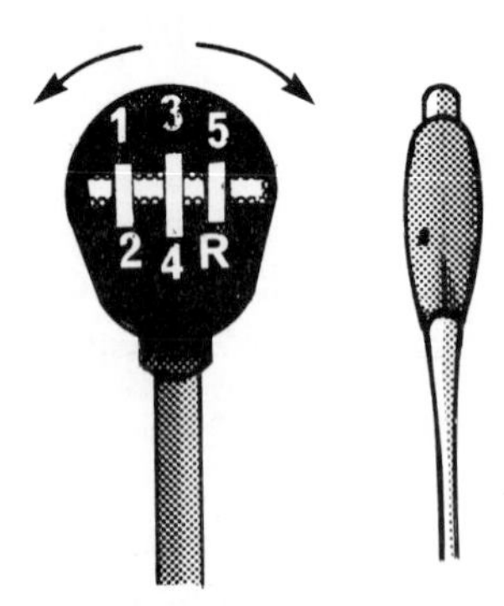

Figure 12. Check that the parking brake is on and the gear lever is in the neutral position before starting the engine.

STARTING THE ENGINE

To start the engine, insert the key fully and whilst gently turning the key clockwise, also turn the steering wheel slightly (to release the steering lock). Then carefully turn the key forward to its next position until the oil, ignition and parking brake warning lights come on. If you turn the key further this will operate the starter motor so release the key as soon as you hear the engine firing. If it does not start first time, do not worry and try again. You are now ready to move off. Let us look at the procedure for moving off, on level ground from a stationary position and how to stop the car shortly afterwards.

MIRRORS/BLIND SPOT

Assume that you are parked at the left-hand side of the road. Before you can drive off from a stationary position you must always check your interior and side mirrors. However the mirrors do not scan the whole area, so there is a blind spot to your off-side (right-hand side). To alleviate this problem you simply look over your right shoulder after you have checked your mirrors before moving away. It is of **vital** importance to make these checks every time you decide to move off (see figure 13). If you fail to do this during your driving test, the examiner will fault you. Before moving off, get into the habit of always looking round after first checking your mirrors in order to avoid a traffic accident.

Figure 13. Don't forget to look over your shoulder and check your blind spot before moving off.

MOVING OFF AND STOPPING

The correct procedure you should carry out before moving off can be remembered by using the following code:

- **PREPARATION**
- **OBSERVATION**
- **MOVE**

Assume you are parked on level ground at the left-hand side of the road, with the parking brake on and the gear lever in the neutral position.

Preparation

Push the clutch right down and hold it there. Place your hand on the gear lever with the palm in the direction you wish to go and gently push the lever to the front left wheel, thus selecting first gear. Set the gas until you hear a steady or lively tone. When this occurs hold your right foot perfectly still. Slowly let the clutch up until you hear the engine note change and freeze your left foot in that position - you are now at **biting point**.

Do not increase the pressure on the gas pedal or let the clutch come up too far, as you may stall your engine. Check your mirrors and if it is safe, release the parking brake and reposition your hand on the steering wheel. If your car moves forward as you release the parking brake, push the clutch down a little until your car stops - this will take power away from the driving wheels.

Observation

Check your mirrors, look over your right shoulder, and check your blind spot (the area not covered by the mirrors). Decide at this point if a signal is necessary.

Ask yourself, *"Is there anyone, including pedestrians who would benefit from my signal?"* If the answer is no, do not signal. Giving a signal for the sake of giving a signal is a complete waste of time, and it may cause danger or confuse other road users. We will deal with the use of signals in more detail later. You must then look forward and check that there is no danger of pedestrians stepping into your path (forward observations).

Move

As soon as it is safe to move off, slowly let the clutch out a little more and the car will slowly move forward. Keep holding the clutch in that position, the **holding point**, until the car builds up sufficient momentum. When the car has built up sufficient momentum, slowly release the clutch and apply gentle pressure to the accelerator. A very useful analogy is to think of a pair of scissors when moving off. You should use all the controls smoothly and keep full control of the car.

When moving off imagine there is a glass of water on the bonnet - if you move off too quickly, you will spill the water. It may take you a long time for your clutch control to become second nature but try to really concentrate on the clutch when moving off from a stationary position as this will eventually lead to smooth and controlled driving. Remember to take your foot off the clutch pedal to avoid wear and tear but keep your foot near the clutch in case you need it later on.

Once you have moved off safely you must check your mirrors and if it is safe, build up more speed to approximately 10 mph. You will hear the engine getting louder - it is now time to change into second gear.

THE SAFETY LINE POSITION

The safety line position is the safest position a car can adopt on the road, in relation to the actual and potential dangers existing at that moment. Actual danger may be a group of children fooling around at the side of the road. Potential danger may be parked vehicles at the side of the road because a pedestrian may walk out in front of your car without looking. Before you decide to move off you must always remember to position your car in the best safety line position to enable you to move off safely.

Once you have moved off, look well ahead and position the car to a safety line position, approximately 90 cm (3 feet) from the kerb. Make sure you allow plenty of room if you have to pass any vehicles which are stationary because a car door may open without any warning.

CHANGING INTO SECOND GEAR

Push the clutch down and come off the gas simultaneously. Place your hand on the gear lever and select second gear. Bring the clutch up and gently apply more gas. Carry out the same procedure (conditions permitting) for selecting third and fourth gear.

USING MIRRORS BEFORE CHANGING DIRECTION

If you have to move to the middle of the road to avoid an obstruction, never change direction too quickly. Always check your mirrors, then Look, Assess and Decide before repositioning your car. Keep a safe distance from the vehicle in front in case the driver brakes suddenly.

STOPPING SMOOTHLY

You will be clearly instructed as to how to stop your car. An example of how your instructor will teach this is as follows (see figure 14). *"Check your mirrors and signal if necessary. Position the car approximately 30 cm (1 foot) parallel from the kerb. Cover the brake, cover the clutch, gently brake, and when the car is at walking pace (about 5 mph), push the clutch down as fast as you can to stop the engine stalling. When the car is just about to stop, ease off the footbrake, and the car will roll to a smooth stop. Apply the parking brake and select neutral. Take both feet off your pedals."* This will initially seem rather difficult but with practice it will eventually become second nature.

PARKING BRAKE BEFORE NEUTRAL

It is important that you get into the routine of applying the parking brake first and then selecting neutral when your car comes to a complete stop. This sequence, (parking brake/neutral), should be used when you have to stop at traffic lights, pedestrian crossings or after pulling up at the side of the road. This is in case your foot accidentally slips off the clutch pedal when you are in gear, causing the car to lurch forward.

Remember the sequence of Mirrors (Look, Assess, Decide), Signal, Manoeuvre. This routine must always be used before you stop your car. If you check your mirrors well before stopping you will be in a position to decide if it is safe to stop. There may be a vehicle following closely behind. Therefore it may be more prudent for you to stop further on, so that the vehicle behind does not hit you. Get into the habit of always using the Mirrors (Look, Assess, Decide) routine before you make any driving decision. We will be looking at this routine in more detail later on.

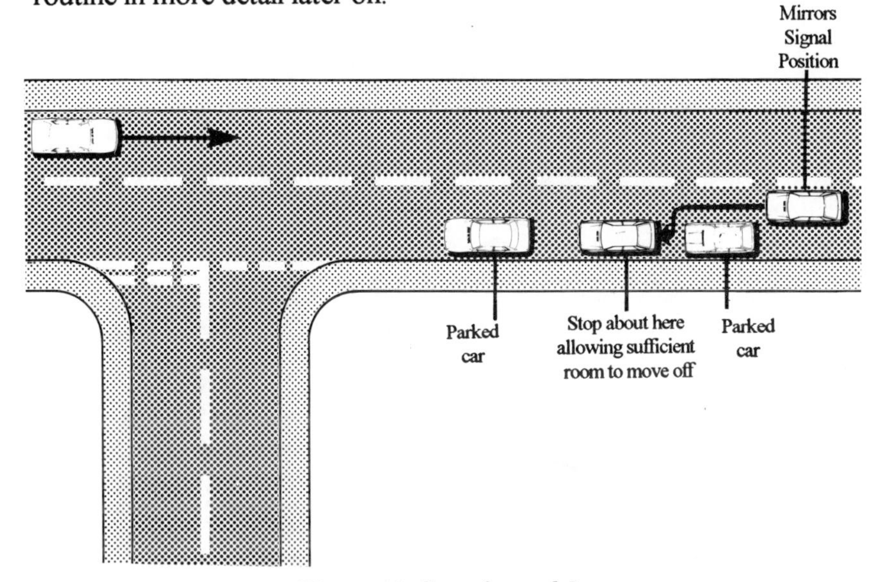

Figure 14. Stopping safely.

STOPPING IN A SAFE, LEGAL AND CONVENIENT PLACE

You should always stop in a safe, legal and convenient place (see figure 16). The Highway Code stipulates many places where it is unsafe to stop: near a school entrance; on a footpath, pavement or level crossing; within 10 metres (32 ft) of a junction, except in an authorised parking space; near the brow of a hill or a hump-back bridge; opposite a traffic island or (if this would cause an obstruction) another parked vehicle; where you would force other traffic to enter a tram lane; where the kerb has been lowered to help wheelchair users; in front of the entrance to a property; in a parking space reserved for specific users, such as orange badge holders or residents, unless entitled to do so. Ensure that you always park your vehicle safely and where it will cause the least inconvenience to others. Walk a few metres rather than cause accidents. Ensure that you stop as close and as parallel to the kerb as possible. Some learners stop so far from the kerb that the examiner needs a 'gang plank' to reach it.

Figure 15. Before moving off or stopping, imagine that there is a glass of water on the bonnet of the car.

Do not squeeze in between two parked vehicles. This will make it very difficult for you to move off again. You must not touch the kerb as this may damage the tyres. A final point on this subject is that you should try to ease off the footbrake just before the car comes to a complete stop (although not on a downhill gradient). This will give you a smoother and more controlled stop because the car will come to a halt under its own momentum.

KEEPING CONTROL

Remember never apply the parking brake when your car is moving as this could cause a skid and may damage your car. It is a popular misconception that you will fail your driving test if you do not change down the gears before stopping. This is absolute bunkum! You can stop in any gear you wish, even at traffic lights, providing that you do not put the clutch down too early. If you leave your gears alone before stopping you can concentrate more on your steering and mirrors. A common fault in learners is to let their steering wander whilst changing gear. If this should happen when you are changing gear, simply tense your right hand slightly before making a gear change - this will help to steady the car when it is moving. You can practice steering with one hand on the steering wheel.

Figure 16. Never stop where you will inconvenience other road users.

STALLING

Do not worry if you stall your engine. Simply apply the parking brake (if necessary) and select neutral before restarting the engine. Once you gain plenty of experience you can start the car if you stall with the clutch pressed fully down in gear - providing you are on level ground.

LOOK WELL AHEAD

It is imperative that you always look well ahead and avoid staring intently at the kerb, down at the bonnet or following the white centre line in the middle of the road whilst driving. Otherwise your car may meander all over the road and an accident may occur (see figure 17).

Figure 17. Keep your eyes on the road.

MOVING OFF FROM BEHIND A PARKED VEHICLE AND ON UPHILL AND DOWNHILL GRADIENTS

After you have practiced moving off, gear changing and making normal stops, your driving instructor will teach you how to move off from behind a parked vehicle or obstruction and on uphill and downhill gradients. You will be asked to carry out one or more of these exercises during your driving test. The examiner will expect you to move off safely, under control and without too much delay. These manoeuvres should never be rushed and you should always remember to take your time. With plenty of practice and patience you will gain more confidence and moving off behind a stationary obstruction (or on an incline) will eventually become second nature. We will start by examining the way you should move off from behind a parked vehicle.

MOVING OFF FROM BEHIND A PARKED VEHICLE

Your car should be positioned on level ground, keeping a safe distance from the vehicle in front so that you can move off without too much delay. I cannot stress enough how important it is for you to take your time, as this manoeuvre is very difficult, i.e. you will be forced to steer round the vehicle and position your car correctly a safe distance from the parked vehicle (see figure 18).

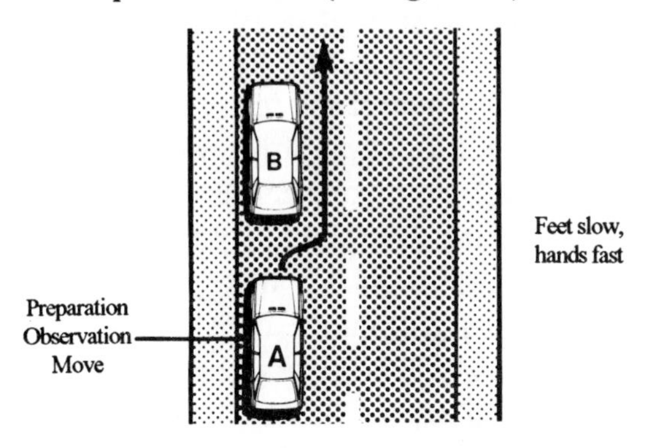

Figure 18. Moving off at an angle.

Before you can move off safely - always follow this procedure:

- **PREPARATION**
- **OBSERVATION**
- **MOVE**

Remember, you should adopt the habit of using the Preparation, Observation, Move sequence every time you wish to move off from a stationary position. When moving off you only have to do one thing at a time so keep calm and concentrate.

Preparation/observation
Simply follow the procedure for moving off on level ground from a stationary position.

Move
Providing there are no pedestrians who might step into your path, slowly let the clutch out a little until the car begins to move forward.

Hold the clutch in that position and turn the steering wheel quickly to the right, until you have cleared the obstruction. Then position your car to a good safety line position, about 90 cm (3 feet) away from any parked vehicles, in case a door opens without warning.

Make sure you keep total control of your car. Keep your *"Feet Slow"* and move your *"Hands Fast"*. Do not release the clutch quickly or your car will lose control and may end up on the other side of the road. Keep a look out for a pedestrian who might step out from in front of the parked vehicle or other vehicles before moving off, especially traffic approaching from the opposite direction. You must not move off if there is any possibility that you may make another vehicle slow down or alter its course. With practice you will gain confidence and this exercise will become second nature. We will now examine how to move off on an incline. Assume that your car is parked on the left-hand side of the road facing uphill (see figure 19).

MOVING OFF UPHILL

Moving off uphill is basically the same procedure as moving off on level ground except that you have to apply more gas. The steeper the hill you are on, the further you will have to press down the accelerator pedal. More gas is required because the engine will have to run faster (work harder), to move the car uphill. Remember the Preparation, Observation, Move routine before moving off.

Preparation

Push the clutch down and select first gear. Set the gas until you hear a steady or lively tone. Slowly let the clutch up until you hear the engine note change. When this happens, keep your feet perfectly still.

Observation

Check your mirrors and if it is safe, release the parking brake and place your hand back on the steering wheel. If the car rolls backwards, simply let the clutch pedal out a little. By letting the clutch out, you have connected power to your driving wheels. If the car moves forward, press the clutch down slightly. Hold the car completely still and count to three. By counting to three you will show the examiner how confident you are with your clutch control and this will prevent you rushing the exercise. Again, look in your mirrors and assess the situation behind and to the offside of your car. Look over your right shoulder and check your blind spot. Decide if a signal is necessary. As soon as it is safe behind you, look forward and ensure that no pedestrians are about to step from the pavement into your path.

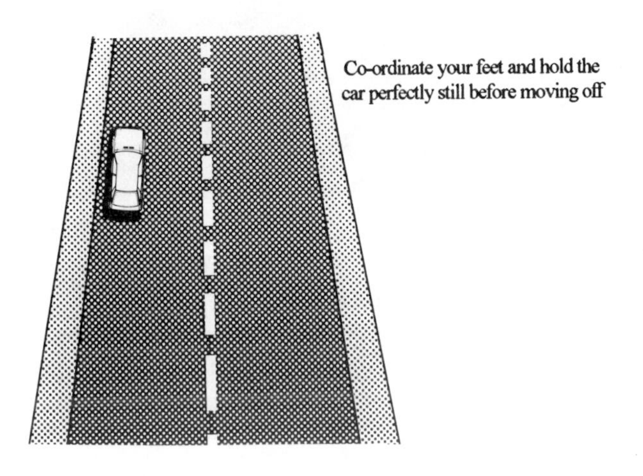

Co-ordinate your feet and hold the
car perfectly still before moving off

Figure 19. Moving off uphill.

Move

Providing that there are no pedestrians who may step into your path, slowly let the clutch out until the car begins to move forward. As soon as this happens, hold the clutch perfectly still until the car has built up momentum. After your car has built up sufficient momentum, slowly release the clutch and press the gas pedal gradually until your car builds up more speed. Take your foot fully off the clutch, and check your mirrors to see if it is safe for you to apply more gas. Now let us look at the way we should move off downhill. Assume that your car is parked at the left-hand side of the road facing downhill (see figure 20).

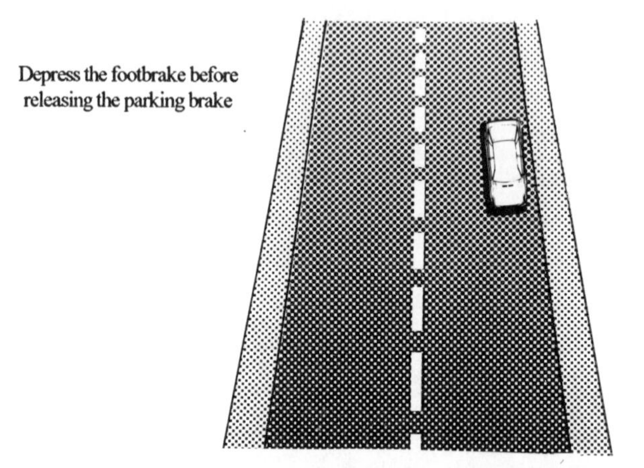
Depress the footbrake before releasing the parking brake

Figure 20. Moving off downhill.

MOVING OFF DOWNHILL

To prevent the car from rolling forward down the gradient, apply the footbrake before you release the parking brake otherwise the car will move forward before you are fully prepared.

- Push the clutch pedal down and select first or second gear.
- Depress the footbrake.
- Release the parking brake, but do not release the footbrake.
- Look in your mirrors and over your shoulder to check your blind spot, to ensure it is safe. Do not forget to look forward to check for any pedestrians who may step into your path.
- As soon as it is safe, take your foot off the brake.
- Let up the clutch smoothly and simultaneously set the gas slightly.

It is important that you do not leave the clutch down too long when moving off otherwise you will be **coasting**. If you leave the clutch down the car's weight will make the car increase speed and you may lose control. When you have mastered the art of moving off at an angle, on a hill up and down, stopping safely, steering, changing gears competently and creeping (slowly edging forward), your instructor will prepare you for the open road. This means dealing with any hazards or road junctions which you may encounter.

MAKING PROGRESS

Your instructor will verbally instruct you on:

- Stopping your car and emerging safely at give way junctions.
- Turning from a main road into a side road.
- Keeping up with the flow of traffic when it is both safe and correct to do so (within your ability).
- Overtaking/passing other vehicles safely.
- Meeting and crossing the path of other vehicles.
- Anticipating the actions of other road users including pedestrians.
- Positioning your car correctly on the road.
- Making effective use of the mirrors.
- Taking correct and prompt action on all traffic signs, road markings or traffic lights.
- Exercise proper care in the use of speed.
- Follow behind another vehicle at a safe distance.

TURNING LEFT FROM A MAIN ROAD INTO A SIDE ROAD

Imagine you have already moved off and you have just selected second gear. An example of the verbal instruction your instructor will give to you on how to turn left from a main road into a side road, and then how to turn right at a give way junction might be, *"I want you to take the next road on the left. Check your mirrors, signal left, keep 90 cm (3 feet) from the kerb, cover brake, cover clutch, check mirrors. Look ahead, look left, and at the corner steer left. When the car is parallel to the kerb steer right to a safety line position. Check your mirrors, a little more gas. Hand on gear lever, palm towards you, clutch down off gas, select third gear, clutch up, more gas".*

TURNING RIGHT FROM A SIDE ROAD INTO A MAIN ROAD

When you are to perform this manoeuvre, your instructor will say, *"At the end of the road turn right, check mirrors, signal right, move to a position just left to the centre of the road. Cover brake, cover clutch. At the white lines I would like you to stop. Gently brake, clutch down, gently brake to a stop. Feet still. Hand on gear lever palm towards me, select first gear. Set gas, check mirrors, look right, look left, look right again. If the road is clear, slowly clutch up until the car moves, feet still, steer right. When the car is parallel to the kerb, steer left, select a safety line position, check your mirrors, and apply a little more gas. Hand on gear lever, palm towards me, clutch down, off gas, select second gear, clutch up, more gas".* When your driving improves, emphasis should be placed on awareness of the actions of other drivers and pedestrians and the correct judgement of speed and distances.

MOVING OFF

QUESTIONS (refer to figures 12 - 20) (See page 245 for answers).

Q1. Which two additional safety checks should you carry out before starting the engine? Fill in the missing words.

Check that the **p**□□□□□□ **b**□□□□ is on, and the **g**□□□ **l**□□□□ is in the **n**□□□□□□ position.

Q2. Which routine should you carry out before moving off? Fill in the missing words.

The **P**□□□□□□□□□□, **O**□□□□□□□□□□□, **M**□□□ routine.

Q3. What should you do if your car moves forward when you release the parking brake when moving off on level ground?

A. Push the clutch down a little until your car stops.

B. Let the clutch out a little until your car stops.

C. Apply the parking brake.

D. Slam on the brakes.

Q4. What is the safety line position?
A. The blind spot.
B. One metre from any obstruction existing at that moment.
C. The safest position a car can adopt on the road.
D. None of these.

Q5. What should you do if your car rolls backwards when you release the parking brake when moving off uphill?
A. Push the clutch down a little.
B. Let the clutch pedal out a little.
C. Push the accelerator down a little.
D. Try to accelerate up the hill.

Q6. Why must you apply more pressure to the gas pedal if you intend to move off on an uphill gradient?
A. The engine will **not** have to work harder to move the car uphill.
B. The engine will have to work harder to move the car uphill.
C. None of these.
D. Otherwise the engine will stall.

Q7. What can cause your engine to stall? Fill in the missing words.
1. **H**□□□□□□ the **p**□□□□□□ **b**□□□□ on for too long.
2. **L**□□□□□□ the **c**□□□□□ pedal come up too far.
3. The **g**□□ **p**□□□□ has not been held **d**□□□ far enough.

Q8. What should you normally do if your engine stalls?
A. Apply the parking brake and select neutral before restarting.
B. Select neutral then apply the parking brake.
C. Apply the footbrake then select neutral.
D. Restart the engine as quickly as possible to avoid embarrassment.

Q9. Should you always signal your intention before moving off from the side of the road?
A. Only signal if you see a vehicle or cyclist approaching.

B. Always signal as a routine.
C. Only if someone will benefit from your signal.
D. Never signal before moving off.

Q10. Could signalling for the sake of signalling be dangerous?
A. This is a foolish practice.
B. This is a safe practice.
C. Signalling all the time will help other road users.
D. None of these.

Q11. Why is it crucial to check the blind spot and then look forward before moving off?
A. To impress the driving examiner.
B. To enable you to check the area not covered by your mirrors.
C. To show that you are a safe and competent driver.
D. To see if you can spot one of your friends.

CHANGING GEAR

QUESTIONS

Q1. How should you change into second gear assuming that you are driving along in first gear?
A. Push down the clutch and operate the footbrake simultaneously.
B. Set the gas and push the clutch down simultaneously.
C. Push down the clutch and come off the gas simultaneously.
D. None of these.

Q2. What may happen if you look down at the gear lever or foot controls whilst driving?
A. You may accidentally speed up the car.
B. You may cause your car to stall.
C. Other drivers may not see you, which may cause them to swerve.
D. You may cause your car to wander and therefore lose control.

STOPPING

QUESTIONS

Q1. How do you stop your car without jerking it?
A. Select first gear just before stopping.
B. Apply the parking brake at the very last second.
C. Ease off the footbrake just before your car comes to a stop.
D. Simultaneously depress the clutch and brake.

Q2. Why is it important to use the mirrors well before stopping?
A. You will be able to see what the rear seat passengers are doing.
B. You will be able to decide if it is safe to stop.
C. You will be able to tell when it is safe to push down the clutch.
D. You will be able to see the driver behind.

Q3. Why is it important to take your time and keep full control of your car before moving off from behind a stationary vehicle?
A. You may cancel your indicator by mistake.
B. None of these.
C. You may turn the steering wheel too fast and the steering mechanism may lock.
D. You may clip the back of the car.

SOME COMMON FAULTS COMMITTED BY LEARNERS: STEERING

- Steering with only one hand on the steering wheel unnecessarily.
- Incorrect or poor grip on the steering wheel.
- Erratic steering.
- Looking at the instructor or hand and foot controls whilst driving.
- Striking the kerb and driving in the gutter.
- Poor forward observations.
- Staring intently at the bonnet, road ahead, kerb, parked vehicle or centre of the road whilst driving.
- Using one hand fixed on the steering wheel whilst turning.

- Not using the "push and pull" method.
- Short non-fluid movements of the wheel.

BEFORE AND AFTER STOPPING

- Not using the Mirrors (Look, Assess, Decide) routine well before stopping.
- Not stopping in a safe, legal or convenient place.
- Not stopping parallel or too far from the kerb.
- Harsh braking before stopping.
- Applying/grasping the parking brake before the car comes to a complete stop.
- Stopping when unsafe to do so.
- Not de-clutching before stopping.
- De-clutching too early or too late before stopping.
- Not realising the engine has stalled.
- Not applying the parking brake and selecting neutral after stopping.
- Removing the foot from the footbrake before applying the parking brake and selecting neutral.
- Failing to cancel the indicator signal after stopping.

Lesson 3 - Making proper use of the mirrors and giving signals

MIRRORS

The first thing you must do before you make any driving decision is to check your mirrors. The mirrors are the eyes in the back of your head. Before you decide to give any signal, change direction, slow down or stop, the mirrors must be checked well in advance. Late use of the mirrors will lead to poorly organised and hurried driving decisions. A good driver will **always** know what is behind him and what is happening around the sides of his car (see figure 21).

There are normally two types of mirrors fitted to modern cars; a flat mirror, which is found in the inside of the car and a convex mirror, which is situated on the outside. When you are driving and you look at your mirrors, the vehicle behind you will seem smaller in a convex mirror so it could be closer than you think. The convex mirror is designed to give you a wider view either side of the car.

Look, Assess, Decide

Before you move off from a stationary position, give any signal, accelerate, change direction, slow down or stop you must make sure you know what is behind you (and if your signal would benefit any other road users including pedestrians). *Don't* look in the mirrors and signal for the sake of signalling. The skill in the use of the mirrors is to take in what you see and act accordingly on the information you have received. A very simple statement but a very common reason why learners fail their driving test.

For example, the learner is driving along and in the distance there is a parked vehicle. The learner checks the mirrors and sees that there is a vehicle following closely behind and it is obvious that it is about to pass the learner. The learner disregards this and moves out, causing the driver behind to slow down or alter his course. Although the learner on this occasion did in fact check the mirrors, he will be faulted for not making "effective use of mirrors". Effective use of mirrors means looking and acting sensibly on what was seen. In other words you must Look, Assess and Decide - do not drive with "blind eyes".

However, it is important to remember that if you are approaching a road junction and there is neither traffic or pedestrians in the vicinity, you should always signal your intention to turn as pedestrians may appear from blind spots.

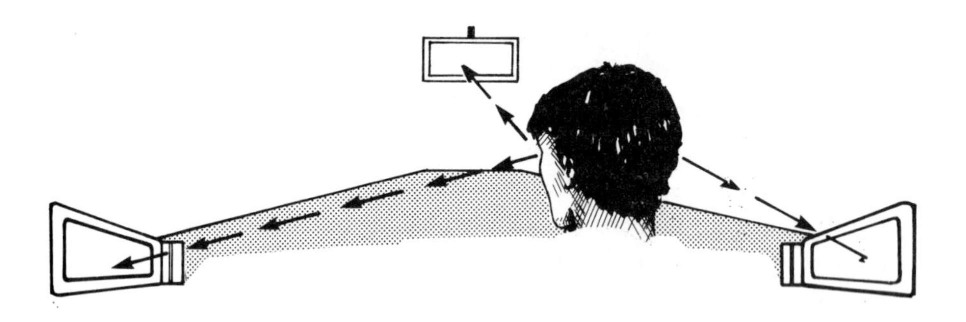

Figure 21. Make effective use of mirrors before making a driving decision.

DO NOT STARE

Avoid staring at the mirrors because you only need to take a quick glance. If you take your eyes off the road for more than a split second the road situation ahead may change and an accident occur.

DO NOT OFFSET THE MIRRORS

Do not try to impress the examiner by offsetting your mirrors so that you have to make an excessive head movement. This may cause your steering to wander. Driving examiners are specifically trained to perceive use of the eyes only. Remember the Mirrors (Look, Assess, Decide), Signal, Manoeuvre routine before you make any decision.

LIMITATIONS OF THE MIRRORS

The mirrors don't give you perfect all round visibility. Before moving off, always check your mirrors and look behind over your right shoulder (your left shoulder if moving off from the right-hand side of the road) to check the area not covered by the mirrors (blind spot).

THE BLIND SPOT

A useful exercise in appreciating the mirrors' limitations is to park at the left-hand side of the road and then watch for a slow moving vehicle appearing in the right-hand mirror. Follow its progress and when the vehicle disappears in this mirror, that is the blind spot.

MIRRORS

QUESTIONS (refer to figure 21) (See page 245 for answers).

Q1. What must you do before making any driving decision?
A. Check your mirrors.
B. Signal.
C. Apply the footbrake.
D. Depress the clutch.

Q2. What may happen if you don't check your mirrors in good time?
A. You may hit the vehicle in front.
B. Nothing will happen.
C. They may not be correctly positioned.
D. You may endanger other road users.

Q3. Where would you normally find a convex mirror?
A. On the outside of the vehicle.
B. On the inside of the vehicle.
C. On the outside and the inside of the vehicle.
D. On the front of the vehicle.

Q4. Why should you avoid staring at the mirrors?
A. Another driver may put on his main beam and blind you.

B. The road situation ahead may change.
C. The mirror may steam up.
D. You may loose control of the car.

Q5. Do the mirrors give you perfect all round visibility?
A. Only when it is light.
B. Yes.
C. No.
D. Only when the road is clear.

Q6. What is the blind spot?
A. A disease that affects drivers eyes as they get older.
B. The area reserved for blind pedestrians.
C. The area not covered by the mirrors.
D. A nickname for the engine.

GIVING SIGNALS
Signals are used to warn other road users of your presence and intentions, which includes pedestrians. There are four types of visible signals you can give whilst driving:

- Direction Indicator.
- Arm Signal.
- Stop lamps.
- Headlights.

And one audible signal (stationary or moving).

- Horn.

Direction indicator
If you give any signal it must be given in good time and in a clear and unmistakable manner. You must signal if it would help other road users, including pedestrians. Many accidents are caused by drivers

and motorcyclists signalling incorrectly and at the wrong time. Making proper use of your mirrors and applying good forward observations when driving will avoid late and unnecessary signalling. Remember the Mirrors (Look, Assess, Decide), Signal, Manoeuvre routine. Always check that your signal has been cancelled after any manoeuvre. If you fail to do this other road users might misinterpret your intentions and an accident may occur.

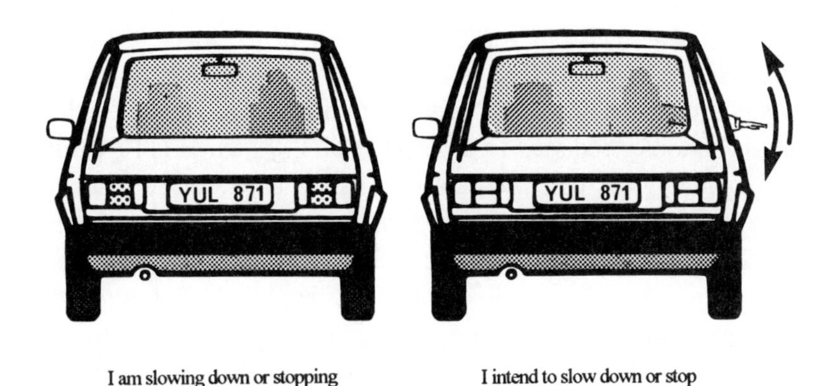

I am slowing down or stopping

I intend to slow down or stop

Figure 22. Giving signals to other road users.

Arm signal

This signal can be useful when approaching a zebra crossing. It warns traffic behind you, and pedestrians, that you intend to slow down. You can use the slowing down arm signal to warn traffic behind you if you are approaching any hazard in the road ahead. This signal should preferably be given early on so as to avoid confusion. Remember you must never use an arm signal to beckon pedestrians to cross the road. However, arm signals may be given to let traffic controllers know your intended direction of travel. These signals are illustrated in the Highway Code. It is imperative that you never mix arm and indicator signals together - this can be highly confusing for other road users.

Stop lamps

The stop lamps are fitted to the rear of a motor car and are illuminated when you press the brake pedal. This signal informs other road users that you are slowing down. Remember to check your mirrors in good time **before** braking smoothly so that you are aware of what is happening both behind you and at the sides of your car. For obvious safety reasons, you must give other drivers time to react to your brake lights.

Headlights

Headlights are normally used at lighting-up time, or at any time when visibility is seriously reduced to a distance of 100 metres (110 yards) or less. However, they can also be used as a signal to warn other road users of your presence; for example, during the hours of darkness, flashing your headlights can be a useful warning preliminary before overtaking another driver. Alternatively during daylight hours you may flash headlights instead of a horn as a warning on motorways or any other fast roads (where other drivers may not hear the horn due to the speed of the vehicles). Flashing your headlights means exactly the same as sounding your horn, i.e. it lets other road users know that you are there. Do not flash headlights to another driver or pedestrian for any other reason. It is dangerous for example to “flash” other drivers to emerge from a side road - they must be allowed to use their own judgement on when it is safe to do so.

Horn

The purpose of the horn is to attract the attention of other road users including pedestrians. The horn should only be sounded as a warning of your presence and it should not be used as a rebuke. It is an offence to sound your horn when your car is moving between the hours of 23.30 and 07.00 (11.30 pm and 7 am) in a built-up area or at any time when your car is stationary. You may disregard this if you have reasonable cause to do so. For example, assume that you are parked at the side of the road between two vehicles, and the vehicle in front suddenly starts reversing towards you. If you believe it is not going to stop, then on this occasion, due to danger, it is permissible to sound the horn to warn the other driver.

SIGNALS

QUESTIONS (refer to figure 22) (See page 245 for answers).

Q1. When should you give a directional indicator signal?
A. If it would help other road users.
B. If it would help pedestrians.
C. If it would help other drivers.
D. Only where absolutely essential.

Q2. Why must you ensure your signal has been cancelled after any manoeuvre?
A. It may blow the indicator bulb.
B. It may cause your battery to go flat.
C. Other road users may misinterpret your intentions.
D. It may confuse oncoming traffic.

Q3. When is it an offence to sound your horn in a built-up area?
A. Between the hours of 22.30 and 7.30 (10.30 pm and 7.30 am).
B. Between the hours of 23.00 and 07.00 (11.00 pm and 7 am).
C. Between the hours of 22.00 and 08.00 (10.00 pm and 8 am).
D. Between the hours of 23.30 and 07.00 (11.30 pm and 7 am).

Q4. What is the purpose of the horn?
A. To beep at another motorist who does not move off a set of traffic lights which have turned to green.
B. To tell someone off.
C. To attract the attention of other road users.
D. To make as much noise as possible.

SOME COMMON FAULTS COMMITTED BY LEARNERS: MIRRORS

- Not using the Mirrors, Signal, Manoeuvre routine.
- Failing to check the mirrors before moving off, increasing speed, signalling, changing direction, slowing down or stopping.
- Not making effective use of mirrors.
- Staring intently at or late use of the mirrors.
- Failing to check the mirrors during normal driving.
- Offsetting the mirror(s) to make an excessive head movement.

Chapter 2

Lesson 4 - Approaching and turning corners

Having mastered the basics of driving, your instructor will teach you a uniform and methodical system of car control. The system of car control you should use before you make any driving decision is Mirrors (Look, Assess, Decide), Signal, Manoeuvre, Position, Speed and Look (M.S.M.P.S.L.). Get into the habit of using this system and learn it by heart because you will be using it many times throughout this book.

A corner is where two roads meet - it is also known as a road junction. Some corners are very sharp and some are just simply bends in the road. You must always remember that once you have decided to turn into the corner, the speed of your car must be completely under your control and you must maintain the same speed throughout the corner. Accelerating into a corner too quickly is a dangerous practice. If your speed is not under complete control you may cause your car to skid or you may drive "blind" into some danger without having time to brake. The important thing to remember is that the sharper the corner, the slower your speed must be; the slower your speed, the lower the gear; the lower the gear, the more control you will have.

It is a popular misconception that the lower the gear the more speed you will have. In reality, a low gear simply allows more control. The amount of gas used to negotiate a corner will depend on the type of road you are on and the condition of the road surface. If you are travelling uphill you may have to use more gas. However, if you are travelling on a downhill gradient, you may simply have to cover the footbrake and by selecting a low gear, the engine in conjunction with the brakes will assist you to negotiate the corner under full control. This is why it is essential to ensure that you do not turn the corner with the clutch down. If you do, the power will be taken from the driving wheels and your car will gain speed (especially if travelling down a hill), and it will be "free wheeling" around the corner. This is commonly known as "coasting". Coasting is a potentially dangerous fault and you could fail your driving test if the examiner sees you doing it.

It would be more prudent to turn the corner much more slowly if the road you are travelling on is covered in snow, or if it has a poor or wet surface. Furthermore, avoid accelerating out of the corner until you have straightened your car in a parallel course to the kerb. In other words it is better to be slow rather than too fast. The examiner will not fault you for turning a corner slowly if you are under complete control. Do not be tempted to speed up round the corner because there is a vehicle following closely behind. If you do so the other vehicle may speed up as well and that will only make the situation worse.

Before we begin to look in detail at the way we should approach and turn corners, you must know the difference between a major and a minor road. A road which is classified as "major" will have a centre line running along the crown (middle) of the road. A road which does not have a centre line is called a minor road. If on a major road you see the gaps in the broken line getting shorter this indicates that danger lies ahead such as a road junction. Imagine you are driving along in fourth gear.

An example of the directions your instructor will give to you on how to approach and turn round a left-hand corner will sound something like this, *"I want you to take the next road on the left. Check your mirrors, signal left, keep about 90 centimetres from the kerb, gently brake, select second gear, check mirrors, look ahead, look left and at the corner steer left. Steer right to a safety line position. Check mirrors, apply more gas, select third gear".*

When your instructor gives this command, the following are the detailed step-by-step sequence of events you should carry out for approaching and turning corners. Again imagine your car is in fourth gear and that you are travelling at 30 mph (see figure 23), with the intention of turning left.

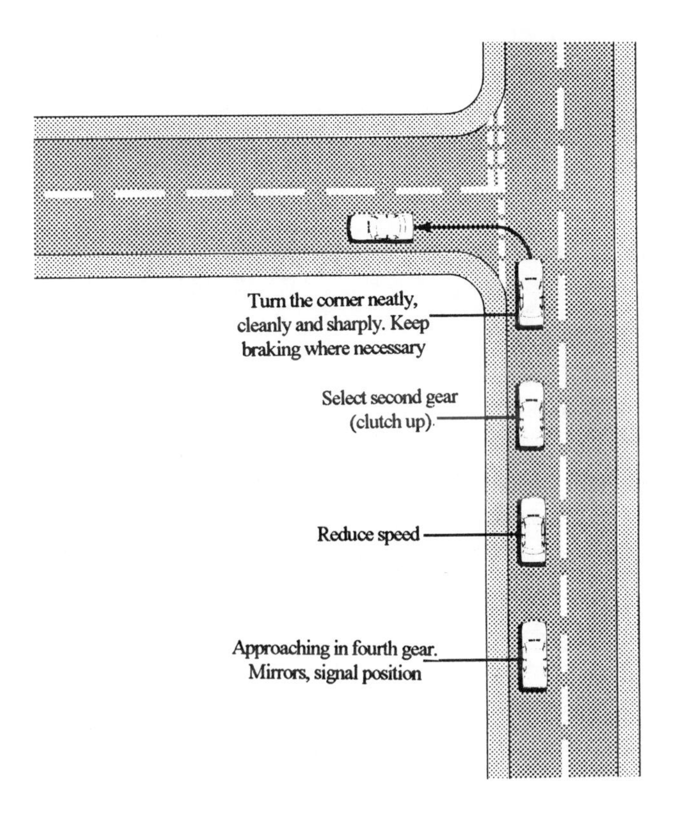

Figure 23. Approaching and turning a corner to the left.

Step 1. ***Mirrors (Look, Assess, Decide)***
You cannot make a safe driving decision unless you know what the traffic behind you is doing so. The mirrors must be checked early. Watch out for cyclists who could be creeping up the inside lane.

Step 2. ***Signal***
If it is safe to do so you should now give a left turn signal. This is to ensure that any drivers behind you, and any pedestrians know where you are going. Give your signal at the correct time; either a late or early signal will only confuse other drivers. After you have signalled your intention to turn left you will be ready to manoeuvre your car into the correct position for the left turn (see figure 24).

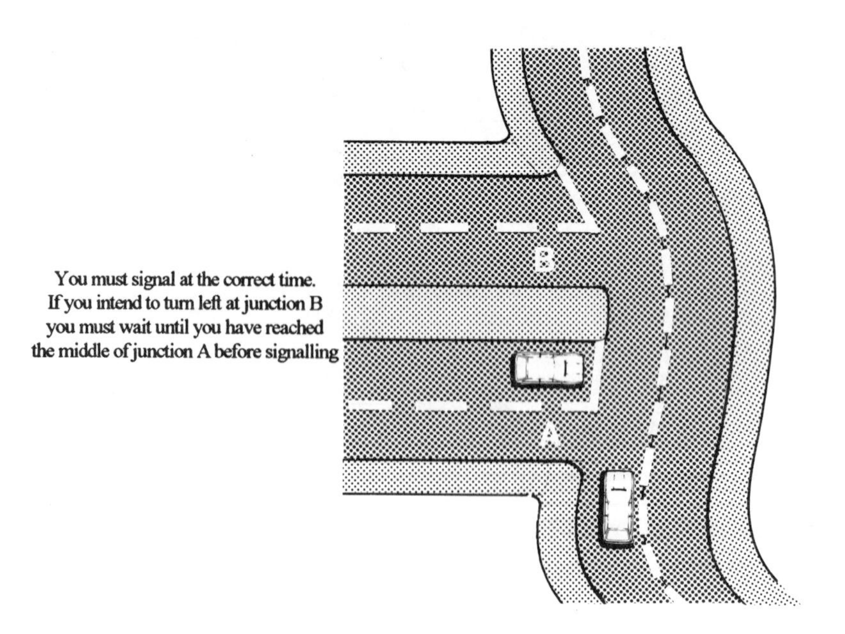

You must signal at the correct time.
If you intend to turn left at junction B
you must wait until you have reached
the middle of junction A before signalling
B
A

Figure 24. Signalling at the correct time.

Step 3. ***Position***

The correct position for a left turn is approximately 90 cm (3 feet) from the kerb. If you are too close your back wheels may strike the kerb. If you are too far from the kerb there is a possibility that another driver or cyclist could illegally overtake you on the left-hand side. Remember you may have to manoeuvre your car round an obstruction to get into the correct position. Once you have moved into the correct position you should reduce your speed on the approach to the corner.

Step 4. ***Speed***

You should slow down with the footbrake to approximately 10 mph (if necessary), and change directly from fourth gear into second gear. Second gear should be selected approximately 10 metres (3 car lengths) from the corner. The clutch at this point must be brought fully up, which will assist you in braking and help to slow down the car. I cannot stress enough that the clutch must be brought fully up throughout the manoeuvre unless you are changing gear. If you do not, you will not have maximum control of your car. You could however change from fourth to third gear, then from third to second gear. The method you use to change down the gears is not of paramount importance to the driving examiner.

Remember, the examiner will be watching that your speed is completely under your control. If you want to change from a higher gear to a lower gear you will have to match the road speed of the car with the speed of the engine. To achieve this, apply pressure to the footbrake. However, you could keep your foot gently on the gas pedal whilst changing gear (sustained revs), if you do not wish to lose any road speed, i.e. when you are just ready to overtake a moving vehicle or driving uphill.

There are no hard and fast rules about the sequence in which gears are used. The **modern** method accepted by the Driving Standard Agency examiners is to change directly from fourth to second gear. Just before the car reaches the turn the car should be parallel to the kerb (do not swing out). If you do swing out, you may end up on the other side of the road and conflict with other traffic.

Step 5. ***Look***

When you have your speed completely under control, you must ensure that you look early as you approach the corner. If you start looking in good time you will be able to see any potential dangers in the road into which you are turning. Be particularly mindful of pedestrians and give way to anyone who is about to step off the pavement or has already stepped onto the road. Your vision may be restricted into your new road and there will be a strong possibility that you may conflict with other traffic.

Remember that your vision may also be obstructed by tall hedges, buildings, parked vehicles or roadside furniture. Before you turn, look in the direction in which you intend your car to go and make the turn neat, clean and sharp. As your car straightens up, it should stay parallel to the kerb. Do not swing inwards to the kerb or outwards to the centre of the road. If you want to avoid striking the kerb with your rear wheels you should start to steer left when the front of your car is just beyond the corner (see figure 25).

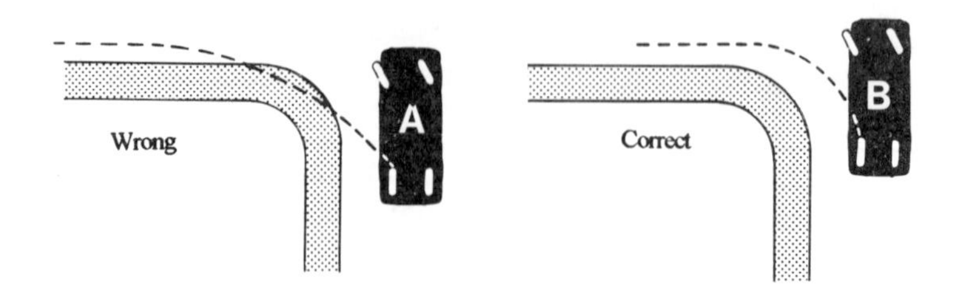

Figure 25. Turning corners. Car A has turned too early. Car B has turned at the correct time.

As soon as you are safely round the corner, cancel your indicator, (if necessary), check your mirrors and apply more gas, (conditions permitting), then select a good safety line position parallel to the new road. Remember, you must never accelerate if another vehicle is overtaking you.

Repeating the Mirrors, Signal, Manoeuvre, Position, Speed and Look routine to yourself will help you to remember and comprehend things more easily. Good driving is based around the ability to perform this exercise properly. When you can undertake approaching and turning corners to a high standard you will have the basic knowledge to deal will many other road situations, such as roundabouts, overtaking, handling other road users, etc. Let us now study the way we should turn right (see figure 26).

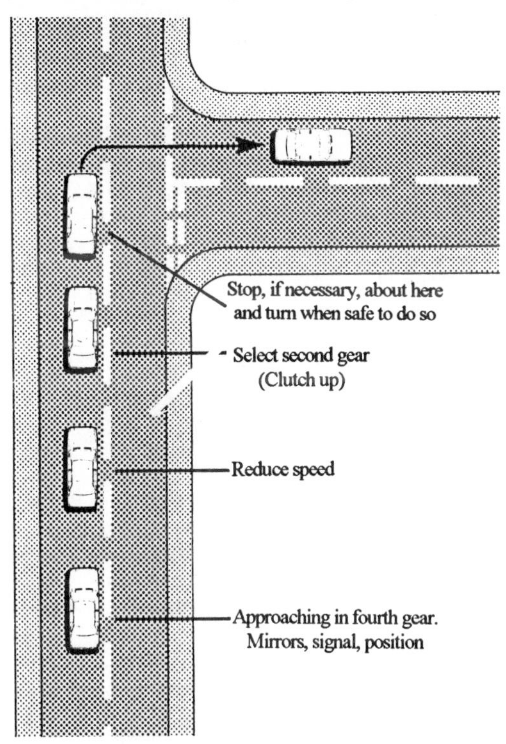

Figure 26. Approaching and turning a corner to the right.

TURNING RIGHT

Step 1

Turning right is potentially hazardous since it may involve crossing the path of oncoming vehicles and the learner must also be mindful of pedestrians crossing the road. Turning right is far more difficult than turning left and there are slight variations. Again, apply the Mirrors (Look, Assess, Decide), Signal, Manoeuvre, Position, Speed and Look routine. You should position the car approximately 30 cm (1 foot) from the centre of the road. However, keep well into the left if turning right out of a narrow road (this is to allow room for other vehicles to turn in) whilst increasing your vision into your new road.

Step 2

Once the position has been established, reduce speed. You must start to look early into the corner to see if there are any potential dangers in or near the side road. Normally second gear should be selected, unless you are turning at a curve in the road, where third gear would be sufficient. However if you have to stop or slow down to under 5 mph to give way to either oncoming traffic or pedestrians crossing the road, first gear should be selected in order to give you greater control of your car (see figure 27).

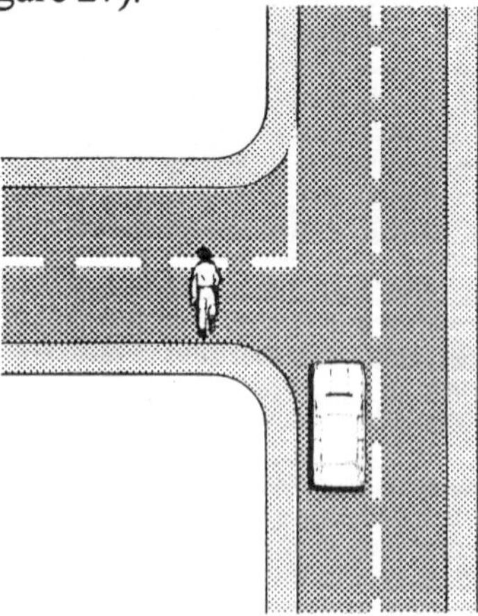

Figure 27. Be prepared to give way to pedestrians.

If you have to stop to give way, the front of your car should be in line with the centre of the road into which you are turning. There is no need to apply the parking brake unless you are on an incline, or you expect to be sitting for any length of time. You must not cross the path of an approaching vehicle if it would cause it to slow down or alter course.

Step 3

Avoid cutting the right-hand corner. This is a dangerous practice because it will put you on the wrong side of the road (see figure 28). Before you turn, make a final right-hand mirror check, in case somebody is foolish enough to overtake you on the right-hand side. Always look into the road you are turning into for any possible danger. Remember to look and assess the situation before you decide if it is safe to make any driving decision. Finally, select a good safety line position once you have entered your new road, and cancel your indicator (see figure 29).

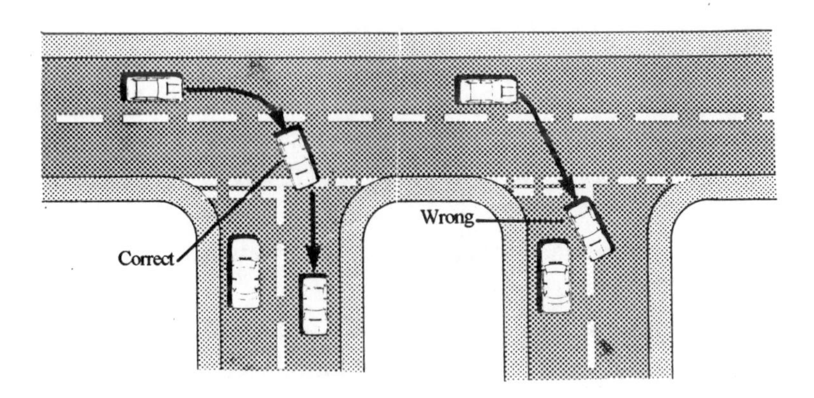

Figure 28. Avoid cutting corners.

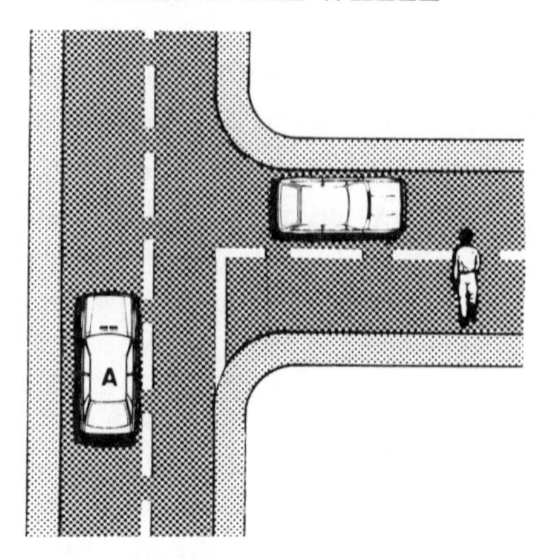

Figure 29. Always look into a new road before turning.

KEEP BRAKING

It is of paramount importance that you do not release the footbrake as you approach a corner (unless you are travelling uphill) because it will lessen your control of your car, particularly of steering and braking. Braking a bit too much is better than sharp and sudden braking at the last moment.

APPROACHING AND TURNING CORNERS

QUESTIONS (refer to figures 23 - 29) (See page 245 for answers).

Q1. What uniformed and methodical system of car control should you use before turning a corner? Fill in the missing words.
The **M□□□□□□** (Look, Assess, Decide) **S□□□□□** **M□□□□□□□□** routine.

Q2. Why is it important to start looking early when approaching a corner?

A. To enable you to change your mind if it is the wrong turning.
B. So that you can see how fast you can turn the corner.
C. To enable you to see any potential dangers in the road.
D. To allow you to tell your passengers what is coming.

Q3. What position should you normally adopt before turning left?

A. Approximately 50 cm (1½ feet) from the kerb.
B. Approximately 30 cm (1 foot) from the kerb.
C. Approximately 2 metres (6 feet) from the kerb.
D. Approximately 90 cm (3 feet) from the kerb.

Q4. How can a badly timed signal confuse other road users?
A. Another driver may misinterpret your intention..
B. Drivers behind you may think that you have left your indicator on by mistake.
C. There is no such thing as a badly timed signal.
D. Other drivers may think that there is a fault with your indicator.

Q5. Why should you keep a safe distance from the kerb before making a left turn?
A. You may miss your turning.
B. Other drivers may think you are stopping at the roadside.
C. Another driver or cyclist may overtake on the left-hand side.
D. So that you don't clip the kerb.

Q6. Why is it important that you turn a corner in the correct gear with the speed of your car completely under your control?
A. You may cause your car to stall.
B. You may cause your car to skid or swing out.
C. You may cause your car to pick up debris lying in the gutter.
D. None of these.

Q7. Why should you never turn a corner with the clutch pedal down?
A. You will be "freewheeling" around the corner.
B. You will be riding the clutch.
C. You will cause unnecessary wear and tear to the clutch plates.
D. You will not be able to change gear quickly.

Q8. Why should you be very careful before making a right turn?
A. In case a dog runs out in front of you.

B. In case someone overtakes you at the junction.
C. In case a drunken pedestrian steps in front of your car.
D. In case it is the wrong turning.

Q9. How can you avoid striking the kerb with your rear wheels whilst turning left?
A. Start to steer left 90 cm (3 feet) beyond the corner.
B. Start to steer left when the front of the car is just before the corner.
C. Start to steer left when the front of the car is just beyond the corner.
D. Start to steer left 180 cm (6 feet) beyond the corner.

Q10. Why is it important not to allow your car to swing inwards to the kerb or outwards to the centre of the road when turning a corner?
A. You will cause unnecessary wear to the tyres.
B. Other drivers may think your steering has failed.
C. You may conflict with other road users.
D. You may stall the car.

Q11. What position should you normally adopt before turning right?
A. Approximately 30 cm (1 foot) from the centre of the road.
B. Approximately 60 cm (2 feet) from the centre of the road.
C. As close to the centre of the road as possible.
D. Approximately 180 cm (6 feet) from the centre of the road.

Q12. Are you permitted to cut right-hand corners?
A. Only during daylight.
B. Never cut right-hand corners.
C. Avoid cutting right-hand corners unless it is completely safe and absolutely necessary.
D. Yes, whenever it is convenient.

Q13. Give three reasons why you should not cut right-hand corners? Fill in the missing words.

1. You will end up on the **w**□□□□ **s**□□□ of the **r**□□□.
2. Your **v**□□□□□ of the new **r**□□□ will be **r**□□□□□□□□□.
3. There is a strong possibility of **c**□□□□□□□□□□ with other **t**□□□□□□ coming out of the road into which you are turning.

SOME COMMON FAULTS COMMITTED BY LEARNERS: APPROACHING AND TURNING CORNERS

- Not using the Mirrors (Look, Assess, Decide), Signal, Manoeuvre routine.
- Not acting properly on information received from the mirrors.
- Giving an incorrect or misleading signal.
- Failing to cancel the signal where necessary.
- Not positioning the car correctly either before or after turning.
- Not reducing speed sufficiently enough before turning the corner, and cutting the corner.
- Selecting a low gear at an excessive speed.
- Selecting the wrong gear for the corner.
- Poor co-ordination whilst braking and changing gear.
- Turning the corner with the clutch held down.
- Looking down when changing gear or changing gear too late.
- Oversteering or understeering/failing to straighten up after turning.
- Failing to keep the correct course before turning.
- Allowing the car to move forward past the turning point, resulting in a “hook” turn.
- Not giving way to pedestrians who are crossing the road either before or whilst turning.
- Not looking early into the side roads on the approach to the corner.
- Not anticipating the actions of pedestrians or stopping needlessly.
- Failing to anticipate the actions of other drivers.
- Not using the “push and pull” method whilst turning.
- Turning in front of closely approaching traffic whilst making a right turn.

Lesson 5 - Dealing with road junctions

Once you have mastered how to approach and turn corners, your driving instructor will teach you how to deal with more complex road junctions. There are many different kinds of road junctions. One essential fact to be remembered is that **all** road junctions are dangerous irrespective of whether you have priority or not. Therefore, you should never be complacent. In this lesson we shall look at a T-junction controlled by give way lines, when the give way lines are against you (see figure 30).

Whilst you are sitting your driving test, the driving examiner will be watching that you carry out the Mirrors (Look, Assess, Decide), Signal, Manoeuvre, Position, Speed and Look routine correctly, as you approach the give way junction. It is essential to ensure that your speed on the approach to the give way junction is completely under your control and that you take **effective observation** before you actually emerge from the give way junction. Two very simple statements, but two very common reasons why learners fail their driving test. When you approach any road junction you must never make the examiner feel uncomfortable or make him doubt that you did not take effective observation before emerging. The full sequence you should adopt is as follows: **Mirrors (Look, Assess, Decide) - Signal - Manoeuvre - Position - Speed - Look**

About 92 metres (100 yards) before a give way junction, the examiner will give you the instruction to turn. Firstly, you must carry out the Mirrors (Look, Assess, Decide), Signal, Manoeuvre routine.

Mirrors

In your first driving lesson you were taught how important it was to check your mirrors in good time before making any driving decision. The mirrors tell you what is happening behind and around the car and if it is safe to give a signal.

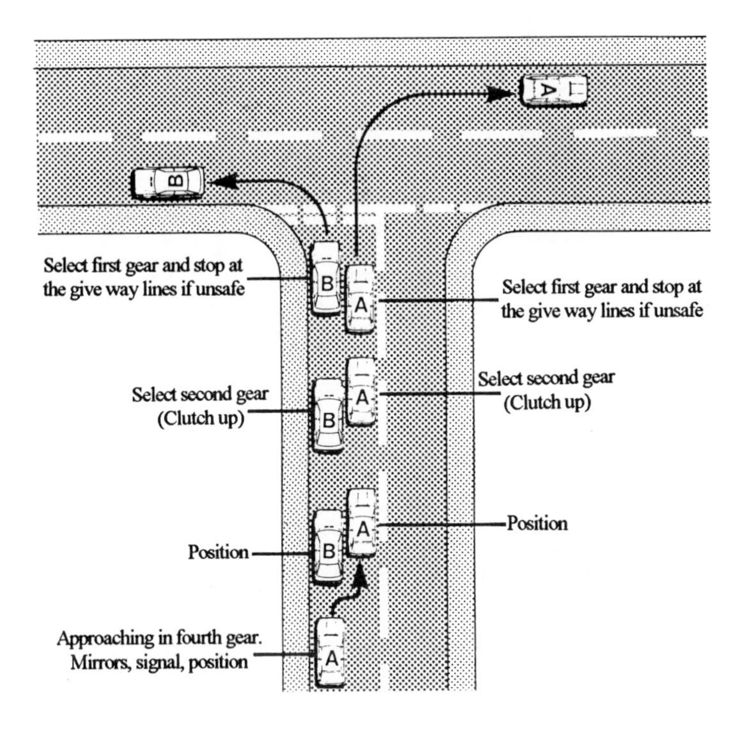

Figure 30. Dealing with road junctions.

Signal

Timing your signal is very important. If there is another vehicle waiting to emerge from a side road and you give a signal too early, the other driver may misinterpret your intention and think that you are going to turn into the road from where he is emerging. This manoeuvre may result in an accident (see figure 24). It would be far safer to delay your signal until you have reached the middle of the side road.

Manoeuvre

Remember that you may have to manoeuvre round an obstruction to get into the correct position. After giving your signal, you should carry out the Position, Speed and Look routine.

Position

If you intend to turn left, you should normally position your car approximately 90 cm (3 feet) from the left-hand kerb. If you intend to turn right, your position should be just left to the crown (middle), of the road. However, if you are in a road which allows one lane of traffic in each direction your position should be well over to the left, to allow other vehicles plenty of room in which to turn. On the other hand, if you are driving along a one way street and you wish to turn right, position your car as far over to the right as possible.

Speed

When you have positioned your car correctly, you should gently apply the footbrake, reduce your speed to approximately 10 mph, and select second gear (making sure that you bring the clutch pedal up). If you leave the clutch down (coasting), you will not have full control of your car and you may speed up if you are travelling down a hill. Second gear should be selected about 3 car lengths from the give way lines. After selecting second gear you should again reduce your speed to approximately 5 mph and select first gear (again bringing the clutch up). Select first gear about 1 car length from the give way line.

Look

Stop your car behind the double broken white give way lines. Check the junction and take effective observation before making a decision to move into the new road.

EFFECTIVE OBSERVATION

You must take effective observation at the junction by checking right, left and right **again** before you enter the main road. However, checking right, left and right again, might not be enough if there are any parked vehicles or roadside furniture obstructing your view. You should "creep" your car forward slowly using clutch control until your car is at point X (see figure 31 and 32).

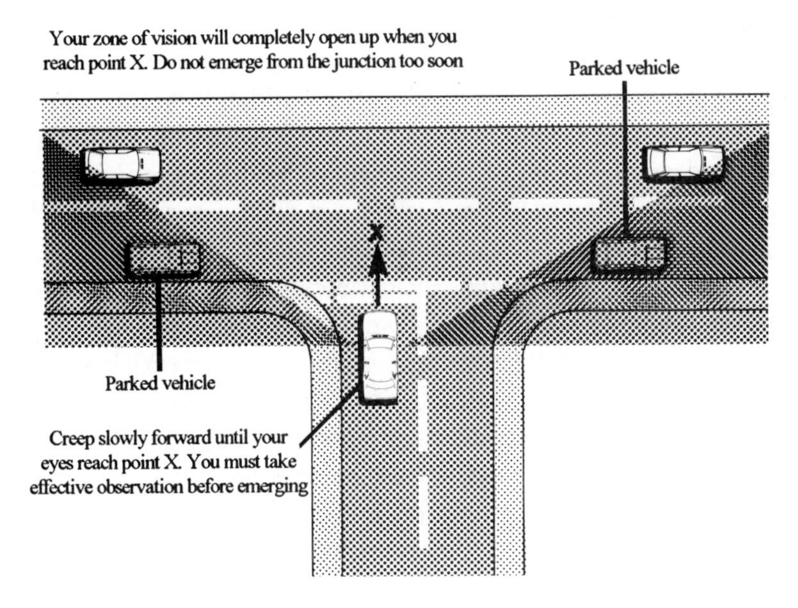
Your zone of vision will completely open up when you reach point X. Do not emerge from the junction too soon
Parked vehicle
X
Parked vehicle
Creep slowly forward until your eyes reach point X. You must take effective observation before emerging

Figure 31. Effective observation before emerging.

SWEET SHOP

Figure 32. To reach the sweet shop safely the child must walk forward and take effective observation by looking both sides of the parked vehicles. The learner driver must adopt the same principle when emerging from a blind give way junction.

WHERE AND WHAT TO LOOK FOR

At point X, you should have a clear view of the main road in both directions and you will be in a much better position to decide when it is safe to emerge. It is very important to know what you are looking for before emerging at a give way junction. You must look out for, and give way to other vehicles, cyclists and pedestrians who may be using the road into which you are turning. Motorcycles and mopeds tend to travel very fast and their riders do not always make themselves visible by wearing brightly coloured clothing. As you look left, remember to check for any vehicles which are overtaking and are on the wrong side of the road. Do not forget that parts of your car can obstruct your view, so take this into consideration at all times.

Watch out for any vehicles that may be emerging from a side road or driveway, because they may be hidden by parked vehicles or roadside furniture. A good tip is to wind your window down (especially in fog or at night) and listen out for approaching traffic. Be alert and proceed (if safe) when you get a signal to move at a junction controlled by a policeman or traffic warden. Once you have decided it is perfectly safe to emerge, turn carefully into the main road. Do not swing out into the middle of the road and take up a good safety line position parallel with the kerb. You must never make another driver or cyclist slow down or change direction (see figures 33a and 33b).

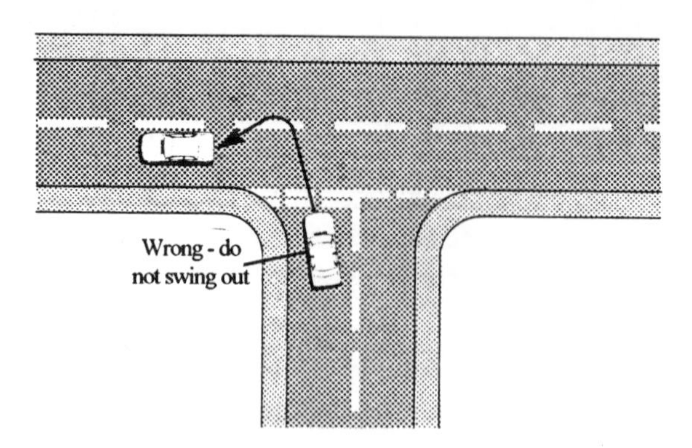

Figure 33a. Turning too wide at a road junction.

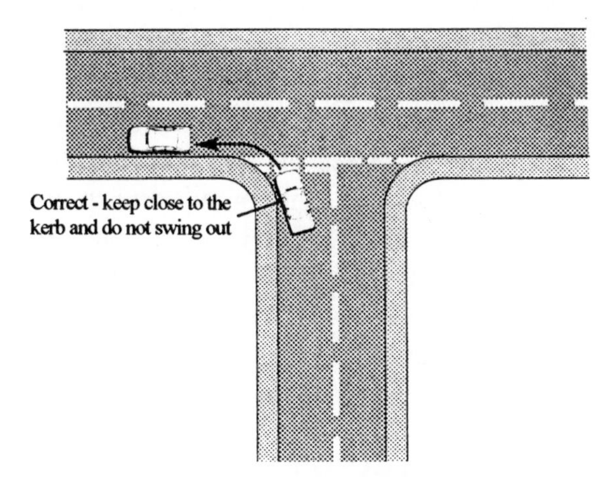
Correct - keep close to the
kerb and do not swing out

Figure 33b. Turning correctly at a road junction.

BE PATIENT

Never be tempted to move out because an impatient motorist has beeped his horn at you. Use your own judgement as to when it is safe. Try however, to anticipate a safe gap in the traffic and emerge at the earliest opportunity. If you do not emerge at the earliest opportunity the examiner may fault you for failing to avoid undue hesitancy.

WHAT THE EXAMINER WILL BE LOOKING FOR

There are two ways in which you can be failed for not taking effective observation before emerging. The first is that you do not check the situation but rather emerge straight out of the junction causing danger to yourself and other road users. The second is that you look, see another vehicle approaching but you mistakenly believe you may emerge from the give way junction before the other vehicle arrives. If you emerge from a give way junction the examiner will watch very carefully that you do not cause the other driver to slow down or change direction - if you do, you will fail your driving test.

KEEP BRAKING

During the earlier lessons, when dealing with approaching and turning corners, I told you how important it was to regulate your speed on the approach to a corner. It is imperative that you keep braking continuously on the approach to the road junction. The amount of pressure you apply to the footbrake will vary according to the type of road on which you are driving (e.g. if you are driving down a steep hill you will have to brake more firmly to keep your car under full control). If you do not apply pressure to the footbrake when you press the clutch down to change gear, power will be taken from the driving wheels and the engine won't be helping the car to slow down. Therefore, you can brake and operate the clutch simultaneously.

EMERGING SAFELY WITHOUT STOPPING

Once you have gained confidence in stopping at give way junctions and emerging with due regard for other road users, you should get into the habit of emerging at give way junctions without actually stopping, providing it is **safe** to do so. Give way means give way; it does not mean stop. Therefore, if you approach a give way junction, you should ask yourself two questions, *"How good is my vision?"* and *"What gear should I select for the junction?"* Always remember that your gear should match your speed and your speed should match your visibility. The secret is to start looking early as you approach the junction. Looking early will give you the best indication as to the gear you will require, and when to make a change.

If your vision is poor and you cannot take effective observation before emerging you should select the lowest gear possible. This is because the lower the gear you use, the more control you will have just when you need it most. Should you decide to keep your car moving whilst you are taking effective observation, you should only emerge without actually stopping when you are satisfied it is completely safe, and that you will not cause any other driver or cyclist to alter their course or slow down. If you have to stop your car at the give way lines, creep slowly forward under clutch control and take effective observation before emerging. You must always be prepared to stop at a give way junction if your vision is obstructed in any way.

TO SUM UP

A word of warning. Never emerge from any give way junction if you see another driver signalling his intention to turn. It is prudent to wait until you receive more positive information before emerging, i.e. wait until the other driver slows down and makes a definite move to turn. He may have left the indicator on by mistake. There is one crucial rule regarding give way junctions. If you are in any doubt and your vision is restricted in any way, you must **STOP** and not emerge from the give way junction until you are quite sure it is safe to do so. Remember the adage; ***"If in doubt - DON'T"*** (see figure 34a and 34b).

Finally, if you approach a T-junction where there are no traffic lights or "**STOP**" or "**GIVE WAY**" signs, you must remember to give way to any vehicle or cyclist in the continuing road at the top of the T (see figure 34c).

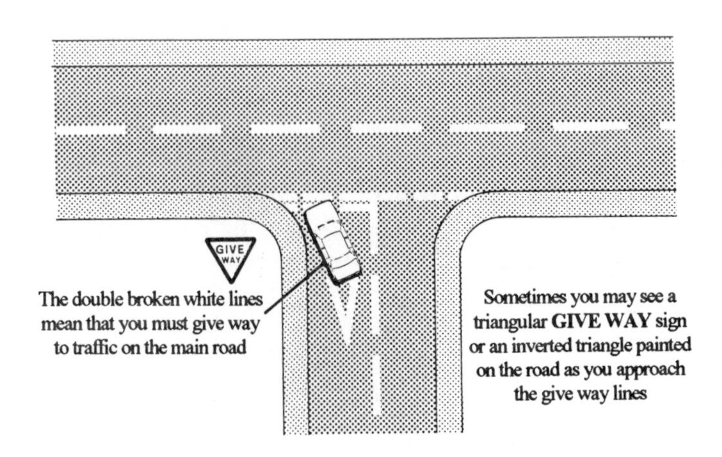

GIVE
WAY
The double broken white lines
mean that you must give way
to traffic on the main road
Sometimes you may see a
triangular GIVE WAY sign
or an inverted triangle painted
on the road as you approach
the give way lines

Figure 34a. A junction controlled by give way lines.

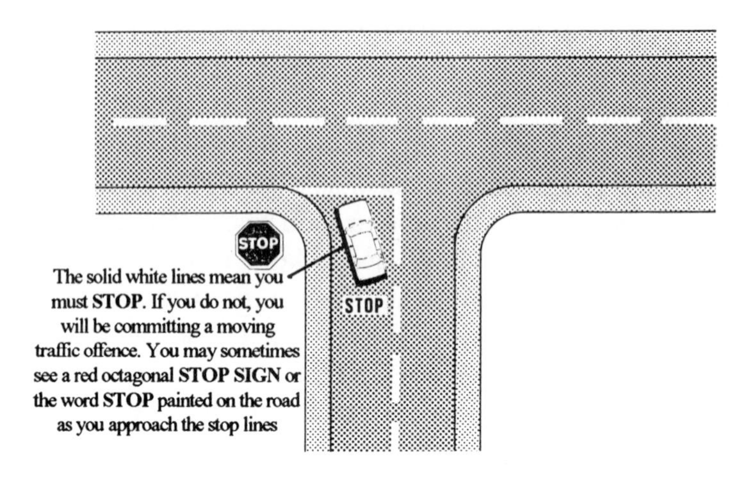

STOP
The solid white lines mean you must **STOP**. If you do not, you will be committing a moving traffic offence. You may sometimes see a red octagonal **STOP SIGN** or the word **STOP** painted on the road as you approach the stop lines
STOP

Figure 34b. A junction controlled by a stop line.

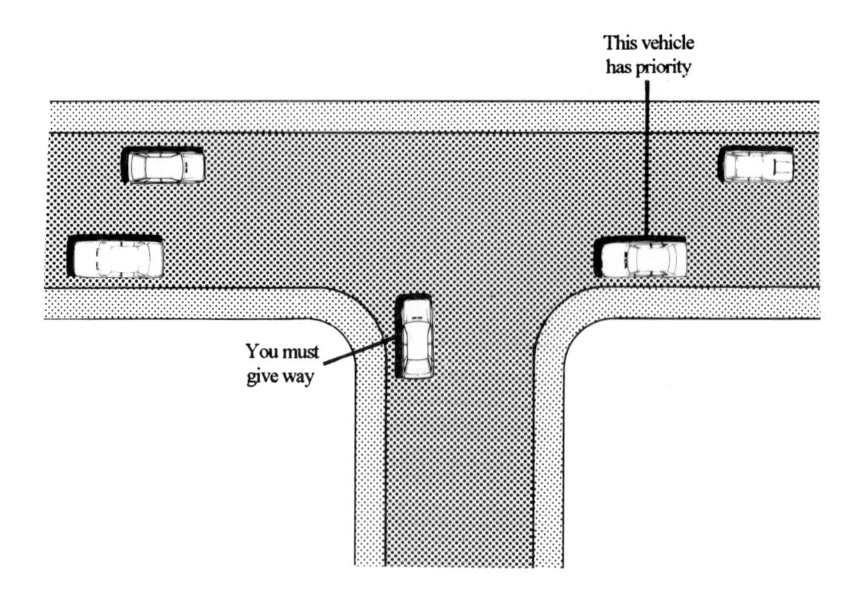

This vehicle has priority

Figure 34c. A T-junction without any road markings.

DEALING WITH ROAD JUNCTIONS

QUESTIONS (refer to figures 30 - 34) (See page 246 for answers).

Q1. What vital thing should you remember about all road junctions?

A. All road junctions are dangerous.

B. Some road junctions are dangerous.

C. Only road junctions without road markings are dangerous.

D. Road junctions with traffic lights are dangerous.

Q2. Why is it very important that your speed is completely under control when approaching a give way junction?

A. Your footbrake will be less effective.

B. You will not have to carry out an emergency stop.

C. You may lose control of your car.

D. You will not be able to move off again at speed.

Q3. What does effective observation before emerging mean?

A. You must check right and left at least 3 seconds before emerging.

B. You must check right and left before emerging.

C. You must check right, left and right again before emerging.

D. You must check right and left at least 10 seconds before emerging.

Q4. Why must you emerge from a give way junction at the earliest opportunity?

A. Other drivers may get frustrated and take silly risks.

B. You may stall your car.

C. You may overheat the engine.

D. You may be late for your appointment.

Q5. What gear would you select when emerging from a give way junction? Fill in the missing words.

Your **g**□□□ should match your **s**□□□□ and your **s**□□□□ should match your **v**□□□□□□□□□.

Q6. Do you always have to stop at a give way junction?
A. Yes, at all times.
B. Never.
C. You only need to stop for one second.
D. No, providing it is completely safe and legal you can emerge without stopping.

Q7. Name two occasions where the examiner may fail you for not taking effective observation before emerging at a give way junction? Fill in the missing words.
1. You do not **c**□□□□ the situation and **e**□□□□□ straight out of the junction causing **d**□□□□□ to yourself and other **r**□□□ users.
2. You see another **v**□□□□□□ approaching but you **m**□□□□□□□□□ believe you may **e**□□□□□ from the give way junction before the other vehicle arrives.

Q8. What is the crucial rule regarding give way junctions?
A. If you are in any doubt, get out of the car and have a good look.
B. If you are in any doubt, you must **STOP**.
C. If you are in any doubt you must use your horn to warn other traffic.
D. If you are in any doubt, slow down.

Q9. What position should you adopt if you are turning right out of a narrow road?
A. You should position your car well over to the left.
B. You should position your car well over to the right.
C. You should position your car in the centre of the left-hand lane.
D. You should position your car well back from the give way lines.

Q10. Why should you keep well left when turning right out of a narrow road?
A. To allow plenty of room for an emergency vehicle to turn into your road.

B. You will be able to see other vehicles turning into your road much better.
C. So that you can move off quickly.
D. Your vision will be increased into your new road and you will allow other vehicles plenty of room to turn in.

Q11. What should you do if you are sitting waiting to emerge from a give way junction and an impatient motorist beeps his horn or "flashes" his lights at you?
A. Wait at the junction to teach the driver behind a lesson, even though the new road is clear
B. Stick your fingers up at him.
C. Be patient and use your own judgment..
D. Get out your car and remonstrate with him.

Q12. Should you emerge from a give way junction if you see another driver signalling his intention to turn?
A. No, you should wait until you receive more positive information.
B. Yes. If another driver is signalling left, it is obvious that driver is going to turn left.
C. Yes. As long as you have not stalled your vehicle.
D. None of these.

Q13. Assume you are driving downhill towards a road junction. What will happen if you push the clutch down and you are not applying firm pressure to the footbrake?
A. Your car will slow down.
B. Your car will gain speed and you may lose control.
C. Your car will stall and you may lose control.
D. Your car may overheat.

Lesson 6 - Dealing with crossroads

A road which crosses the path of another road is called a crossroad. There are many different types of crossroads. It is important to remember that all crossroads are dangerous and they must be treated with caution. Although you may have priority there is nothing to stop a vehicle or cyclist pulling straight out in front of you. You must **always** take effective observation before emerging. Generally speaking, the smaller the road, the more dangerous the crossroad - but **never** be complacent. In the following paragraphs we will examine various types of crossroads. In order to understand this section, it is important to remember that a road which is classified as "major" will have single broken lines marking the middle of the road, whilst a road which does not have single broken lines marking the middle of the road is called a "minor" road. Remember, if you see the gaps in the broken line getting shorter, this indicates that **danger** lies ahead such as a road junction or bend. First, we will look at the way one should deal with the major crossroad.

THE MAJOR CROSSROAD

Proceeding straight ahead

As you approach the junction with the intention of proceeding straight ahead, apply the 3 steps of the Mirrors (Look, Assess, Decide), Signal, Manoeuvre routine (see figure 35).

The mirrors must be checked in good time so that you know who is behind you and what the vehicles following are doing. Since in this instance you intend to go straight ahead, you should try to avoid giving a change of direction signal unless it is absolutely necessary, otherwise other road users might be misled into thinking that you intend to turn at the junction. It is imperative that you cancel the signal as soon as practically possible if you do have to change course. Break down the manoeuvre itself into the 3 steps of the Position, Speed and Look.

Position

You should position your car approximately 90 cm (3 feet) from the kerb, unless you have a legitimate reason for changing your position.

Speed

Once your position is established you should keep your speed constant and **never** accelerate into the crossroad. Racing into a crossroad is a dangerous and foolish practice.

Look

Give the crossroad a quick check to the right, left, and right again, in case another vehicle or cyclist decides to pull out in front of you. If this ever happens at least you will have time to take evasive action. You should normally proceed through the crossroad in fourth gear.

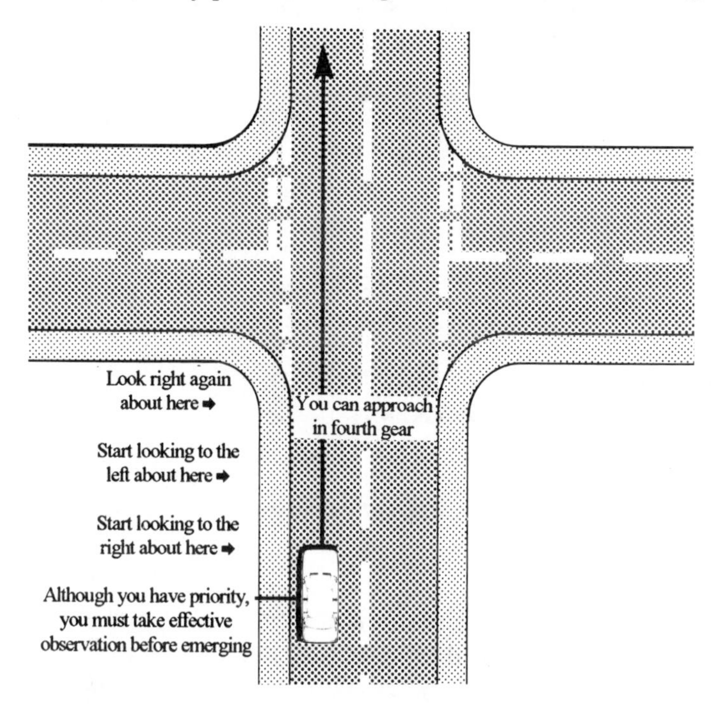
Look right again about here ➡
You can approach in fourth gear
Start looking to the left about here ➡
Start looking to the right about here ➡
Although you have priority, you must take effective observation before emerging

Figure 35. Proceeding straight ahead at a major crossroad.

THE MINOR CROSSROAD

Proceeding straight ahead

If you want to proceed straight ahead at a minor crossroad, you should follow the same procedure as you would do for proceeding straight ahead at a major crossroad. Apply the three steps of the Mirrors (Look, Assess, Decide), Signal, Manoeuvre routine breaking down the manoeuvre itself into the three steps of the Position, Speed and Look. The only difference is that you should change down to third gear on the approach to the crossroad, and look right, left and right again before you emerge (see figure 36).

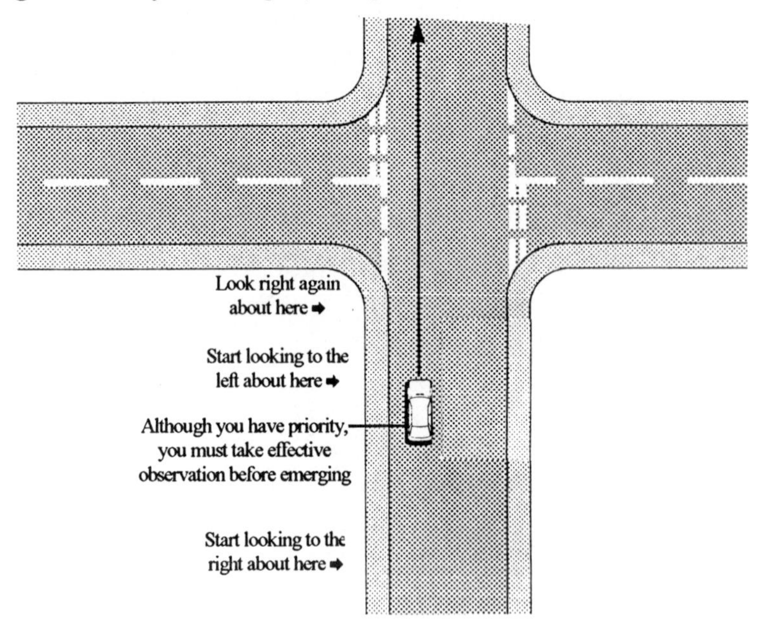
Look right again
about here
Start looking to the
left about here
Although you have priority,
you must take effective
observation before emerging
Start looking to the
right about here

Figure 36. Proceeding straight ahead at a minor crossroad.

The point of no return

If you reach the point of no return at the crossroads, and a vehicle or cyclist decides to pull out, third gear will give you more acceleration power to get out of trouble. Dropping down a gear will also help you regulate your speed on the approach to the crossroad.

THE UNCONTROLLED CROSSROAD

An uncontrolled crossroad is a road junction where there are no road markings or signs to indicate who has priority. This is potentially the most dangerous type of junction because traffic may emerge from any direction. Treat this type of junction as though you have give way lines against you. You **must** stop if there is any doubt that it is not safe to proceed. You will be surprised how many people just drive straight through without even slowing down, thinking that they have priority (see figure 37).

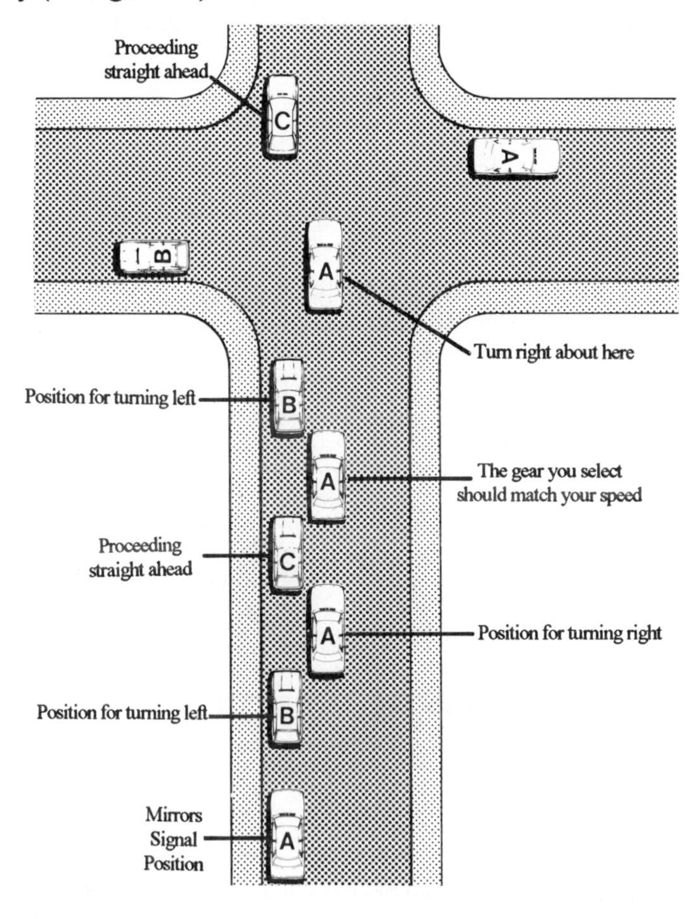

Figure 37. Dealing with an uncontrolled crossroad.

How to turn right

Turning right at crossroads can be very tricky because another driver may be coming towards you with the same intention of turning right. Again use the Mirrors (Look, Assess, Decide), Signal, Manoeuvre, Position, Speed and Look routine. You should check your mirrors in good time and signal right when it is safe to do so. Now position your car about 30 cm (1 foot) from the centre of the road. If you are turning right from a narrow road and you position your car well over to the left, this will allow other vehicles to turn into your road and your vision will be increased into your new road. You must now look well ahead and be prepared to give way to oncoming vehicles approaching from the opposite direction.

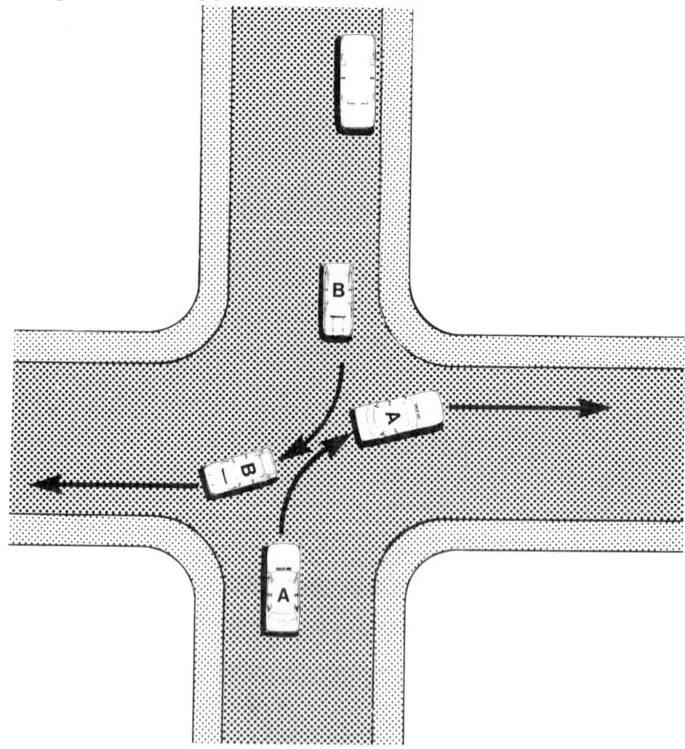

Figure 38. Turning nearside to nearside at a staggered junction.

Turning offside to offside or nearside to nearside

If another vehicle is coming towards you with the intention of turning right, you will have to make the decision of either turning offside to offside (driver's side), or nearside to nearside (passenger's side). The easiest way to get round this problem is to try to make eye-to-eye contact with the other driver. Endeavour to take the initiative over the other driver by placing your car in the position for turning right which suits you best. You should normally turn offside to offside if you are turning right at a large crossroad, and nearside to nearside if you are turning right at a small crossroad. In other words the larger the crossroad the more room you will have to turn behind the other vehicle. If you are turning at a staggered junction you should normally turn nearside to nearside, but do not rely on this happening. Always watch what the other driver is going to do and act accordingly (see figure 38).

Advantages and disadvantages

The advantage of turning nearside to nearside is that your vision is not restricted into the road into which you are turning. The advantage of turning offside to offside is that you can see traffic hidden behind the oncoming vehicle. The disadvantage of turning nearside to nearside is that you may find it difficult to see traffic hidden behind the oncoming vehicle. The disadvantage of turning offside to offside is that other vehicles can block your vision into your new road. Sometimes road markings will guide you in which way to turn, so act accordingly (see figure 39a & b).

Life saver

As soon as it is safe to turn right at the crossroad **always** check your mirrors in case someone is foolish enough to overtake you on the right-hand side. Avoid cutting the corner and give way to pedestrians who may be crossing the road. Remember do not attempt to turn right unless you can complete the movement safely.

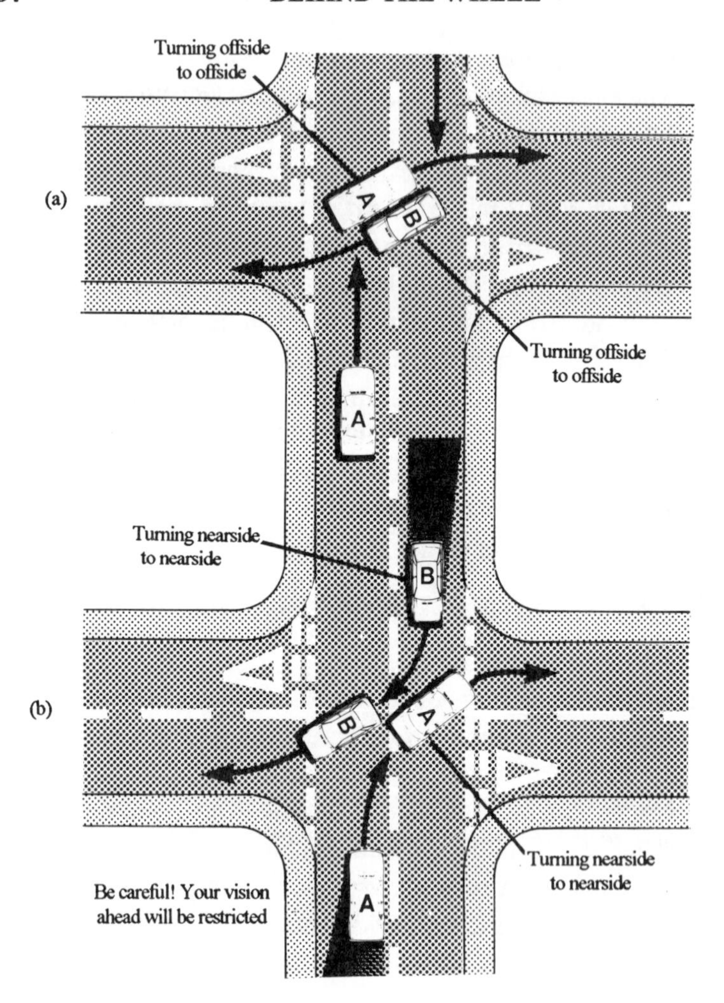

Figure 39a. Turning offside to offside at a major crossroad.
Figure 39b. Turning nearside to nearside at a major crossroad.

DEALING WITH CROSSROADS

QUESTIONS (refer to figures 35 - 39) (See page 246 for answers).

Q1. What is a crossroad?

A. A road which leads to a church.

B. A road which crosses the path of a Y junction.

C. A road which crosses the path of another road.

D. A road where there have been many accidents.

Q2. What very important point should you remember about all crossroads?

A. All crossroads are dangerous whether you have priority or not.

B. Only crossroads that have road markings are dangerous.

C. Only unmarked crossroads are dangerous.

D. They always have traffic lights.

Q3. Name three types of crossroad? Fill in the missing words.

1. **M**□□□□ crossroad.
2. **M**□□□□ crossroad.
3. **U**□□□□□□□□□□□ crossroad.

Q4. What is a major crossroad?

A. A junction that leads to a military barracks.

B. A junction with no centre line along the centre of the road.

C. A junction with a centre line along the centre of the road.

D. A junction with a fly over.

Q5. What does the centre line running along the middle of the road indicate?

A. That you do **not** have priority over the minor road.

B. That you have priority over the minor road.

C. That an uncontrolled crossroad lies ahead.

D. That you must never overtake.

Q6. What is a minor crossroad?

A. A junction where children can cross safely.

B. A junction with a centre line along the middle of the road.
C. A junction with no centre line along the middle of the road.
D. A junction without a fly over.

Q7. State two reasons why you should select third gear when approaching a minor crossroad with the intention of proceeding straight ahead? Fill in the missing words.
1. This helps you to **r**□□□□□□□ your **s**□□□□ on the approach.
2. You will have the **p**□□□□ to **a**□□□□□□□□□ out of any trouble.

Q8. Why should you take effective observation before proceeding straight ahead at a major crossroad?
A. In case you want to go faster to get through the crossroads.
B. You don't have to take effective observation if you have priority.
C. In case another vehicle or cyclist pulls out in front of you.
D. So that you don't have to stop if no traffic is coming.

Q9. What is an uncontrolled crossroad?
A. An uncontrolled crossroad is a junction with no road markings or signs to indicate who has priority.
B. A junction with road markings and signs to indicate who has priority.
C. A junction which is not manned by a policeman/traffic warden.
D. A junction with a pedestrian crossing.

Q10. Should you always stop your car at an uncontrolled crossroad?
A. Never.
B. Yes. In case another driver approaching from the opposite direction barges straight through.
C. No. You have priority at every uncontrolled crossroads.
D. No. Only if your view is obstructed and you cannot see if it is completely clear.

Q11. When would you give a slowing down arm signal whilst approaching an unmarked crossroad?
A. If you palm of your hand is sweaty.
B. If someone is following closely behind you and you intend to slow down or stop.
C. If there are no pedestrians or vehicles in the vicinity.
D. If your indicators are defective.

Q12. What disadvantage may you encounter if you turn offside to offside at a crossroad?
A. You may find it difficult to see approaching traffic.
B. Your vision into the side road may be restricted.
C. You may stall your car.
D. You may loose control of your car.

Q13. What disadvantage may you encounter if you turn nearside to nearside at a crossroad?
A. A pedestrian could walk into the path of your vehicle.
B. Your vision into the side road may be restricted.
C. You may find it difficult to see approaching traffic.
D. You may loose control of your car.

Q14. What gear should you select if you are turning right at an uncontrolled crossroad?
The **g**□□□ you choose should **m**□□□□ your **s**□□□□ and your **s**□□□□ should **m**□□□□ your **v**□□□□□□□□□.

SOME COMMON FAULTS COMMITTED BY LEARNERS: JUNCTIONS AND CROSSROADS

- Not using the Mirrors (Look, Assess, Decide), Signal, Manoeuvre routine.
- Not complying with a mandatory "Stop" sign/road marking.
- Not regulating speed correctly on the approach.
- Not taking effective observation before emerging.

- Not judging the speed and distance of other traffic and emerging when unsafe.
- Stopping with the front of the car past the kerbline of the junction when unsafe.
- Not positioning the car correctly before or after turning.
- Emerging from the junction in the wrong gear.
- Cutting the corner.
- Failing to give way to pedestrians who are crossing the road.
- Not taking effective observation when dealing with a minor or major crossroad.
- Not emerging from the junction when a suitable gap appears.
- Not anticipating the actions of other road users.
- Turning in front of closely approaching traffic when turning right.

Chapter 3

Lesson 7 - Reversing in a straight line

Before you can be taught how to reverse round a corner or turn your car round using forward and reverse gears, you must learn how to reverse in a straight line. Learning how to reverse in a straight line correctly will give you confidence and teach you skills which are necessary to successfully develop low speed control when driving backwards, and using the steering wheel in reverse. Many learner drivers wrongly imagine that in reverse the car travels the opposite way to that in which you turn the steering wheel. Reversing is a simple exercise to perform if you think logically and take your time.

Always remember that before you reverse, it must be legal, safe and convenient. You may release your seat belt for ease of movement and select reverse gear. Set the gas until you hear a steady or lively tone, slowly let the clutch up until the engine note changes, and "freeze" your left foot in that position. Look at your steering wheel and imagine it as a clock face, with the top of the wheel as 12 o'clock. You can modify the basic holding position by using your right hand only at the 12 o'clock position. Whilst you are reversing in a straight line you can place your left hand on the back of the passenger seat.

GETTING THE BEST VIEW

Imagine the car is parked on level ground at the left-hand side of the road. Turn well round in your seat and look out of the rear window (see figure 40). Draw an imaginary line down the centre of the window and through the car between the passenger and driver's seat.

You are sitting on one side of the imaginary line and your driving instructor is sitting on the other side. Keep looking backwards and remember to think logically. If you want your instructor's side of the car to go towards the kerb then steer towards your instructor. On the other hand, if you want to steer away from the kerb, then steer towards yourself. The secret is to keep looking out of the rear window. Do not look forward to see where the front of the car is going as this will only confuse you and you will lose your sense of direction.

Figure 40. Reversing in a straight line.

Carry out all round observations and give way to other road users because you will be travelling in the wrong direction. Providing it is clear, start to let the clutch come up a little more until the car begins to move backwards. If you feel you are moving too fast, simply push the clutch down a little to slow down. Continue to reverse, slipping the clutch as necessary to control your speed, but do not bring the clutch up too far or you will fly backwards out of control. Keep looking backwards, aiming your view high along the road using peripheral vision and do not stare at the kerb. A useful exercise is to steer towards the kerb (before 12 o'clock or towards your instructor), and watch the rear of your car move towards the kerb. Then steer away from the kerb (after 12 o'clock or away from your instructor) and watch the rear of the car move away from the kerb.

A very important point to remember is that when the car is driven forward you can see your car turning with the steering. However, whilst reversing, you have to wait for the steering to take effect. A second essential point when attempting this manoeuvre, is that you should always remember which way your front wheels are pointing. Do you remember that in the previous lessons you were taught the Preparation, Observation, Move routine before moving off? You can use the same routine when your instructor teaches you how to reverse in a straight line.

REVERSING IN A STRAIGHT LINE

*QUESTIONS (refer to figure 40)**(See page 246 for answers).*

Q1. What is the general rule regarding reversing?

A. There are no general rules regarding reversing.

B. You must make sure no pedestrians are standing near the car.

C. You must make sure no emergency vehicles are behind you.

D. You must make sure that there is no-one behind you.

Q2. Why should you be mindful of children before reversing?

A. In case a child kicks a ball and smashes the rear window.

B. Children are hard to see.

C. If you do not look out the rear window the police will charge you for dangerous driving.

D. In case some distraction is nearby.

Q3. Which way should you be looking when you are driving backwards?

A. You look out of the rear window.

B. You should look at the interior mirror.

C. You should look at the interior and outside mirrors.

D. You should over either shoulder.

Q4. Which routine should you carry out before you reverse in a straight line? Fill in the missing words.
The **P**□□□□□□□□□□, **O**□□□□□□□□□□, **M**□□□ routine.

Q5. Which way should you steer if you want the rear of your car to go towards the kerb, if you are driving backwards on the left-hand side of the road?
A. The steering wheel will turn itself to go towards the kerb.
B. Pull your right hand down towards the kerb.
C. Pull both hands towards the kerb.
D. Pull your left hand down towards the kerb.

Q6. What may happen if you do **not** adopt a comfortable seating position before carrying out the manoeuvre?
A. The seatbelt may lock and it could strangle you.
B. You will find the exercise easy to perform.
C. You may develop backache.
D. You will find the exercise difficult to perform.

Lesson 8 - Turning round using forward and reverse gears

The idea of this manoeuvre is to turn your car round to face the opposite direction using forward and reverse gears, under control and with due regard for other road users. The reason for this manoeuvre is to show the examiner that you can use and co-ordinate all the major controls of the car within a limited space (i.e. the space between the two kerb stones). When you are sitting your driving test it is essential that you do not touch the kerb stones during this manoeuvre. This is a helpful exercise if there are no side roads for your car to reverse into. Always remember that it is an offence to reverse your car for longer than is necessary.

This manoeuvre is commonly known as a 3-point turn. This is wrong. In the test, the examiner may ask you to turn your car round and face it in the opposite direction by means of forward and reverse gears. He will expect the car to be turned round reasonably accurately, but not necessarily in 3 distinct manoeuvres. You are allowed to take 5, possibly 7 turns. This is dictated by the width of the road, and the overall length of your car.

The priority in this exercise is on safety and control. If the examiner thinks that the road is wide enough to be done in three movements then he would expect it to be done in three movements. Before commencing the turn in the road you must ask yourself three things:

- Is it legal?
- Is it safe?
- Is it convenient?

Never attempt to do the exercise in a one way street or any place where it would inconvenience other drivers or pedestrians. You must make sure you keep away from roadside furniture such as lamp-posts and pillar boxes as these might distract you.

Let us see how you should carry out this manoeuvre during your driving test (see figure 41). You must feel as comfortable as possible in your seat and remove your seatbelt if you wish. The best way to remember how to do this exercise is to split the manoeuvre into three stages. Stage one is where the manoeuvre starts. The driving examiner is particularly looking for observation and control.

OBSERVATION AND CONTROL

Before and during the manoeuvre you must carry out both the static and moving observations. You must not move off unless it is completely **safe** to do so and you must be prepared to stop and give way to any other drivers or pedestrians when the car is in motion. To control your car, you must move it slowly by co-ordinating your clutch, accelerator, and steering together. Before moving off at all three stages, remember the following code:

- **PREPARATION**
- **OBSERVATION**
- **MOVE**

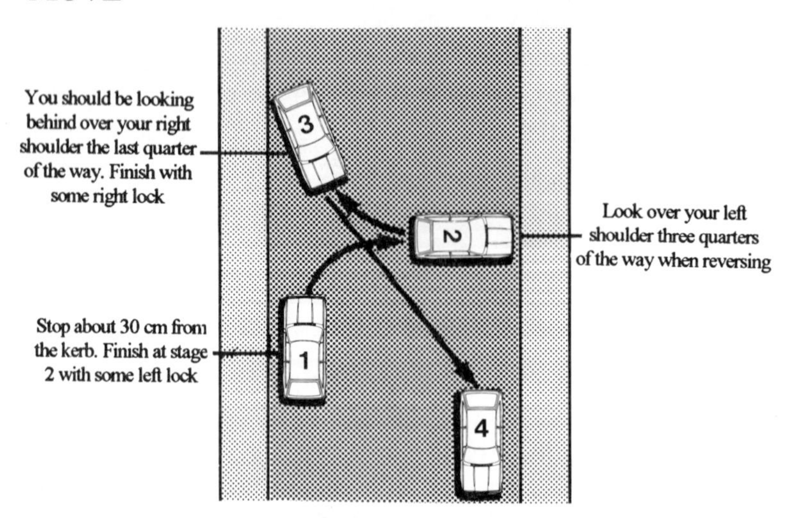

Figure 41. Turning round using forward and reverse gears.

Stage 1- *Preparation*

Firstly, you must look at the "camber" of the road to judge how much power your car will need for the manoeuvre. In most roads, because of drainage, the highest point is in the centre (or "crown"). The crown slopes at either side right to the gutters and the degree of slope from the crown to the gutter is known as the camber. Some cambers are quite steep and other cambers are so small that for all intents and purposes you may as well be on level ground. Clearly, the steeper the camber you are on, the more gas you will require to keep good control of your car. You must:

- Select first gear.
- Set the gas, until you hear a steady or lively tone.
- Slowly let the clutch out until the engine note changes and keep the feet still. Release the parking brake.

Observations and Move

Carry out all round observations. Providing the road is clear, begin to move the car forward slowly keeping good control of the clutch. Turn the steering wheel briskly to the right and aim to get your car at a right angle across the road. As the car crosses the crown (middle) of the road, push the clutch down as fast as possible and gently brake and stop the car about 30 cm (1 foot) from the kerb. Do not strike the kerb otherwise you may either cause damage to your tyres or mount the kerb. You should try to turn the steering wheel at least once to the left, so that by the time your car stops, the wheels are straight ahead or possibly with a bit of a left lock on. Apply the parking brake.

You are now at stage 2. Remember the rule: ***"Keep the feet slow and move the hands fast".***

Stage 2 - *Preparation*

- Select reverse gear.
- Set the gas until you hear a steady or lively tone.

- Slowly release the clutch until the engine note changes and keep the feet still. Release the parking brake.

Observations and Move

Carry out all round observations and if it is safe, you will have to do a slight hill start because of the camber of the road. Look over your left shoulder because that is the direction in which the car is going. Slowly let the clutch out and turn the steering wheel briskly to the left. Again, remember to move your hands fast and keep your feet slow. As the car comes across the camber of the road, push the clutch down as fast as possible, look over your right shoulder and turn the steering wheel back to the right and gently brake to a stop. Therefore when the car stops about 30 cm (1 foot) from the kerb, it will be at an angle with the front wheels again facing slightly to the right. Apply the parking brake. You are now at stage 3.

Stage 3 - *Preparation*

- Select first gear. Again because of the camber, a slight hill start will have to be carried out.
- Slowly let the clutch out until the engine note changes - feet still. Release the parking brake.

Observations and Move

Carry out all round observations and if it safe, move off under full control and stop at the other side of the road - unless the examiner tells you to proceed. Don't forget to put on your seatbelt and look over your right shoulder to check the blind spot **before** moving away from the side of the road.

TO SUM UP

The secret of this manoeuvre is to maintain low-speed control. Don't panic if you see another vehicle approaching although you must give priority to other vehicles. If another vehicle is in the distance you should carry on but take your time and do not rush the exercise otherwise you may lose control of your car. This is a difficult exercise to perform and may take time before being executed competently.

TURNING ROUND USING FORWARD AND REVERSE GEARS
QUESTIONS (refer to figure 41)(See page 246 for answers).

Q1. When can the turn in the road manoeuvre prove useful?
A. If you are forced to reverse your car for more than 300 metres.
B. If the kerb is more than 30 cm (1 foot) high.
C. When there are no side roads for you to reverse into.
D. If the kerb is more than 90 cm (3 feet) wide.

Q2. Why is it important to check the camber of the road before commencing the turn in the road exercise?
A. To see how much power your car will need for the exercise.
B. To see if there is any loose gravel.
C. To check that no debris is lying in the gutter.
D. None of these.

Q3. What two types of observations should you carry out when performing this manoeuvre? Fill in the missing words.
1. **S**□□□□□ observations.
2. **M**□□□□□ observations.

Q4. In which direction should you be looking when you are reversing backwards?
A. Whichever is the most comfortable.
B. Observe out of the front window.
C. Use all your mirrors to reverse backwards.
D. Observe out of the back window.

Q5. What are the advantages of keeping your "feet slow" and moving your "hands fast"?
A. You will have total control of your car.
B. To keep your feet and hands warm if it is cold.

C. So that you can carry out the manoeuvre as fast as possible.
D. So that you don't stall the car.

Q6. What procedure should you adopt before commencing this exercise and during all three stages of the manoeuvre? Fill in the missing words.
The **P**□□□□□□□□□, **O**□□□□□□□□□□, **M**□□□ routine.

Q7. Can you release your seatbelt before carrying out the manoeuvre?
A. Yes. You may do so only when it is dark.
B. No. It is illegal.
C. Yes. At any stage.
D. Only if you have a certificate of exemption.

SOME COMMON FAULTS COMMITTED BY LEARNERS: TURNING ROUND USING FORWARD AND REVERSE GEARS

- Not co-ordinating the accelerator, footbrake, clutch or parking brake with steering.
- Stalling the engine due to poor co-ordination.
- Striking the kerb or mounting the pavement.
- Not observing properly before and during the manoeuvre.
- Turning the steering wheel too slowly and not achieving reasonable accuracy.
- Not acting properly when other road users arrive.
- Turning the car round using too many movements.
- Turning the steering wheel the wrong way.
- Failing to release the parking brake.
- Stopping needlessly.
- Not giving way to other vehicles and pedestrians.

Lesson 9 - Reversing to the left

After you have learned how to turn your car round using forward and reverse gears, your instructor will teach you how to reverse round a corner from a main road into a side road. This must be carried out under control with due regard for other road users. Before you can reverse round the corner you must ask yourself three things:

- Is it safe?
- Is it legal?
- Is it convenient?

Never attempt to do this exercise in either a one way street or from a side road into a main road or at a crossroads because you will only inconvenience other drivers and pedestrians. During your driving test the examiner may stop you before a corner and say, *"I would like you to reverse into this road on the left. Drive past it, stop, then back in and continue to drive in reverse gear for some distance, keeping reasonably close to the kerb."* or words to that effect.

You are stopped before the corner for 3 reasons:

- To decide which type of corner it is. There are 2 different types:
1. A sharp corner which we call a right angled or club corner.
2. A big round sweeping curve, which we call a 'bell-mouth' corner. (These are handled differently for two reasons with regard to accuracy and this will be covered later).
- To ensure that when you drive forward you can look into the side road to make sure it is clear of any obstructions such as parked vehicles and children playing on the road.
- You are given the chance to position the car properly for doing the reverse. You should position the car about 60 cm (2 feet) from the kerb and approximately 1½ car lengths past the corner parallel with the kerb.

When you are sitting your driving test the driving examiner will pay particular attention to the control and observations displayed by you before and throughout the manoeuvre. Let us look at how we should handle the car during the exercise.

CONTROL

You must co-ordinate the use of the foot and hand controls so that you move the car smoothly and accurately. Many learners fail their driving test due to lack of control, because they "rushed" round the corner when they saw another vehicle coming. Do not put yourself under pressure. All you have to do is simply **stop** and give way.

OBSERVATIONS

There are certain observations you must carry out before and during the reverse. Basically the observations are divided into two parts: the static observation and the moving observation. Before reversing the car you must ensure that all-round observations are carried out. You must give way to any other road users including pedestrians. Remember that you are the one who is reversing against the flow of traffic. Whilst the car is on the move, you should be continually on the look out for other vehicles arriving, pedestrians crossing or any other form of danger which may require you to stop. If either another vehicle or pedestrian arrives and you are going to cause any inconvenience to them, you must **STOP!** You are causing inconvenience to everybody else and not the other way around. As soon as the examiner gives you the instruction to reverse to the left, the following step-by-step sequence of events should take place. This manoeuvre is carried out in three easy stages.

Stage 1 (see figure 42).

Assume that the examiner has stopped you on the left-hand side of the road prior to the junction into which you are going to reverse. Prepare the car for moving off, carry out all the normal observation procedures and move off when it is safe to do so. Drive past the junction, checking to confirm that there are no parked vehicles. Signal if necessary halfway across the junction to avoid confusion. If you signal too early another driver may think that you may be turning into the side road. Remember to use the Mirrors (Look, Assess, Decide), Signal, Manoeuvre routine before stopping.

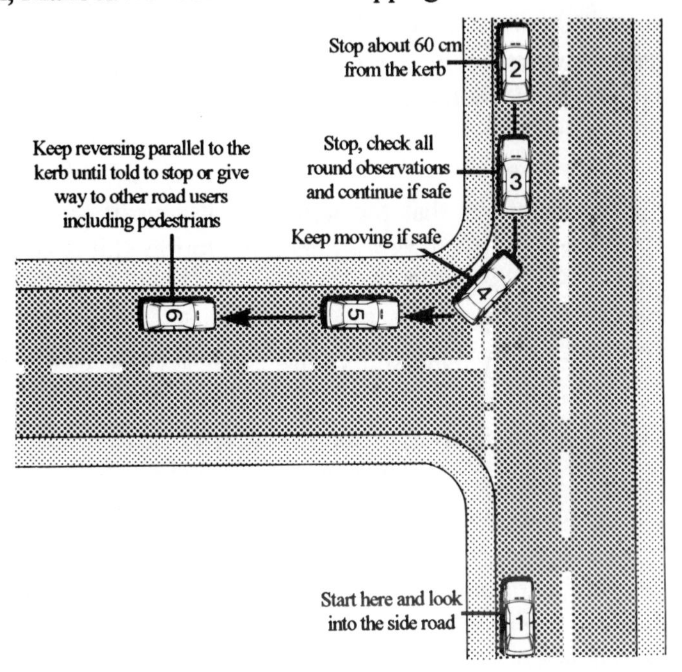

Figure 42. Reversing to the left.

Stage 2

Stop the car approximately one and a half car lengths beyond the junction and position the car parallel to the kerb approximately 60 cm (2 feet) away. If you position the car too close to the kerb you will find it difficult to negotiate the corner as the camber could drag in the wheels. Apply the parking brake and select neutral. Release your seat belt if desired, turn yourself well round in the seat and look over your left shoulder. Place your hands on the steering wheel at the quarter to three or ten to two position.

Remember that during the straight reverse, you may modify the basic holding position when reversing in a straight line, by holding the wheel with your right hand firmly around the 12 o'clock position (and rest your left hand on the passenger seat). Prepare the car for moving off and carry out all round observations. If safe, set the gas to a steady or lively tone and reverse slowly under full control, slipping the clutch as necessary. Always keep a look out and be prepared to stop and give way to any other road users.

Stage 3

As soon as you can see that the kerb has disappeared in the rear window, look forward to check for oncoming traffic. If it is safe, keep reversing (look over your left shoulder out the back of the car) and start to follow the kerb round. Remember to check over your right shoulder to observe any blind spots. This is because the front of your car will swing out to the centre of the road which may result in an accident. Imagine the position of the rear nearside wheel, just behind the back seat, to the edge of the kerb, and keep that wheel parallel to the kerb. You must turn the steering wheel sufficiently to get you round the corner. The sharper the corner, the more you will have to turn to get your car round. When your car is nearly parallel to the kerb, steer away from the kerb, and endeavour to keep your car about the same distance from the kerb when you started and parallel to it.

Remember, if you initially turned the steering wheel quickly to get round the corner, you will have to steer quickly to straighten up. *"Keep the feet slow and move the hands fast"*. Continue to reverse in a straight line for some distance away from the junction (conditions permitting) and adjust the steering if necessary but don't speed up. Then gently brake to a stop. You should finish adjacent to the kerb but not too close as you may cause your car to pick up debris or even strike the kerb. Apply the parking brake and select neutral. If any vehicle drives into your path, either simply stop and give way, or if you happen to be blocking the junction, stop and then drive forward far enough to clear the junction. **Always** act sensibly on what you see.

TO SUM UP

Once you have gained more experience you can practice reversing on up and downhill gradients. Remember to look out of the back window as much as possible otherwise you will lose your sense of direction. You need only look forward to watch out for other road users. Avoid looking at the front of your car whilst reversing. If you look out of the back of your car the front of your car will automatically follow you round. Would you look backwards to see where the back of your car is, if you were driving forwards turning left from a main road into a side road?

Always remember to check in front of you occasionally and be prepared to stop and give way to other road users. After completing the reverse, you may be "keyed-up". It is at this point that many learners make mistakes. You must remember to fasten your seatbelt, check your mirrors, and look over your right shoulder to check your blind spot, before moving off again. With a "club corner" as compared to a "bell-mouth", you will have to turn the steering wheel down towards the kerb more quickly because of the tightness of the corner. Therefore it is clear that you must turn your steering wheel in the opposite direction until you have straightened your front wheels. This enables you to reverse accurately and parallel to the kerb. Remember the examiner is only interested in your overall control and observations throughout the manoeuvre.

REVERSING TO THE LEFT

QUESTIONS (refer to figure 42)(See page 246 for answers).

Q1. Give three reasons why the driving examiner will ask you to stop before a corner? Fill in the missing words.

1. To decide which **t**□□□ of corner it is.

2. To ensure that when you drive **f**□□□□□□ you can look into the side road to make sure it is **c**□□□□ of any **o**□□□□□□□□□□.

3. To give you the chance to **p**□□□□□□□ your car properly for doing the **r**□□□□□□.

Q2. What specific points will the examiner be looking for throughout the reversing exercise? Fill in the missing words.
The **c**□□□□□□, **o**□□□□□□□□□□ and **a**□□□□□□□ displayed by you.

Q3. What are the two types of observations you should carry out when performing the reverse exercise?
1. The **s**□□□□□ observations.
2. The **m**□□□□□ observations.

Q4. What routine should you use before reversing?
The **P**□□□□□□□□□□, **O**□□□□□□□□□□, **M**□□□ routine.

Q5. Why is it important to keep your car under low-speed control whilst reversing?
A. You may overheat the engine.
B. You may knock a pedestrian down.
C. You may stall the car.
D. You may lose control of your car.

Q6. What should you look out for when your car is reversing?
A. Cyclists.
B. Your rear window does not steam up.
C. Disabled people crossing.
D. Other vehicles arriving or any other danger.

Q7. What should you do if you see another vehicle or pedestrian?
A. Carry on because you have priority.
B. You must stop.
C. Beep your horn to warn them of your presence.
D. Speed through your manoeuvre.

Q8. Why **must** you look forward just before reversing around a corner?
A. The front of your car may strike a pedestrian standing in the road.
B. The front of your car will swing inwards.

C. The front of your car will swing out.
D. The front of your car may mount the kerb.

Q9. How do you know how much steering to apply to enable you to negotiate the corner to achieve reasonable accuracy?
A. The sharper the corner the more you will have to turn.
B. Turn the steering wheel a full 2 turns.
C. Turn the steering wheel a full 2 ½ turns.
D. Turn the steering wheel about 3 turns.

Q10. Why should you keep looking out of the back window as much as possible whilst reversing?
A. If it is raining, a passing motorist may spray your rear window.
B. You may knock a pedestrian down standing behind your car.
C. Otherwise you will lose your sense of direction.
D. It is the most comfortable and convenient position.

Q11. Why should you always remember to check in front of you occasionally whilst reversing?
A. To look out for emergency vehicles.
B. To look out for stray animals.
C. A drunken pedestrian may have staggered into the path of the car.
D. To see any approaching traffic and give way where necessary.

Q12. What must you remember to do before moving off after completing the reverse? Fill in the missing words.
1. Put on your **s**□□□□□□□.
2. Check your **m**□□□□□□ and look over your **r**□□□□ shoulder to check your **b**□□□□ **s**□□□.

Q13. How may you keep low-speed control whilst reversing?
A. Apply more acceleration.
B. Slip the clutch where necessary.
C. Always apply the footbrake.
D. Always alternate between the accelerator and clutch.

Lesson 10 - Reversing to the right

An examiner may ask you to reverse to the right during your driving test if you are driving a van or a vehicle with limited nearside vision. He would most certainly ask you to do this manoeuvre if you were driving a close-sided vehicle for example. It is, of course, much easier to reverse round a right-hand corner than a left-hand corner, because the kerb can be seen all the way round, and it is much easier to judge the distance from the kerb. Like the left-hand reverse, this exercise is split into three stages. The examiner will stop you on the left-hand side of the road a short distance before the turning. He has stopped you for the same reasons as in the reverse to the left.

The examiner will then say to you, *"I would like you to reverse into that road on the right. Continue driving on the left until you have passed it then move across to the right and stop. Reverse and continue to drive in reverse gear well down the side road, keeping reasonably close to the right-hand kerb"*. Let us look at the step-by-step sequences of events that should occur at the different stages of the manoeuvre.

Stage 1

Prepare your car for moving off. Carry out all round observations and if it is safe to proceed, move forward and carry out the Mirrors, (Look, Assess, Decide), Signal, Manoeuvre routine and position your car just left of the centre of the road. You must look into the side road and judge the type of corner, for the same reasons as the reverse to the left. Indicate if necessary half way across the junction into which you are going to reverse.

When you are past the junction move into a position approximately 2 car lengths from the corner, about 60 cm (2 feet) parallel from the kerb. Be careful, because you have moved to the wrong side of the road. If you move over too early you will endanger traffic emerging from the side road (see figure 43).

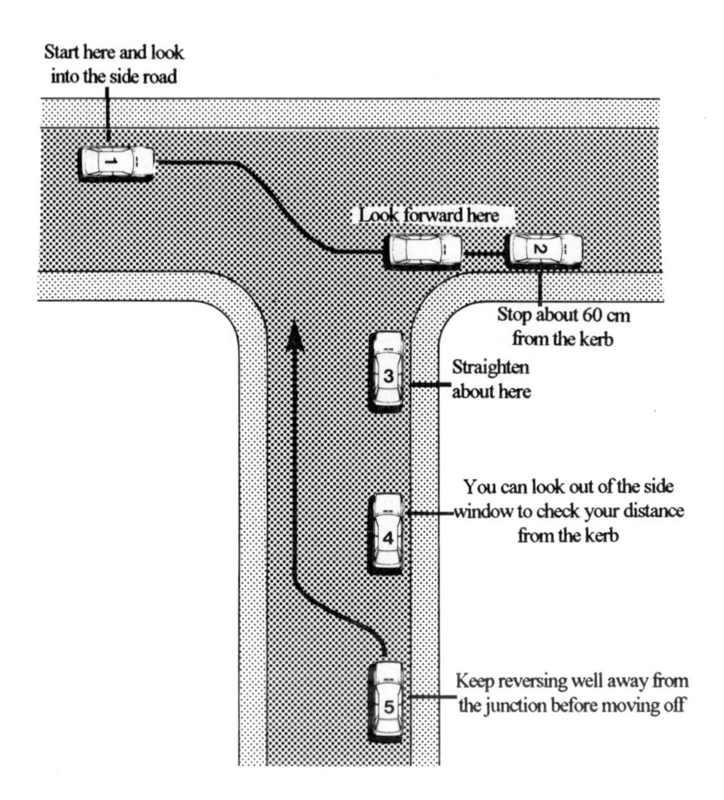

Figure 43. Reversing to the right.

Stage 2

When you are in the correct position, apply the parking brake and select neutral. Release the seatbelt for ease of movement. You may wind your window down to listen out for other traffic. Select reverse gear and keep your feet perfectly still. Turn yourself well round in the seat and carry out all round observations. Remember you must keep a constant look out for the presence of other vehicles and pedestrians. If anybody arrives who may be an inconvenience, you must stop and give way. If it is safe, set the gas to a steady or lively tone and release the parking brake. Look over your left shoulder out of the rear window.

If it is safe, reverse slowly under full control, slipping the clutch as necessary. Occasionally look forward and check for oncoming traffic. As soon as you reach the point where you want to turn, check ahead because when you start to steer, the front of your car will swing out. At this point you should also check over your right shoulder and look at the road into which you are going to reverse. As soon as it is safe (make a final check over your left shoulder or nearside mirror) keep looking over your right shoulder and continue reversing slowly, using clutch control and follow the kerb around. As the car becomes almost parallel again, look over your left shoulder to look out of the rear window, and straighten up the wheels.

Remember, the sharper the corner you have reversed round, the faster you will have to turn the steering wheel to straighten up (but don't increase speed). If you don't straighten up the front wheels quickly enough you will strike the kerb.

Stage 3

Continue to reverse (keep looking out of the rear window) in a straight line keeping reasonably close to the kerb, for at least 4-5 car lengths (conditions permitting) from the junction and then gently brake to a stop. Apply the parking brake and select neutral. The reason you reverse so far back is so that you will be well away from the junction, and in a safer position before you move off again. Before you move off, don't forget to check over your left shoulder and nearside mirror, as the blind spot on this occasion is on the left-hand side. When you drive off, move over to the correct side of the road before you get to the junction.

It is important to remember that looking over the right shoulder only whilst reversing would be dangerous because the area behind and to the left of your car would remain unchecked. You must keep a constant look out in all directions for other vehicles and pedestrians.

REVERSING TO THE RIGHT

QUESTIONS (refer to figure 43) (See page 246 for answers).

Q1. Why should you look into the side road before reversing around the corner?

A. To ensure it is clear of any obstruction.

B. To check the height of the kerb.

C. To check that the corner is not too sharp.

D. To ensure that you don't mount the kerb.

Q2. Give 3 places where you should avoid carrying out this exercise? Fill in the missing words.

1. In a **o**□□ **w**□□ **s**□□□□□.
2. From a **s**□□□ road into a **m**□□□ **r**□□□.
3. At a **c**□□□□□□□□□.

Q3. Why is it important to check the area to the left-hand side of your car when reversing to the right around a corner?

A. The area to the right of your car would remain "blind".

B. To ensure that you don't reverse into any puddles.

C. In case you hit a pedestrian standing on the road.

D. The area to the left of your car would remain "blind".

Q4. What observations should you carry out before moving off after completing the reverse to the right?

A. Check your blind spot.

B. Check your mirrors and then look over your right shoulder.

C. Check your mirrors and then over your left shoulder.

D. Check that you have done up your seat belt.

Q5. Why should you keep reversing for at least five car lengths from the junction before stopping?

A. So that you can move off quickly.

B. You will be able to check your blind spot much easier.

C. In case you stall your car.

D. You will finish the manoeuvre well away from the junction.

Q6. Approximately what position should you adopt before reversing round the corner?
A. 2 car lengths from the corner, about 60 cm (2 feet) from the kerb.
B. 3 car lengths from the corner, about 90 cm (3 feet) from the kerb.
C. 6 car lengths from the corner, about 60 cm (2 feet) from the kerb.
D. A car length from the corner, about 30 cm (1 foot) from the kerb.

Q7. What may happen prior to reversing if you move over to the wrong side of the road too early?
A. You may hit a cyclist riding on the road.
B. You may endanger traffic emerging from the side road.
C. You may miss your turning.
D. You may take your turning too fast.

SOME COMMON FAULTS COMMITTED BY LEARNERS: REVERSING AROUND A CORNER

- Failing to check into the side road when driving past the corner.
- Not adopting the correct position prior to reversing.
- Reversing too fast. Stalling the engine.
- Failing to keep full control of the clutch.
- Not observing properly before and during the manoeuvre.
- Not giving way to other vehicles and pedestrians.
- Striking the kerb or mounting the pavement.
- Not acting properly when other road users arrive.
- Reversing around the corner too widely or not correcting in time.
- Turning the steering wheel too early and stopping needlessly.

Lesson 11 - Reverse parking between two vehicles

Reverse parking is a manoeuvre many drivers cannot perform properly - they commonly hit the kerb and sometimes another vehicle's bumper. The reason for this is normally because the driver tries to park his car either too quickly or in far too small a space. It is a fairly simple manoeuvre to perform providing you take your time and attempt to park your car in a space at least 1½ times the length of your own vehicle. Parking between two vehicles should be practiced many times until you can do it competently (see figure 44).

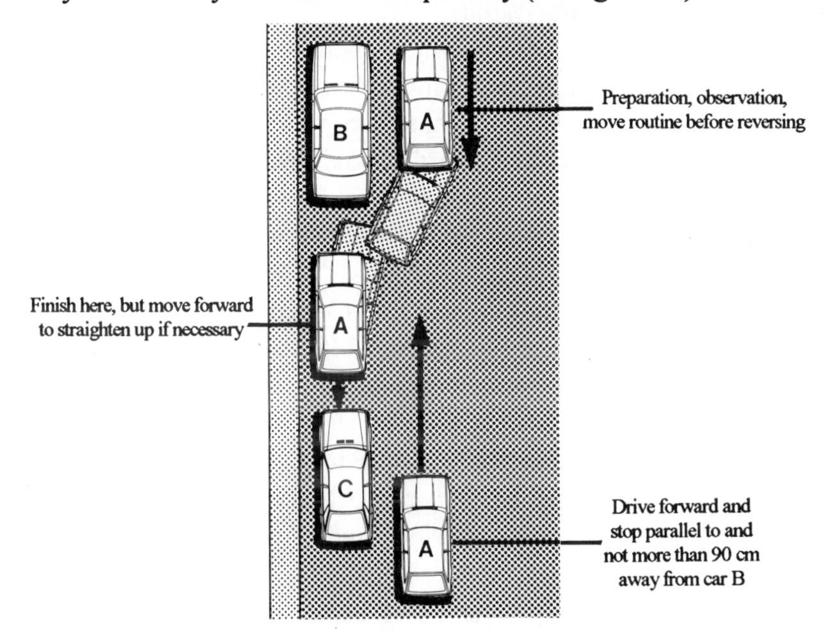
B
A
Preparation, observation, move routine before reversing
Finish here, but move forward to straighten up if necessary
A
C
A
Drive forward and stop parallel to and not more than 90 cm away from car B

Figure 44. Reverse parking between two vehicles.

Firstly, find a quiet road with 2 vehicles parked approximately 2 car lengths apart. Remember, before you attempt any manoeuvre it must be safe, legal and convenient. With practice you will be able to reduce the distance between the two vehicles to 1½ lengths. To successfully accomplish this manoeuvre, drive forward and position your car level or slightly ahead of the first vehicle and parallel to it. Make sure you are approximately 90 cm (3 feet) away from the side of this vehicle.

Release your seat belt for ease of movement if you wish, and carry out the Preparation, Observation, Move routine (see lessons 7-10). Make sure that you are turned well round in your seat and reverse back slowly, turning your steering wheel slightly to the left. You should attempt to place the left part (driver's side) of your rear window at the front nearside (passenger's side) headlight of the rear parked vehicle. Remember that the front of your car will swing out to the centre of the road during the manoeuvre and therefore be dangerous to any passing traffic.

You should check over your right shoulder to observe any blind spots. If you are causing any inconvenience to other road users whilst reversing, pause until it is safe to continue. When the front of your car has cleared the rear of the forward parked vehicle, turn the steering wheel quickly to the right. Continue reversing and when your car is nearly straight, steer left to straighten the front wheels.

REVERSE PARKING BETWEEN TWO VEHICLES

QUESTIONS (refer to figure 44) (See page 246 for answers).

Q1. What is the object of reverse parking?

A. Park the car.

B. Park on the left-hand kerb and parallel to it.

C. Park as quickly as possible with good observations.

D. Park as close as possible to the left-hand kerb and parallel to it.

Q2. When should you **not** reverse park between two parked vehicles?

A. If it would cause an obstruction to any person or vehicle.

B. If there is a school in the vicinity.

C. After 11.30 pm (23.30 hrs.).

D. After 12.00 pm (midnight).

Q3. How close should you park to another vehicle when parked parallel to the kerb?

A. About 2 metres between you and any vehicle in front or behind.
B. About 1 metre between you and any vehicle in front or behind.
C. About 30 cm between you and any vehicle in front or behind.
D. About 60 cm between you and any vehicle in front or behind.

Q4. What routine would you use before commencing the exercise? Fill in the missing words.
The **P**□□□□□□□□□, **O**□□□□□□□□□□, **M**□□□ routine.

Q5. What position approximately should you adopt before parking between two vehicles?
A. 30 cm (1 ft) from the first vehicle and about half way along it.
B. 60 cm (2 ft) from the first vehicle and about 1 car length in front.
C. 90 cm (3 ft) from the first vehicle and about half way along it.
D. 120 cm (4 ft) from the first vehicle and about half way along it.

Q6. What part of your car should you line up with the front nearside headlight of the rear parked vehicle to achieve reasonable accuracy?
A. The nearside (passenger's side) rear window in line with the nearside headlight of the rear parked vehicle.
B. The offside (driver's side) rear window in line with the nearside headlight of the rear parked vehicle.
C. The left-hand mirror in line with the nearside headlight of the rear parked vehicle.
D. The interior mirror in line with the nearside headlight of the rear parked vehicle.

Q7. Are you permitted to reverse your car a very short distance between two parked cars in a one way street?
A. Yes. But only after 6 pm (18.00 hrs.).
B. Yes. But only after 7 pm (19.00 hrs.).
C. Yes. But you must attempt the manoeuvre in less than 60 seconds.
D. No. One way means one way and one way only.

Chapter 4

Lesson 12 - Judging speed, making progress and general road positioning

EXERCISING PROPER CARE IN THE USE OF SPEED

It is a popular misconception that if a learner on a driving test has failed because of speeding, the speed limit has been broken. Of course this is possible, but it could also be that during the driving test, in the examiner's opinion, the learner was driving too fast for the conditions at the time. A possible example might be the learner passing a school at 30 mph with children running riot on the pavement. The examiner may fail him because of this - a more appropriate speed may be 20 or possibly 10 mph. You must always build up a judgement of what is **safe**, not what is legal.

A SAFE SPEED

Speed is far and away the most common cause of **death** on the roads. A safe speed is one at which the driver can stop under full control in a safe position on the road, well within the distance known to be clear. Different types of weather conditions, the state of the road and any hazards on the road will affect the speed of your car. You should slow down and make sure you can stop safely, well within the distance you can see to be clear. If you are travelling on any roads outside built-up areas it does not mean you can go as fast as you wish. You must obey the speed limits for the roads you are travelling on and the rules laid down in the Highway Code. Never accelerate into any hazard and be prepared to select a lower gear as the situation demands.

THE OVERALL STOPPING DISTANCE

The overall stopping distance at 30 mph is approximately 23 metres (75 feet). On a wet slippery road, it is **double** that distance. Imagine you are driving your car along a quiet road at 30 mph in good conditions and all of a sudden a child runs out in front of you. By the time your brain acknowledges this information and you react by braking to a stop, you would have travelled a distance of approximately 23 metres (75 feet). Remember that when you are driving, your car will travel 1½ times its speed in one second (see figure 45). On a dry road, a good car with good brakes and tyres will stop in the distances shown. Remember these are shortest stopping distances which will increase greatly with wet and slippery roads, poor brakes, tyres and tired drivers.

mph	THINKING DISTANCE		BRAKING DISTANCE		OVERALL STOPPING DISTANCE	
	m	*ft*	*m*	*ft*	*m*	*ft*
20	6	20	6	20	12	40
30	9	30	14	45	23	75
40	12	40	24	80	36	120
50	15	50	38	125	53	175
60	18	60	55	180	73	240
70	21	70	75	245	96	315

Figure 45. Shortest stopping distances.

KEEP YOUR DISTANCE

On the open road and in good conditions, always keep a safe distance from the vehicle in front. Either a distance of one metre for each mile per hour of your speed or a two second time gap in case the driver ahead brakes suddenly. This will also leave space for an overtaking vehicle to pull in. On wet or icy roads the gap should be at least doubled. Drop back if an overtaking vehicle pulls into the gap in front of you (see figure 46).

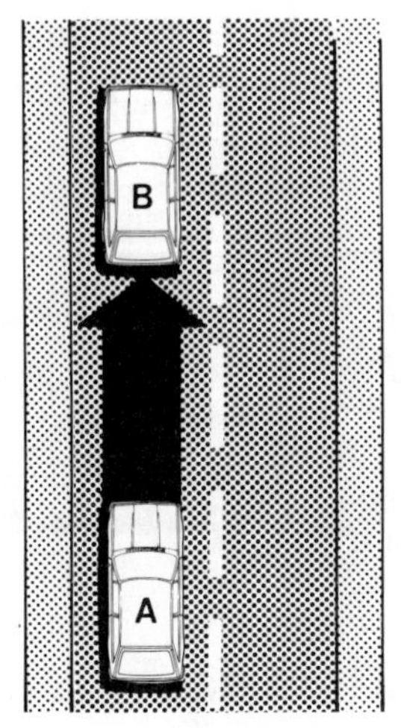

Figure 46. Keeping your distance.

THE TWO-SECOND RULE

Imagine you are following a vehicle and it has just passed a roadside feature such as a lamp-post in the pavement. If you reach the lamp-post before being able to repeat slowly, ***"one second, two seconds"***, then you are driving too close to the vehicle in front.

PEDESTRIANS

Take account of pedestrians and animals and be prepared to slow down or possibly stop if they run out in front of you without any warning. Elderly people, who are less alert, need more time to cross the road so give them plenty of time. **Never** put them under pressure to cross the road quickly or leave them stranded in the middle of the road. Children are unpredictable and they rely on **you** for their safety (see figure 47).

HAZARDS

Always look well ahead and be ready to slow down and change down gears to deal with any hazards that you may come across. Never drive so fast that you cannot stop in the distance that you can see to be clear ahead of you. Do not be tempted to keep up with other drivers travelling faster. Exercising proper care in the use of speed will get you there even if it means arriving late. It is better to arrive late for an appointment than never arriving at all.

Figure 47. You must exercise proper care in the use of speed.

THE MACHO DRIVER

The problem with many young male drivers is that they feel under pressure from their friends and their culture in general to be aggressive and macho when driving. Such ideas are reinforced by computer games which encourage young boys to overtake at great speeds and generally risk their lives for high scores. This behaviour is not conducive to sensible driving when they come to face life on the real roads. When they "die" playing the computer games they only lose one "life"; on the real roads they only have one life. Be wise with speed, any fool can drive fast enough to be dangerous.

JUDGING SPEED

QUESTIONS (refer to figures 45 - 47)(see page 246-247 for answers).

Q1. What is the speed limit in a built-up area with street lights?
A. 50 mph.
B. 40 mph.
C. 20 mph.
D. 30 mph.

Q2. How would you define a dangerous speed?
A. Passing an ice cream van at 30 mph.
B. A speed over 70 mph.
C. A speed which is dangerous for the conditions.
D. A speed over 50 mph.

Q3. State two reasons why it is important to obey speed limits? Complete the missing words.
1. It is a **l**□□□□ **r**□□□□□□□□□□.
2. **S**□□□□ **l**□□□□ are an important method of **r**□□□□□□□□□ traffic so that the roads are **s**□□□ for everyone.

Q4. Give three examples of when travelling at 30 mph in a built-up area could be dangerous? Complete the missing words.
1. When **p**□□□□□□ an ice-cream van and if **c**□□□□□□□ are in the vicinity.
2. When **d**□□□□□□ in poor **w**□□□□□□ or **r**□□□ conditions.
3. If **p**□□□□□□ a **s**□□□□□ with children running riot on the pavement.

Q5. How many metres would your car travel in one second if you are driving at a speed of 30 mph?
A. About 36 metres (120 feet).
B. About 12 metres (40 feet).
C. About 24 metres (80 feet).
D. About 14 metres (45 feet).

Q6. What distance should you stay behind the vehicle in front if you are driving on the open road in good conditions?
A. A gap of 1 metre for each mile per hour of your speed.
B. A gap of 2 metres for each mile per hour of your speed.
C. A gap of 3 metres for each mile per hour of your speed.
D. A gap of 4 metres for each mile per hour of your speed.

Q7. Fill in the missing figures. Your overall stopping distance will be:
1. □□ metres or □□ feet at 30 mph.
2. □□ metres or □□□ feet at 50 mph.
3. □□ metres or □□□ feet at 70 mph.

SOME COMMON FAULTS COMMITTED BY LEARNERS: CARE IN THE USE OF SPEED

- Driving too fast for the prevailing road or traffic conditions.
- Breaking the speed limit.
- Driving at an unsafe speed for the weather conditions.

MAKING PROGRESS

It can be highly dangerous not to make progress. Other drivers may get frustrated and take silly risks to overtake you. If you are sitting your driving test there are two ways in which you can be failed for not making normal progress.

The first way is that you are travelling too slowly for the road and traffic conditions. For example, if you are driving along a road at 20 mph with a 30 mph speed limit, and in the opinion of the examiner you could easily have travelled safely at 30 mph, you may be faulted for not making progress. Effort must be made by you to use the accelerator to build up the speed of your car, changing up through the gears where necessary. You must endeavour to keep up with the flow of traffic, within the speed limits. Do not stay too long in first or second gear as you may hold up other traffic. Do not reduce speed too early on the approach to a turn because other drivers may dart in front of you. Avoid weaving in and out between parked vehicles at short intervals. By doing this you will show the examiner that you are looking well ahead. Remember a good driver always looks well ahead and positions the car correctly after turning.

The second way of failing to make normal progress is by undue hesitancy. For example, you are sitting at a give way junction, waiting for a gap in the traffic to appear - a gap then appears, but you do not take advantage of it and instead decide to wait. You must not be overcautious to the point of becoming a nuisance. Try to keep your car moving at give way junctions if it is safe to do so. Give way junctions mean give way - they do not mean stop. Other drivers may get frustrated and take silly risks to overtake you.

AVOID UNDUE HESITANCY

Always remember to release your parking brake at either traffic lights, pedestrian crossings or when moving off on a hill. Try anticipating the opposite lights changing - you may select first gear, but don't release the parking brake until your lights change to green. Don't hang around waiting for something to happen during any of the manoeuvres because this is also a progress fault. A high percentage of driving test candidates fail for undue hesitancy or not driving at realistic speeds for the conditions because they desperately try to please the examiner by attempting to show how careful they are. This is the wrong approach.

DRIVE NORMALLY

If the speed limit for the road signs says 60 mph and it is safe to drive at 60 mph then make the effort to drive at the permitted speed. The faster you travel, the further you will have to look ahead. Poor forward observations will result in late and hurried driving decisions. Try to drive normally and don't be tempted to exceed the speed limit to keep up with other drivers because they are travelling faster (see figure 48).

Figure 48. Making progress.

MAKING NORMAL PROGRESS

QUESTIONS (refer to figure 48) (See page 247 for answers).

Q1. Why is it important to make normal progress to suit varying road and traffic conditions whilst driving?

A. Other drivers may overtake.

B. Other drivers may get out of their cars and beat you up.

C. Other drivers may smash their vehicle into the rear of your car.

D. Other drivers may get frustrated and take silly risks.

Q2. For what reason do a high percentage of learner drivers fail their driving test for undue hesitancy?

A. They try to bribe the examiner.

B. They try to please the examiner by being over-cautious.

C. They stop at every stop sign.

D. They travel at 25 mph.

Q3. Give two reasons why it is important to overtake safely when progress is severely held up by slow moving vehicles? Complete the missing words.
1. To **m**□□□ **p**□□□□□□□.
2. To **a**□□□ **h**□□□□□□ up other drivers.

Q4. Will the driving examiner fail you for driving at the permitted speed, if you see a road sign stating 50 mph and it is safe to drive at that speed?
A. Yes. You cannot drive more than 30 mph in your driving test.
B. No. The examiner may fail you for not making progress if you do not drive at the permitted speed.
C. No. As long as you do not drive on the motorway by mistake.
D. Yes. You must always drive at 5 mph below the stated speed limit.

Q5. What may happen if you reduce your speed too early on the approach to a turn?
A. Other drivers may nip in front of you.
B. Other drivers may smash into the rear of your car.
C. A pedestrian may run across the road in front of your vehicle.
D. You may stall your car.

Q6. Give two reasons why you should avoid weaving in and out between parked vehicles at short intervals?
1. To **s**□□□ the **e**□□□□□□□ you are **l**□□□□□□ well ahead.
2. To **a**□□□□ **c**□□□□□□□□ other drivers.

SOME COMMON FAULTS COMMITTED BY LEARNERS: MAKING PROGRESS

- Not driving at a speed appropriate to the road and traffic conditions.
- Not moving off at road junctions when a safe gap appears.
- Staying in a low gear too long.
- Reducing speed too early whilst approaching a road junction.

- Not maintaining the correct speed whilst driving.
- Taking too long preparing to move off at road junctions or during any of the manoeuvring exercises.

GENERAL ROAD POSITIONING

In olden days, horsemen would protect themselves by riding on the left-hand side of the road, close to thick wooded hedgerows. Since the majority of people were right-handed, they would draw their swords with their right hands in order to defend themselves if they were attacked by an enemy. To this day, we still drive on the left-hand side of the road.

The first rule of the road is to keep to the left. In normal driving the correct position from the kerb is approximately 90 cm (3 feet). If you get any closer than that there is either a danger of picking up debris from the gutter or even striking the kerb. However, if the road is clearly marked into lanes you should keep to the centre of the lane at all times. This means that you could be as close as 45 cm (1½ feet) from the kerb when in the left lane. You may have to give up your "keep to the left" position if there is a possibility of danger ahead. For example, if children are fooling around at the side of the road it would be far safer to move into the outside lane.

If you are approaching traffic lights, crossroads or roundabouts and you intend to proceed straight ahead, you would normally keep to the left unless road markings direct you otherwise. If you are turning right from a main road into a side road, you should position your car just left to the centre of the road, unless you are turning right out of a narrow road, in which case you should keep well left.

If you are travelling in a one way street, you may have to move over to the right-hand lane (see figure 49), or possibly obey road signs and markings in order to reach your destination (see figure 50). Traffic often moves quickly in one way streets and you should watch out for vehicles overtaking you on either side of your car. Do not forget to position your car in the right-hand lane of a dual carriageway if you intend to turn right.

CUTTING CORNERS

It is highly important to avoid cutting right-hand corners. This is a dangerous practice because it puts you on the wrong side of the road, and there is a possibility of conflicting with a vehicle coming out of the road into which you are turning.

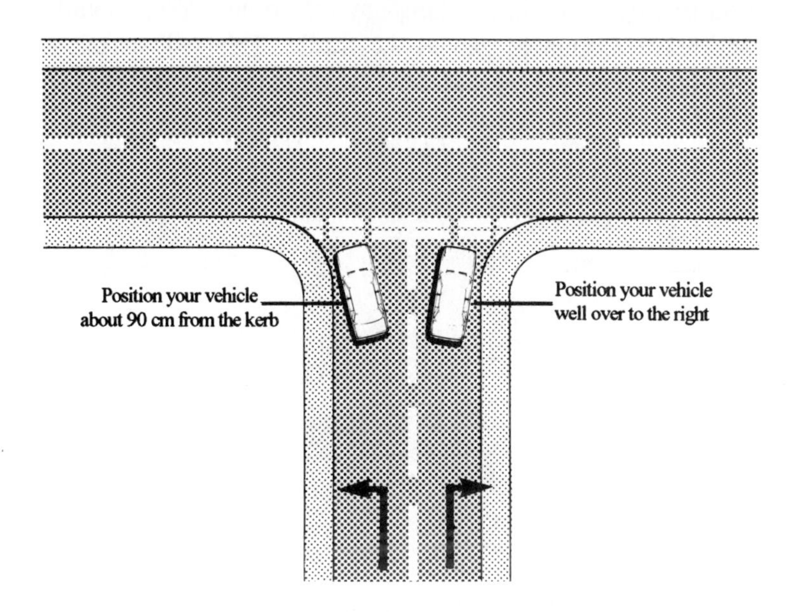
Position your vehicle
about 90 cm from the kerb
Position your vehicle
well over to the right

Figure 49. A one way street turning right or left.

PASSING PARKED VEHICLES

When passing parked vehicles you may have to lose your "keep left" rule. Keep at least 90 cm (3 feet) away because a pedestrian may walk out from behind a parked vehicle or a car door may open into your path. A good tip to remember is that for every 10 mph you are travelling slower, you can be 30 cm (1 foot) closer to any parked cars. Let us be more specific. If you are travelling at 20 mph on a narrow road you could be as close as 60 cm (2 feet), or if you are travelling at 10 mph you could be as close as 30 cm (1 foot). Cyclists need special attention. Give them plenty of room when overtaking because they could swerve or fall off at any time. Before you decide to move back into the left-hand lane, look well ahead to see if it is worthwhile and do not wander in and out if there are more parked vehicles ahead. If you are not causing any danger to other traffic or pedestrians, you should remain where you are. When driving in queues it is courteous and good driving to avoid blocking any side roads. You should hold back and leave a suitable gap in the traffic. This will permit other traffic to enter and leave the side road without any hindrance.

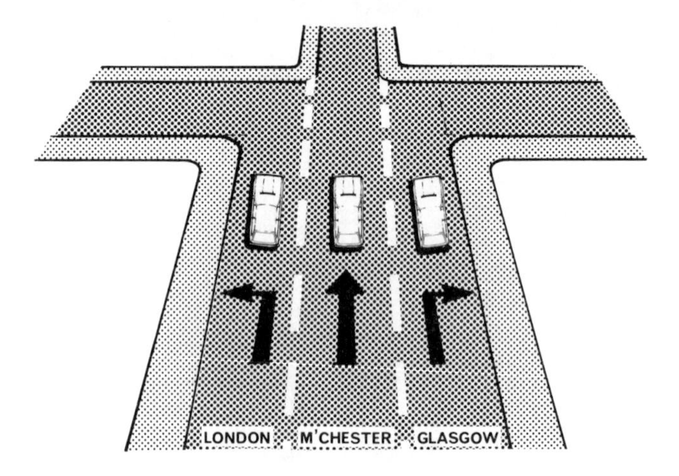

Figure 50. Sometimes you will have to obey road markings in order to reach your destination.

Do not be a road hog by not exercising proper lane discipline. If you drive in the centre of the road all the time for no apparent reason, other drivers may get frustrated and will possibly overtake you in the inside lane. Avoid weaving in and out between parked vehicles because this will only confuse other road users. However, if another vehicle is travelling close behind you and it is obvious that the driver wants to overtake, you should move over to the left if it is safe. Finally, you must never change lanes unnecessarily, or without using the Mirrors (Look, Assess, Decide), Signal, Manoeuvre routine. Try to drive in the middle of your selected lane and if possible avoid straddling lane markings (see figure 51).

Figure 51. General road positioning.

GENERAL ROAD POSITIONING

QUESTIONS (refer to figures 49 - 51) (See page 247 for answers).

Q1. Give four occasions when you may lose your "keep to the left" position? Complete the missing words.

1. If you are **t**□□□□□□ **r**□□□□.
2. If you wish to **a**□□□□ a **f**□□□□□ **l**□□□.
3. If the **r**□□□ **m**□□□□□□□ or **s**□□□□ instruct you to do so.
4. If there is any **f**□□□ of **d**□□□□□ ahead.

Q2. What is the first rule of the road?

A. Overtake when safe to do so.
B. Keep to the right during normal driving.
C. Keep to the left during normal driving.
D. Overtake whenever possible.

SOME COMMON FAULTS COMMITTED BY LEARNERS: POSITIONING AND PASSING STATIONARY VEHICLES

- Not keeping left during normal driving.
- Driving too far from the kerb.
- Straddling lanes when it is unsafe.
- Hogging the middle of the road.
- Driving with the wheels in the gutter or too near to the kerb.
- Changing lanes unnecessarily.
- Weaving in and out between parked vehicles.
- Not returning to the left after overtaking when it was safe.
- Failing to position the car correctly when dealing with traffic lights, pedestrian crossings, roundabouts, one way streets and dual carriageways.
- Failing to keep a safe distance from the vehicle in front.
- Driving too close to parked vehicles.
- Not allowing sufficient clearance when passing cyclists.

Lesson 13 - Overtaking, meeting and crossing the path of other vehicles

OVERTAKING OTHER VEHICLES SAFELY

Many serious and fatal traffic accidents are caused by overtaking because you will be driving on the wrong side of the road, towards oncoming traffic. It is therefore crucial that you only overtake when it is perfectly safe to do so. Never overtake unless you are sure there is no danger to others as well as to yourself. Before you start to overtake, make sure that the road is clear far enough ahead and behind you. Remember to use the Mirrors (Look, Assess, Decide), Signal, Manoeuvre routine. On fast roads, vehicles may be coming up from behind much more quickly than you imagine. Also make sure that the lane into which you intend to move is clear far into the distance. Before overtaking any vehicle you must ask yourself:

- Would I be breaking the law if I overtake?
- Can I overtake safely?
- Does my car have enough speed and power to overtake?
- Can I safely get back into my own lane on time?
- Do I have a safe gap to move back in?
- Is it necessary?

Remember the golden rule, ***If in doubt : DON'T.*** There are two types of overtaking you may perform; overtaking a moving vehicle and passing a stationary vehicle or obstruction. First let us look at the procedure you should carry out before overtaking a moving vehicle.

OVERTAKING A MOVING VEHICLE

When you approach the rear of the slower moving vehicle make sure you keep a safe distance behind it. Remember that the Highway Code states that you should keep a safe distance behind another vehicle. If an overtaking vehicle does pull in front of you - drop back. In the earlier lessons I told you that you should use the Mirrors (Look,

Assess, Decide), Signal, Manoeuvre, Position, Speed and Look routine before you make any driving decision. However, before overtaking we reverse this and instead adopt Position, Speed, Look, Mirrors (Look, Assess, Decide), Signal, Manoeuvre. You must first **POSITION - HOLDBACK**, no less than two seconds back from the vehicle ahead, keeping out just left to the centre of the road so that you can see past the vehicle in front. If you find yourself travelling at the same speed as the moving vehicle, you may have to drop a gear(s) to match your speed. You must also have the correct acceleration to get past the vehicle in front. You must be aware of the acceleration capability of your car so that you can move out of the "danger period" as soon as possible (see figure 52).

Look well ahead for oncoming traffic, junctions or hazards before you decide to overtake. If it is completely safe ahead, behind, and to the sides of your car you should then overtake the vehicle with determination. Remember, you are on the wrong side of the road so spend as little time there as possible. Hold a parallel course until the vehicle you have overtaken is visible in your interior mirror. By doing this, you will have moved back in, well ahead of the overtaken vehicle and you will not have caused it to slow down or change direction. This will also allow space for another overtaking vehicle to pull in. Do not signal your intention to move back in after overtaking because other drivers expect you to drive on the left-hand side of the road.

Signalling left could make other drivers or pedestrians mistakenly believe that you intend to turn left (if there is a side road ahead) or stop on the left-hand side of the road. Signalling for the sake of signalling is a dangerous practice. Check your mirrors and increase a gear, conditions permitting. Make sure you gauge the length of the vehicle you wish to overtake. If the vehicle you are overtaking is a Large Goods Vehicle you should hold well back to give yourself the best possible view so that you can overtake once you can see that there are no hazards ahead.

Be very careful because large vehicles can often obscure hazards. If you gauge the length of the vehicle correctly you will be able to judge how much further you will have to travel before you can pull back onto your own side of the road safely. Never overtake unless you have considered how quickly the combined speed will close the gap you have chosen to overtake. When you are overtaking a Large Goods Vehicle, keep both hands firmly on the steering wheel to avoid your car being "knocked" by any side draught. Take special care when you see a vehicle displaying an "L" plate or a foreign number plate. This could indicate an inexperienced driver or one unused to driving on the left-hand side of the road.

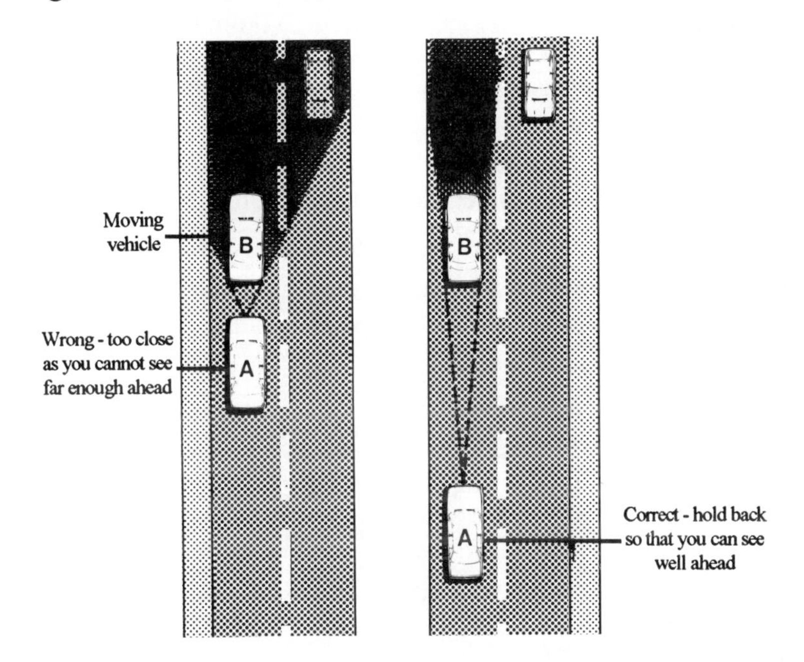

Figure 52. Overtaking a moving vehicle.

Never overtake if you think the other vehicle may speed up. For example, on a downhill gradient or if there is any possibility that you may meet another vehicle coming from the opposite direction, slow down or alter your course. When overtaking, always carefully consider the speed of any approaching vehicle as well as that of your own car and be aware of how quickly the gap between the two will close. Ensure that the road is wide enough before you overtake - it is no use trying to squeeze through a small gap. The other driver may lose control of the steering and you would have no escape route, especially as there may be a pedestrian walking on the pavement. If you decide to brake, another vehicle may have moved in behind your car. The important point is to never overtake if you are in any doubt. Think before you act. Remember, deliberation eliminates uncertainty. When safe, go.

OVERTAKING A CYCLIST

When overtaking cyclists you must always give them plenty of room, as they have a tendency to wobble, swerve or change direction without warning. Let us look at the procedure you should carry out before passing a stationary vehicle or obstruction.

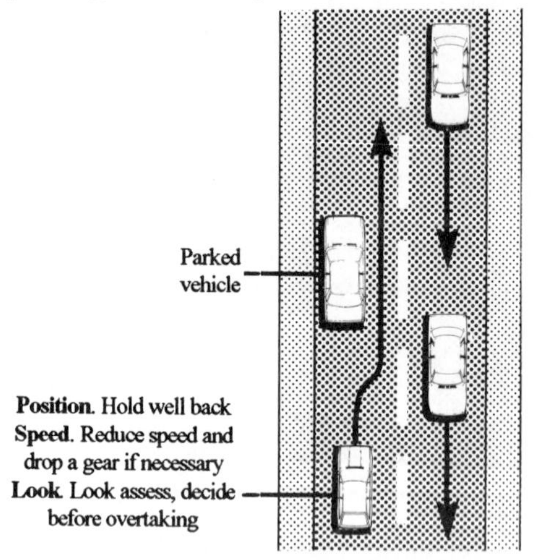
Parked vehicle
Position. Hold well back
Speed. Reduce speed and drop a gear if necessary
Look. Look assess, decide before overtaking

Figure 53. Passing a stationary vehicle.

PASSING A STATIONARY VEHICLE

When approaching a parked vehicle, make sure you carry out the Position, Speed, Look, Mirrors (Look, Assess, Decide), Signal, Manoeuvre routine. You must Look, Assess and Decide if it is completely safe before you make any overtaking decision. It is imperative that you check your mirrors early. Remember not to signal unless someone else is going to benefit. If you give an unnecessary right turn signal, it could indicate to another driver that you intend to turn right if there is a junction ahead.

You must look well ahead. If it is safe, move out from the obstruction as early as possible, leave plenty of room and watch out for pedestrians who may step out from in front of parked vehicles. Watch out for the parked vehicle's door opening, and keep a good safety line position - the safest position to adopt on the road in relation to the actual and potential danger existing at that moment (see figure 53).

ACTUAL AND POTENTIAL DANGER

Actual danger when passing a stationary vehicle could be a person sitting in the driving seat of the car who may decide to open the car door without looking. Potential danger could be passing a parked vehicle from behind which a pedestrian may walk out. With plenty of driving experience you will build up a judgment of when it is safe to pass stationary vehicles. The main thing you must remember is that when you are passing a stationary vehicle and another vehicle is approaching in the opposite direction, it is surprising how quickly the road shortens.

Again, you must consider how quickly your combined speed will close the gap you have chosen to overtake in. A motor vehicle travelling at 30 mph travels a distance of approximately 14 metres (45 feet) in one second. It is therefore important that you judge the speed of the oncoming vehicle. Overtaking could be the last decision you will ever make if it is the wrong one. Remember the golden rule, ***If in doubt : DON'T*** (see figure 54).

HOLDING BACK

There are three types of situation: where you can go, where you cannot go and where you *"don't know"*. The *"go"* and *"don't go"* situations are self-explanatory. However, if you feel that you do not have enough information to make a safe driving decision, then you must hold back *"don't know"* until you receive more knowledge of the road situation so that you may make a responsible decision. In other words, you must never overtake until you are perfectly sure that you can carry out the manoeuvre safely.

Figure 54. If in doubt, don't overtake.

OVERTAKING OTHER VEHICLES SAFELY

QUESTIONS (refer to figures 52 - 54) (See page 247 for answers).

Q1. Why can overtaking be a dangerous manoeuvre to perform?

A. Your indicator may not work.

B. None of these.

C. You will be driving on the wrong side of the road towards oncoming traffic.

D. Overtaking is never dangerous.

Q2. What should you ask yourself before overtaking any vehicle?

1. Would I be **b**□□□□□□□ the **l**□□ if I **o**□□□□□□□?
2. Can I **o**□□□□□□□ **s**□□□□□?

3. Does my car have **e**□□□□□ **s**□□□□ and **p**□□□□ to overtake?
4. Can I **s**□□□□□ get back into my own lane in **t**□□□?
5. Do I have a **s**□□□ **g**□□ in which to move back?
6. Is it **n**□□□□□□□□?

Q3. What is the golden rule before overtaking?
A. If in doubt, **DO IT** but only when safe.
B. If in doubt, **DO IT**.
C. If in doubt, accelerate past the vehicle with determination.
D. If in doubt, **DON'T**.

Q4. How should you overtake a moving vehicle safely? Complete the missing words.
When you **a**□□□□□□□ the **r**□□□ of the slower moving vehicle, make sure you keep a **s**□□□ **d**□□□□□□□ behind it. Adopt the **P**□□□□□□□, **S**□□□□, Look, **M**□□□□□□ (Look, Assess, Decide), **S**□□□□□, **M**□□□□□□□□ routine. Overtake with determination when it is completely **s**□□□.

Q5. When is it safe to move back in after overtaking?
A. As soon as you see the vehicle you have overtaken appear in the left-hand mirror.
B. As soon as you see the vehicle you have overtaken appear in all your mirrors.
C. As soon as you see the vehicle you have overtaken appear in the left and interior mirrors.
D. As soon as you see the vehicle you have overtaken appear in your interior mirror.

Q6. State two reasons why you should leave plenty of room when passing parked cars? Fill in the missing words.
1. Pedestrians may **s**□□□ out from behind **p**□□□□□ **c**□□□.
2. A **d**□□□ may **o**□□□ without **w**□□□□□□.

Q7. What two things should you do whilst overtaking a Large Goods Vehicle? Fill in the missing words.

1. Make sure you **g**---- the **l**----- of the **v**------.
2. Keep **b**□□□□ hands **f**□□□□□ on the **s**□□□□□□□ **w**□□□□ to avoid your car being "**k**□□□□□□" by any side **d**□□□□□□.

Q8. Why keep well back before overtaking another vehicle?

A. To give yourself the best possible view beyond the vehicle you are going to overtake.

B. To give yourself the best possible view behind the vehicle you are going to overtake.

C. So that the driver in front can see you better.

D. So that you can overtake at speed.

Q9. State two reasons why you should wait until you see the vehicle you have overtaken appear in your interior mirror, before moving back into your side of the road? Complete the missing words.

1. This will **a**□□□□ space for another **o**□□□□□□□□□ vehicle to **p**□□□ **i**□.
2. You will not **c**□□□□ the vehicle you have overtaken to **s**□□□ **d**□□□ or **c**□□□□□ **d**□□□□□□□□.

Q10. Ahead of you, you see a small gap between two vehicles parked on the other side of the road with just enough room for two cars to get through. At that moment another vehicle is coming towards you and it is obvious that he intends to drive through the small gap. Why should you avoid driving through the small gap at the same time as the other vehicle?

A. If either of the parked cars move off an accident may occur.

B. None of these.

C. You may have to brake suddenly.

D. You will have nowhere to go if the other driver comes through the gap at the same time and loses control or a car door opens.

Q11. What does the "don't know" (hold back) situation mean?

A. This is a sign of someone with no consideration for others.
B. This is a sign of a responsible, patient and confident driver.
C. This is a sign of an unconfident and nervous driver.
D. This is a sign of a learner driver.

SOME COMMON FAULTS COMMITTED BY LEARNERS: OVERTAKING

- Not making effective use of the mirrors before and after overtaking.
- Overtaking at an unsafe or illegal place.
- Breaking the speed limit.
- Not holding far enough back from the vehicle or cyclist before overtaking.
- Cutting back in too quickly or too early after overtaking.
- Not allowing a safe clearance when overtaking a moving or stationary vehicle.
- Not allowing sufficient clearance to cyclists.
- Not selecting the correct gear prior to overtaking.
- Forcing other traffic from the opposite direction to swerve or slow down.
- Failing to overtake with determination.
- Failing to hold a parallel course when overtaking.
- Failing to anticipate the actions of other road users.
- Signalling unnecessarily before or after overtaking.
- Failing to be decisive.

MEETING OTHER VEHICLES SAFELY

When you are driving on a narrow road you may come across a situation where you will meet other vehicles (see figure 55). This situation usually arises when driving in a built-up area and you can see that there are two parked vehicles ahead. One at the left-hand side of the road and the other vehicle at the right-hand side, possibly parallel with each other. This can be termed a "bottleneck". A problem arises because if another vehicle is approaching and, because of timing, both vehicles may reach the bottleneck at the same time. Most learners find it difficult to appreciate that they may have to slow down further back and if necessary, stop. The one thing you must not do is speed up and try and get through the gap before the other driver. This is very dangerous because the other driver might do the same and this often results in an emergency stop being carried out at the last moment.

If this happens to you on your driving test you may fail for not meeting other vehicles safely. To get round this problem you should look well ahead and apply the Mirrors (Look, Assess, Decide), Signal, Manoeuvre routine and change down a gear(s) if your speed drops. By changing down a gear(s) this will prove to the examiner that you are both looking ahead and aware of hazards on the road. Remember, a hazard is anything which contains danger. If the above situation arises and you are in any doubt about getting through the gap in time, you should hold your car well back from the parked obstruction. By holding well back, your vision is improved past the vehicle and it will be both easier and safer for you before moving off.

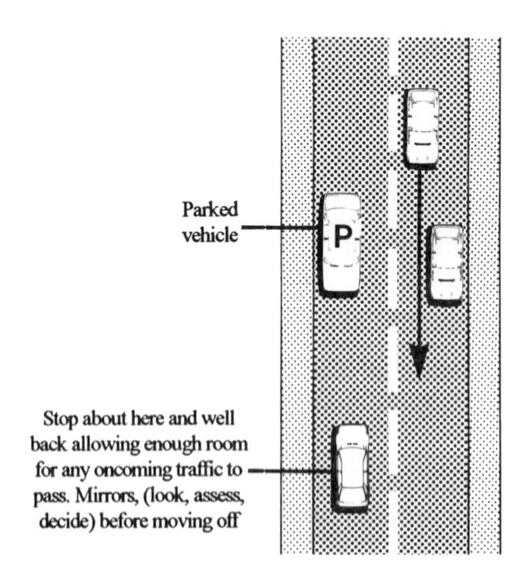
Parked vehicle
P
Stop about here and well back allowing enough room for any oncoming traffic to pass. Mirrors, (look, assess, decide) before moving off

Figure 55. Meeting another vehicle.

In narrow roads you may come across a situation where another vehicle is approaching from the opposite direction and there is only one parked vehicle (or obstruction) on the other side of the road, yet it is still causing a constriction of traffic. On this occasion you normally have priority, unless the other vehicle has already started to move out. Oncoming traffic may not **always** give you priority.

Figure 56. Do not be the meat in the sandwich!

THE MEAT IN THE SANDWICH

There's an old saying, ***"Never be the meat in the sandwich"*** (see figure 56). Never get caught in between two vehicles as anything may happen and you could be trapped with no place to go. A good driver always looks well ahead, scans the area for any possible signs of danger and acts as the situation demands.

MEETING OTHER VEHICLES SAFELY

QUESTIONS (refer to figures 55 and 56)(See page 247 for answers).

Q1. Where are you most likely to meet other vehicles whilst driving?

A. This situation usually arises in a one way street.

B. This situation usually arises on a very wide road.

C. This situation usually arises in a built-up area..

D. This situation usually arises on a narrow road.

Q2. How should you meet another vehicle safely? Fill in the missing words.
Apply the **M□□□□□□ (L□□□, A□□□□□□, D□□□□□□), S□□□□□, M□□□□□□□□□** routine. Slow down, hold back, and if necessary, **s□□□□**.

Q3. What must you **never** do when meeting other vehicles if there is a "bottleneck" ahead?
A. Slow down and barge through the gap before the other driver.
B. Speed up and barge through the gap before the other driver.
C. Stall the car.
D. None of these.

Q4. Why could it be dangerous trying to barge through the gap before the other driver?
A. Insurance policies don't cover this situation.
B. The other driver might execute an emergency stop.
C. The other driver may be a joy rider and ram his vehicle into yours.
D. The other driver might do the same and this often results in an emergency stop being carried out at the last moment.

Q5. What may happen on your driving test if you meet another vehicle and you have to carry out an emergency stop?
A. None of these.
B. You may be failed for not applying the footbrake in good time if an emergency stop arises.
C. You may be failed for not meeting other vehicles safely.
D. You will automatically fail.

Q6. Do you have priority when there is a vehicle or obstruction on the other side of the road?
A. Normally, unless the other vehicle has already started to move out.
B. Oncoming vehicles have priority over learner drivers.
C. Yes.
D. None of these.

SOME COMMON FAULTS COMMITTED BY LEARNERS: MEETING OTHER VEHICLES

- Poor forward observations leading to late driving decisions.
- Failing to be decisive.
- Failing to provide adequate clearance to approaching traffic.
- Failing to anticipate the actions of other road users.
- Not using the Mirrors (Look, Assess, Decide), Signal, Manoeuvre routine.
- Meeting other vehicles too fast.

CROSSING THE PATH OF OTHER VEHICLES SAFELY

When you are turning right from a main road into a side road you sometimes have to give way to oncoming vehicles. However, you must judge the speed of the approaching vehicle and decide whether if it is safe to turn in front of it. If you are in any doubt, you must wait until the oncoming vehicle has passed. The best way for you to judge if it is safe to turn is to ask yourself, *"Is there any possibility that I may make the oncoming vehicle slow down or alter its course?"* If the answer is yes, then you must wait. However if the answer is no, then you may turn in front of the other vehicle. You cannot turn if there is a pedestrian either crossing or about to cross the road into which you are turning.

Always be prepared to give way and to make a final right-hand mirror check before you actually decide to turn, in case someone is foolish enough to overtake you at the junction. If you do not proceed when it is safe, the examiner may fail you for not making progress (see figure 57).

Another way to decide if it is safe to proceed is to ask yourself, *"If I was a pedestrian standing on the pavement could I walk across the road in time without making the driver slow down or alter its course?"* If the answer is no, then you must wait and give way. Do **not** take a chance. Always look well ahead and judge the road and traffic situation. Here are some questions for you to think about:

- What type of vehicle is it? If it's a milk float and the vehicle is some distance away is it a good idea to wait?
- You look ahead and see in the distance that a bus is approaching your car. A pedestrian is standing at the side of the road, hailing the bus to stop. The bus slows down, signals and makes it obvious that it is going to pull up for its passenger before reaching your car. Should you proceed if there are no pedestrians crossing the road into which you are turning?
- You have been sitting patiently for a couple of minutes, waiting for a safe gap in the slow moving traffic ahead and at that moment the vehicle nearest to your car stalls. Should you proceed if there are no pedestrians crossing into the road into which you are turning?

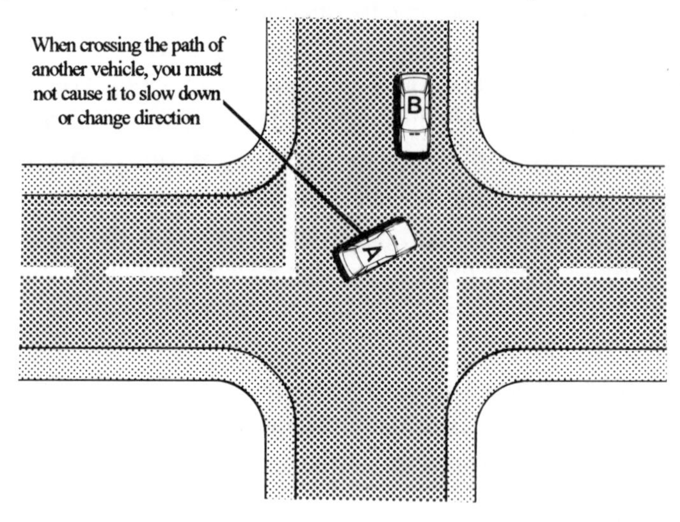
When crossing the path of
another vehicle, you must
not cause it to slow down
or change direction
B
A

Figure 57. Crossing the path of another vehicle.

TO SUM UP

Imagine you are a pedestrian about to cross the road. To cross safely you correctly judge the speed and distance of any approaching traffic. Likewise, as a driver, you should try to develop similar judgement skills before crossing the path of other vehicles. Remember the golden rule: ***If in doubt* - Don't**.

CROSSING THE PATH OF OTHER VEHICLES

QUESTIONS (refer to figure 57) (See page 247 for answers).

Q1. What must you **never** do when turning right in front of traffic?

A. Make any oncoming vehicles slow down or alter their course.

B. Make oncoming vehicles flash their lights at you.

C. Turn right in front of other traffic.

D. Speed up.

Q2. If you are sitting your driving test, could the driving examiner fail you for not turning in front of other traffic if it is safe to do so?

A. No. You must wait until all oncoming vehicles have passed you for at least 10 seconds.

B. No. You can take as long as you want before turning.

C. Yes. The examiner may fail you for undue hesitancy.

D. No. You should wait until a driver invites you to turn.

Q3. What must you be careful of before turning right if there is no oncoming traffic?

A. Animals.

B. Pedestrians already crossing the road.

C. Fire Engines.

D. Stray horses.

Q4. Which golden rule must you obey if you are not completely sure if it is safe to turn in front of other traffic?

A. Go.

B. Don't.

C. Apply the parking brake and select neutral.

D. Go quickly.

Q5. Why should you make a final right-hand mirror check before you actually decide to turn right in front of other traffic?

A. In case someone overtakes you at the junction.

B. To look out for pedestrians.

C. To make sure the right-hand mirror has not steamed up.
D. None of these.

Q6. Which are the best ways to decide if it is safe to turn in front of other traffic? Fill in the missing words.
1. "Is there any **p**□□□□□□□□□□ that I may make the **o**□□□□□□□□□□ vehicle **s**□□□ **d**□□□ or **a**□□□□ its course".
2. "If I was a **p**□□□□□□□□□ standing on the **p**□□□□□□□ could I **w**□□□ across the road in **t**□□□ without making the other driver **s**□□□ down or **a**□□□□ its course".

SOME COMMON FAULTS COMMITTED BY LEARNERS: CROSSING THE PATH OF OTHER VEHICLES

- Cutting in front of closely approaching traffic.
- Making other vehicles stop, reduce speed or swerve.
- Not looking for danger into the side road before turning.
- Not giving way to pedestrians and being indecisive.

Chapter 5

Lesson 14 - Dealing with traffic lights and pedestrian crossings

DEALING WITH TRAFFIC LIGHTS

Traffic lights are a set of coloured lights normally found at road junctions and they are used to control the flow of traffic. It is important that you observe traffic lights early and treat them with caution. Let us look in detail at the correct procedure we should adopt when approaching traffic lights. The sequence of traffic light signals is as follows:

- RED means "STOP", wait behind the stop line on the carriageway.
- RED and AMBER also means "STOP". Do not pass through or start until GREEN shows.
- GREEN means you may go on if the way is clear. Take special care if you mean to turn left or right and give way to pedestrians who are crossing.
- AMBER means "STOP" at the stop line. You may go on only if the AMBER appears after you have crossed the stop line or are so close to it that to pull up might cause an accident.

PROCEEDING STRAIGHT ON AT TRAFFIC LIGHTS

When you approach a set of traffic lights situated at a road junction with the intention of proceeding straight ahead, you should approach in the left-hand lane (see figure 58). However, there are exceptions to this rule. They are as follows:

- When turning right at traffic lights.
- If you wish to avoid a filter lane.
- Traffic signs or road markings dictate otherwise.
- A parked vehicle or obstruction is blocking the left-hand lane.
- If the right-hand lane is more convenient, i.e. a row of vehicles waiting to turn left is causing a queue.

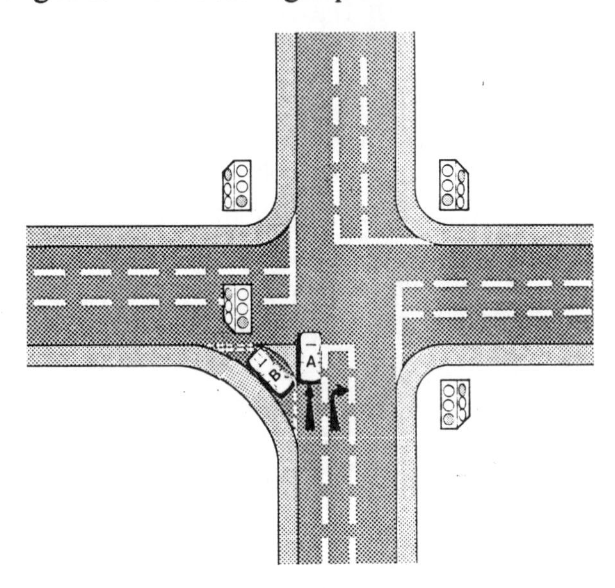

Figure 58. Be prepared to stop at give way lines if it is not safe to proceed.

As previously mentioned you should approach the traffic lights with caution and select third gear approximately 23 metres (75 feet) before the lights. By selecting third gear, you will be regulating your speed correctly on the approach and you will be able to accelerate out of any trouble should the lights change to amber at the point of no return. Don't forget to quickly glance right, left, and right again in case someone ignores a red light and mistakenly crosses your path.

TURNING RIGHT AT TRAFFIC LIGHTS

Turning right at traffic lights presents learners with many problems (see figure 59). However, if you keep calm, think clearly and concentrate it will be relatively simple. When you are approaching a set of traffic lights in fourth gear. As soon as you are given the instruction to turn right, you should adopt the Mirrors (Look, Assess, Decide), Signal, Manoeuvre routine in good time. When the traffic lights are showing red, you must stop just behind the solid white line and wait until the green light appears. When the green light comes on, do not proceed unless the way is clear.

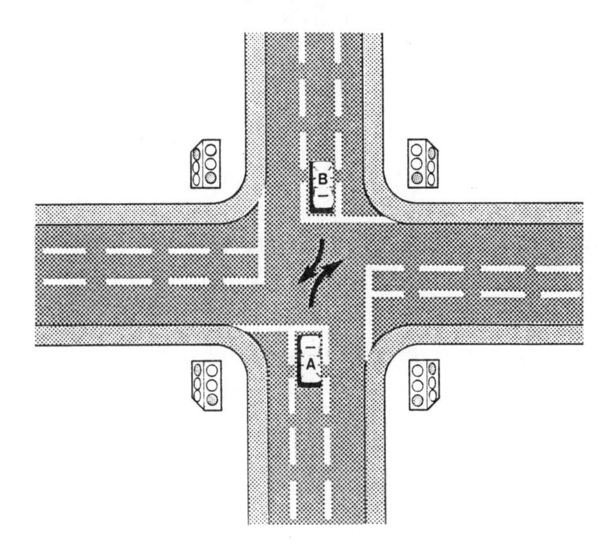

Figure 59. Turning right at traffic lights nearside to nearside as directed by road markings.

TURNING OFFSIDE TO OFFSIDE OR NEARSIDE TO NEARSIDE

If other vehicles are turning right from the opposite direction, wait until it is safe and then move forward and turn right either offside to offside or nearside to nearside. Deciding which way to turn will depend entirely on the layout of the junction. Some junctions have road markings showing that you should turn in front of the traffic opposite. If you obey the road markings you will have no problem, providing you give priority to oncoming vehicles, and give way to pedestrians who are crossing the road into which you are turning.

LOOK, ASSESS, DECIDE

If you check your mirrors in good time you will be able to decide if it is safe to stop if the traffic lights change from green to amber. **Always** get into the habit of checking your mirrors and use the Look, Assess, Decide routine whilst approaching traffic lights. This will enable you to make the correct driving decision if a difficult situation arises without warning. Finally, if you want to turn left at traffic lights remember to watch out for cyclists creeping in up the inside lane. **Always** be prepared to stop and give way to pedestrians who are crossing the road.

Some traffic lights have a slip road leading to the left (see figure 58). Use the slip road if you wish to turn left and give way where necessary. If you are turning left or right at a junction controlled by lights you may see a green arrow. A green arrow may be provided in addition to the full green signal if movement in a certain direction is allowed before or after the full green phase. If the way is clear you may go but only in the direction shown by the arrow. You may do this whatever other lights may be showing.

DEALING WITH TRAFFIC LIGHTS

QUESTIONS (refer to figures 58 and 59) (See page 247 for answers).

Q1. Why is it important to make effective use of the mirrors when approaching a traffic light on green?

A. To decide if it is safe to stop if the lights change from green to amber.

B. To decide if it is safe to stop if the lights change from green to red.

C. To decide if it is safe to slow down if the lights change from green to amber.

D. None of these.

Q2. What lane should you normally take when you approach a set of traffic lights with the intention of proceeding straight ahead?

A. You should normally approach in the fast lane.

B. You should normally approach in the right-hand lane.

C. You should normally approach in the left-hand lane.
D. You should normally approach in any lane.

Q3. Give five exceptions to the "keep left" rule.
1. When **t**□□□□□□ **r**□□□□ at **t**□□□□□□ **l**□□□□□.
2. If you wish to **a**□□□□ a **f**□□□□□ **l**□□□.
3. Traffic **s**□□□□ or road **m**□□□□□□□ dictate otherwise.
4. A **p**□□□□□ vehicle or **o**□□□□□□□□□□ is **b**□□□□□□□ the left-hand **l**□□□.
5. If the right-hand lane is more **c**□□□□□□□□□.

Q4. Who should you be particularly mindful of when turning left at traffic lights?
A. Buses stopping at the side of the road.
B. Large Goods Vehicles.
C. Small cars creeping up on the inside lane.
D. Pedestrians who are crossing the road.

Q5. What should you do if you are turning left at traffic lights and there is a green filter arrow in your favour?
A. You may proceed even if the main lights are depicting red.
B. You may proceed but you must give way to buses and trams.
C. You must stop and wait until the green filter arrow disappears.
D. Wait for the main green light to confirm your right of way.

Q6. Why would the driving examiner not normally use the word traffic lights before he asks you to turn?
A. It is the examiner's responsibility to notice that traffic lights are coming up and to warn you.
B. It is your responsibility to notice that traffic lights are coming up and to act accordingly.
C. None of these.
D. It may be confusing.

SOME COMMON FAULTS COMMITTED BY LEARNERS: TRAFFIC LIGHTS

- Not using the Mirrors (Look, Assess, Decide), Signal, Manoeuvre routine.
- Not taking effective observations when emerging through a green light.
- Not observing or complying with a filter light.
- Not anticipating the actions of oncoming traffic when turning right.
- Failing to comply with a red traffic light.
- Approaching traffic lights too fast.
- Failing to recognise that the traffic lights have changed to green.
- Not taking the correct action when the traffic lights change from green to amber.

DEALING WITH PEDESTRIAN CROSSINGS

When you are driving in a busy area, you are likely to come across a pedestrian crossing. Pedestrians have certain rights of way at pedestrian crossings. You should always be looking well ahead and be prepared to slow down or stop to give way to pedestrians if there is any possibility that a pedestrian could step onto the crossing. It is of paramount importance that you show caution because the pedestrian may be blind, deaf or handicapped. You must regulate your speed correctly on the approach to the crossing. If you don't, you may have to give way to a pedestrian at the last moment with your car screeching to a halt. This may result in another vehicle crashing into the rear of your car. Remember, pedestrian crossings are sometimes found shortly after you have emerged from a junction (or turned a corner) and you may be coming from a "blind spot".

On the approach to a pedestrian crossing you should apply the Mirrors (Look, Assess, Decide), Signal, Manoeuvre routine. If you cannot see the kerb properly because of parked vehicles or some other type of obstruction you should show caution by selecting third gear. This also applies if there are pedestrians near or at the crossing.

Third gear is selected because it gives you more control over your car on the approach to the crossing, and you will be able to accelerate out of any trouble much faster, if you reach the point of no return. There are 4 kinds of pedestrian crossings; pelican, zebra, puffin and toucan.

Pelican crossing
Pelican means:

- **PEDESTRIAN**
- **LIGHT**
- **CONTROLLED CROSSING**

A pelican crossing is a marked area controlled by a set of coloured lights, where pedestrians may cross the road. You will also see zig zag road markings and a row of studs across the road. The row of studs indicate the area to be used by pedestrians. The sequence of traffic lights at a pelican crossing is:

- Red: for **"STOP"**.
- Flashing amber: give way to pedestrians who are already on the crossing.
- Green: you may go on if the way is clear, but you must give way to pedestrians who are still on the crossing.
- Amber: "Stop" at the stop line. You may go only if the AMBER appears after you have crossed the stop line, or if you are so close to it that to pull up might cause an accident.

On the approach to a pelican crossing, you should apply the Mirrors (Look, Assess, Decide), Signal, Manoeuvre routine. Should the traffic lights depict green, you must regulate your speed on the approach to the crossing and be prepared to give way to pedestrians who are crossing or attempting to cross. Remember, a green light does **not** give you the authority to proceed, so act sensibly.

Finally, a straight (not staggered), pelican should be treated as one crossing even when there is a central refuge, and you must wait for pedestrians coming from the far side of the refuge. But if the crossing is staggered (separate crossings, one each side of the refuge but not in a straight line) be prepared to give way to pedestrians when they are on your side of the crossing.

Zebra crossing

The zebra crossing is normally marked by zig zag lines on both sides of the crossing, with flashing beacons at either side of the pavement, black and white panels running across the length of the road and rows of studs along the edge of area to be used by pedestrians. So there is no excuse for not seeing them.

When approaching a zebra crossing, the Mirrors (Look, Assess, Decide), Signal, Manoeuvre routine should be applied. Check the mirrors early so that the situation behind you may be assessed and allow you time, if necessary, to roll down your window and give a slowing down arm signal. This is a very important signal to give because it both warns following vehicles of your intention to slow down and gives pedestrians confidence that you are preparing to stop your car for them. Stop just before the white give way lines and give children and elderly people plenty of time to cross. Do not rev your engine as this may frighten them.

You must not overtake either the moving motor vehicle nearest the crossing or the leading vehicle which has stopped to give way to a pedestrian on the crossing. Even when there are no zig zag lines, never overtake just before a zebra crossing. In traffic queues, leave pedestrian crossings clear.

Puffin crossing

Puffin means:

- **PEDESTRIAN**
- **USER**
- **FRIENDLY**
- **INTELLIGENT**

Puffin crossings are designed to improve safety by helping traffic flow more freely. An infra-red scanner automatically detects when pedestrians are moving on the crossing. This will stall the green light until the pedestrian has reached an area of safety. If there are no pedestrians in the radius of the detector, the green signal will remain in favour of any traffic.

Since the signals are operated in this fashion, the traffic lights will **not** show any flashing amber signal and so any traffic will be able to move with the minimum amount of delay.

Figure 60. Act properly at pedestrian crossings.

Toucan crossing

Toucan crossings are designed for pedestrians and cyclists to cross and ride together respectively. The signals are push button operated and have no flashing amber phase. When you approach a toucan crossing, watch out for traffic signals and zig zag road markings and be prepared to give way to cyclists as well as pedestrians.

A couple of final warnings. **Never** wave pedestrians to cross as they may take your signal for granted, cross without looking and get knocked down by some fool who may be overtaking you. Secondly, never become impatient and start revving your engine loudly at pedestrians to try to get them to cross quicker because they may be elderly or handicapped and need more time to cross.

I once saw a driver being hit over the head by an old lady with a brolly for doing this (see figure 60) and don't be tempted to overtake when approaching a pedestrian crossing (see figure 61). Finally, should you see either a policeman or traffic warden controlling traffic they should be dealt with in accordance with their signals.

Figure 61. Regulate your speed correctly when approaching a pedestrian crossing.

DEALING WITH PEDESTRIAN CROSSINGS

QUESTIONS (refer to figures 60 and 61) (See page 247-248 for answers).

Q1. Where may you encounter pedestrian crossings?

A. Only near road junctions.

B. Only near shopping centres.

C. In built-up areas.

D. Only in city centres.

Q2. What should you be prepared to do when approaching pedestrian crossings?
A. Look in all your mirrors.
B. Speed up and accelerate through the crossing .
C. Stop at every pedestrian crossing.
D. Slow down or stop to give way if there is any possibility a pedestrian could step onto the crossing.

Q3. What does pelican mean? Fill in the missing words.
P□□□□□□□□□, **L**□□□□, **C**□□□□□□□□□.

Q4. What could happen if you do not regulate your speed correctly on the approach to the crossing?
A. Your brakes may fail.
B. You may not be able to stop if necessary.
C. An old lady may hit you on the head with her brolly.
D. You may stall your car.

Q5. Which routine should you apply when dealing with a pedestrian crossing? Fill in the missing words.
M□□□□□□ , **S**□□□□□, **M**□□□□□□□□ routine.

Q6. If you are driving along in fourth gear and can't see the kerb properly on the approach to a pedestrian crossing because of parked vehicles, you must...?
A. Show caution by slowing down and selecting an appropriate gear.
B. Speed up in case pedestrians emerge from behind parked cars.
C. Slow down and select first gear.
D. Slow down and select second gear.

Q7. Name 4 types of pedestrian crossing? Fill in the missing words.
1. **P**□□□□□□ crossing.
2. **Z**□□□□ crossing.
3. **P**□□□□□ crossing.

4. T□□□□□ crossing.

Q8. What are the sequence of traffic lights at a pelican crossing starting from red?
A. Red - amber - green - flashing amber - red.
B. Red - flashing amber - green - red.
C. Red - flashing amber - green - amber - red.
D. Red - amber, flashing green - flashing amber - red.

Q9. What does flashing amber mean?
A. Give way to cyclists.
B. The amber light is broken.
C. Give way to the elderly.
D. Give way to pedestrians.

Q10. Are cyclists permitted to ride across at a toucan crossing?
A. No. Unless told to do so by a policeman or traffic warden.
B. No. Under no circumstances.
C. Yes. Pedestrians and cyclists get the green signal together.
D. Yes. At all times.

Q11. What does puffin mean?
A. Pedestrian, user-friendly, intelligent.
B. Pedestrian, exhausted.
C. Pedestrian, mad, dumb.
D. Pedestrian, fresh, insensitive.

Q12. Why must you never encourage pedestrians to cross?
A. In case pedestrians think you are making a rude gesture.
B. In case the pedestrian feels intimidated.
C. In case the pedestrian hurries across and falls.
D. In case they take your signal for granted and another driver knocks the pedestrian down.

Q13. Give 2 reasons why you should give a slowing down arm signal when you are approaching a zebra crossing? Fill in the missing words.
1. It warns **f**□□□□□□□□ vehicles of your **i**□□□□□□□□ to **s**□□□ down.
2. It gives **p**□□□□□□□□□□ **c**□□□□□□□□□ that you are **p**□□□□□□□□ to **s**□□□ your car for them.

Q14. Where should you stop at a zebra crossing?
A. Stop just before the white zig-zag lines.
B. Stop just before the white give way lines.
C. Stop just after the give way lines.
D. Stop on the crossing.

Q15. Give three reasons why you should wait until the crossing is completely clear? Fill in the missing words.
1. It is a **l**□□□□ requirement.
2. A pedestrian may **t**□□□ **b**□□□.
3. There is also the possibility of **s**□□□□□□ else **s**□□□□□□□ onto the **c**□□□□□□□.

SOME COMMON FAULTS COMMITTED BY LEARNERS: PEDESTRIAN CROSSINGS

- Not using the Mirrors (Look, Assess, Decide), Signal, Manoeuvre routine.
- Approaching the crossing too fast.
- Failing to anticipate the actions of pedestrians.
- Not stopping at the crossing where necessary.
- Not allowing pedestrians sufficient time to finish crossing.
- Beckoning pedestrians to cross.
- Not proceeding at a pelican crossing when the traffic lights turn to flashing amber.
- Overtaking on the approach to or at the crossing.

Lesson 15 - Dealing with roundabouts

A roundabout is a road junction at which traffic moves one way around a central island. Roundabouts can be many different shapes and sizes but they are designed to help traffic flow by mixing streams of traffic with the minimum amount of delay. As with any other road junction, it is very important that you use the Mirrors (Look, Assess, Decide), Signal, Manoeuvre routine when approaching a roundabout. You must be prepared to give way to traffic from your immediate right. Using the "clock method", let us see how you should deal with a roundabout depending on which direction you wish to travel (see figure 62).

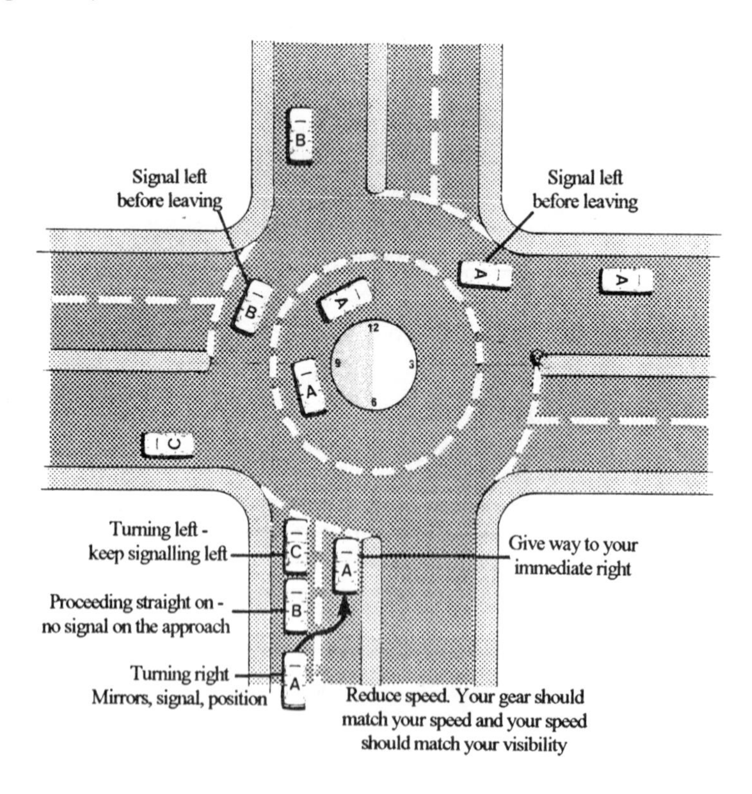

Figure 62. Dealing with a roundabout.

TURNING LEFT (BEFORE 12 O'CLOCK)

As soon as the examiner gives you the instruction to take the next road leading off to the left, the following sequence of movements should take place: **Mirrors (Look, Assess, Decide)**. The mirrors should be checked early, in order that you might assess the situation. Be mindful of the situation both behind and to the sides of the car.

Signal

Signal left to inform other drivers and pedestrians of the direction you intend following.

Manoeuvre and Position

Now position your car approximately 90 cm (3 feet) from the kerb. Try to keep this distance from the kerb and avoid wandering. Remember however that you may have to manoeuvre your car around an obstruction.

Speed

Gently reduce the speed of your car. Start looking early to your right and monitor the amount of traffic already on the roundabout as well as other vehicles emerging into the roundabout. Decide the principal gear you should take to negotiate the roundabout. The gear you select should match your speed and your speed should match your visibility. If it is not safe to proceed at the roundabout you must **stop** and give way.

Remember a give way junction means give way; you do not have to stop - only stop if it is necessary. If you stop needlessly you may hold up other traffic, causing inconvenience or even an accident and you may fail your driving test for undue hesitancy. When it is safe to proceed you should stay in the left-hand lane and keep to this lane throughout the roundabout.

If conditions dictate (for example if the left-hand lane is blocked), approach in the right-hand lane and keep to that lane whilst negotiating the roundabout.

GOING FORWARD (AROUND 12 O'CLOCK)

When going forward, first check the mirrors and do not signal. Position your car in the left-hand lane, and simply follow the set sequence of movements outlined above. However, if the left-hand lane is blocked, position your car in the right-hand lane. Remember, before leaving the roundabout, check the mirrors, and if it is safe, use the left turn indicator just before the exit you wish to take. Also try to select the left-hand lane when leaving the roundabout. If there are more than two lanes at the entrance to a roundabout, select the clearest and most convenient route for the exit you want.

TURNING RIGHT (AFTER 12 O'CLOCK)

If you wish to turn right, check the mirrors and signal right. However on this occasion you must position your car in the right-hand lane when it is safe and keep to that lane throughout the roundabout. Changing lanes unnecessarily is a dangerous practice and it should be avoided at all costs. Before you actually leave the roundabout, check the mirrors and if it is safe, use the left turn indicator at the exit prior to the one you wish to take. You normally have priority when coming off the roundabout. However, to be completely safe you should check your left-hand mirror and over your left shoulder (to check the blind spot), in case another driver is driving round the roundabout in the left-hand lane and it is clear that he is not going to give way. If this happens, you should slow down to let him past if practicable or alternatively drive all the way round the roundabout and leave at the appropriate exit when it is safe. Finally, you should leave in the left-hand lane of your exit unless road conditions dictate otherwise.

Be careful because a driver's zone of vision on the approach to a roundabout can be obstructed by roadside furniture. If in doubt, always **STOP** and give way to traffic from the immediate right. Finally, don't assume when driving on a roundabout that you will continue to have priority. You may occasionally see road signs or markings telling you that you have to give way to other traffic.

THE MINI-ROUNDABOUT

Mini-roundabouts usually consist of a small island or white painted circle in the centre of the junction. The same rules apply at a mini-roundabout as at any other roundabout. You must give way to traffic from your immediate right and travel in a clockwise direction on the roundabout. If you are turning right, use the same procedure as for a normal roundabout. Never be tempted to cross over the small island or the white painted circle. Watch out for large vehicles negotiating the roundabout. They need plenty of room so you should hold back and proceed when the danger has passed.

An additional point to remember is that because mini-roundabouts are very small it is sometimes difficult when turning right to steer and change your signal from right to left. If there is any possibility that you might lose control of your car by taking your hand off the steering wheel to change your signal, you should just keep both hands on the steering wheel and not signal. Do not give up the safety of your car for the sake of an indicator signal.

DEALING WITH ROUNDABOUTS

QUESTIONS (refer to figure 62) (See page 248 for answers).

Q1. Should you give a right turn signal on entering a roundabout with the intention of turning right.?

A. Yes. Other drivers may think you are proceeding straight ahead.

B. No. Only signal right before leaving.

C. No. Only signal right if there is a vehicle behind you.

D. Yes. But only if you see a police car in your rear-view mirror.

Q2. When should you normally give way at a roundabout?

A. You don't have to give way at a roundabout.

B. You should normally give way to traffic from your left.

C. You should normally give way to traffic from your right.

D. You should normally give way to traffic from both directions.

Q3. What gear should you select to negotiate a roundabout?

A. Third gear.

B. First gear if your visibility is good.
C. Second gear if your visibility is good.
D. The gear to match your speed.

Q4. What should you do if it is safe to proceed at a roundabout?
A. You should check that you have signalled.
B. You should enter the roundabout at the earliest opportunity.
C. You should make sure you have selected first or second gear.
D. Check your mirrors one more time.

Q5. What should you do if it is not safe to proceed at a roundabout?
A. You should accelerate around the roundabout.
B. You must stop and give way.
C. Select second gear and approach the roundabout with caution.
D. None of these.

Q6. What may happen if you stop needlessly at a roundabout?
A. You may stall your car and it may take some time to restart.
B. You will confuse other drivers on the roundabout.
C. You may hold up other traffic needlessly.
D. You will take longer to reach your destination.

Q7. Why **must** you look early when approaching a roundabout?
A. To allow you to monitor traffic on the roundabout and act accordingly.
B. To allow you to see emergency vehicles on the roundabout.
C. To allow you to speed up and drive quickly onto the roundabout if you see another motorist driving slowly.
D. To allow you to select the appropriate gear.

Q8. How would you treat a mini-roundabout?
A. You must stop at every mini-roundabout and give way to other traffic from your right.
B. You can drive over a mini-roundabout.

C. Using the same rules as with any other roundabout.
D. With extra caution.

Q9. Why is it important to make effective use of your mirrors and then check over your left shoulder before leaving the roundabout when you are turning right at a roundabout?
A. None of these.
B. You don't have to check before leaving the roundabout. You have priority whilst driving on the roundabout.
C. To ensure that there are no Large Goods Vehicles approaching.
D. In case another driver is driving round the roundabout in the left-hand lane and he is not going to give way to you.

SOME COMMON FAULTS COMMITTED BY LEARNERS: ROUNDABOUTS

- Not using the Mirrors (Look, Assess, Decide), Signal, Manoeuvre routine.
- Not giving way to traffic from the immediate right.
- Not emerging onto the roundabout when a suitable gap appears.
- Not looking early enough to monitor traffic whilst approaching the roundabout. Negotiating the roundabout in the wrong gear.
- Not positioning the car correctly before or during negotiating the roundabout.
- Changing lanes unnecessarily when negotiating the roundabout.
- Emerging into the roundabout when it is unsafe.
- Not leaving the roundabout by the clearest, most convenient exit.
- Signalling too early or too late when approaching or leaving the roundabout. Failing to anticipate the actions of other road users.

Lesson 16 - Dealing with box junctions and dual carriageways

BOX JUNCTIONS

Some road junctions, particularly busy junctions controlled by traffic lights, are called box junctions. At box junctions, criss-cross yellow lines cover the centre of the junction and are designed to permit the free flow of cross traffic. The golden rule is **never** enter a box junction unless your exit road is clear. There is one exception to this rule. If you want to turn right and your exit road is clear, you may enter the box junction even though you are obstructed by oncoming traffic. In this situation, you should position your car and wait in the area marked with yellow lines until there is a safe gap to complete your turn. If there is another vehicle in front of you waiting to turn right, you may wait behind this vehicle. However, be careful because another vehicle coming towards you may want to turn right as well and you must not obstruct it from doing so. Position your car for turning right in the same way as you would for a normal right turn, unless road signs or markings direct otherwise (see figure 63).

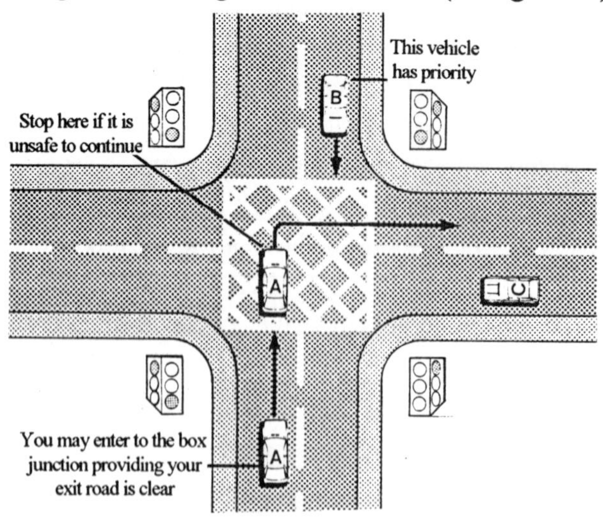

Figure 63. Dealing with box junctions.

DEALING WITH BOX JUNCTIONS

QUESTIONS (refer to figure 63)(See page 248 for answers).

Q1. What is the golden rule at a box junction?

A. Always enter a box junction.

B. Never enter a box junction.

C. Never enter a box junction if you can see oncoming traffic.

D. Never enter a box junction unless your exit road is clear.

Q2. What is the exception to this rule?

A. If you want to turn right and your exit road is clear you may enter the box even though you are obstructed by oncoming traffic.

B. If you want to turn right and there is no oncoming traffic.

C. There is no exception.

D. None of these.

Q3. What position should you normally adopt before turning right at a box junction?

A. In the left-hand lane.

B. As you would for a normal right turn unless road signs or markings direct you otherwise.

C. About 30 cm (1 foot) from the centre of the road, but do not enter the criss cross box.

D. About 60 cm (2 foot) from the centre of the road, but do not enter the criss cross box.

DUAL CARRIAGEWAYS

A dual carriageway is a two-lane road (or more), normally divided by a central reservation, where traffic travels in different directions on either side of the reservation. Dual carriageways present some learners with problems. A pupil of mine once commented, *"Dealing with a dual carriageway is like meeting a migraine"*. Learner drivers have problems at dual carriageways because they become overwhelmed with so much fast moving traffic and visual stimulation going on around them (information overload). They therefore end up missing things that they should be observing. The information overload situation can be avoided if you look well ahead, scan the area and be selective in what you see. Because traffic may move very quickly on dual carriageways, it is vital that you make full use of your mirrors. Keep a good look out for road markings or traffic signs telling you that the dual carriageway is coming to an end so that you will have plenty of time to adjust your speed to suit the new conditions (see figure 64).

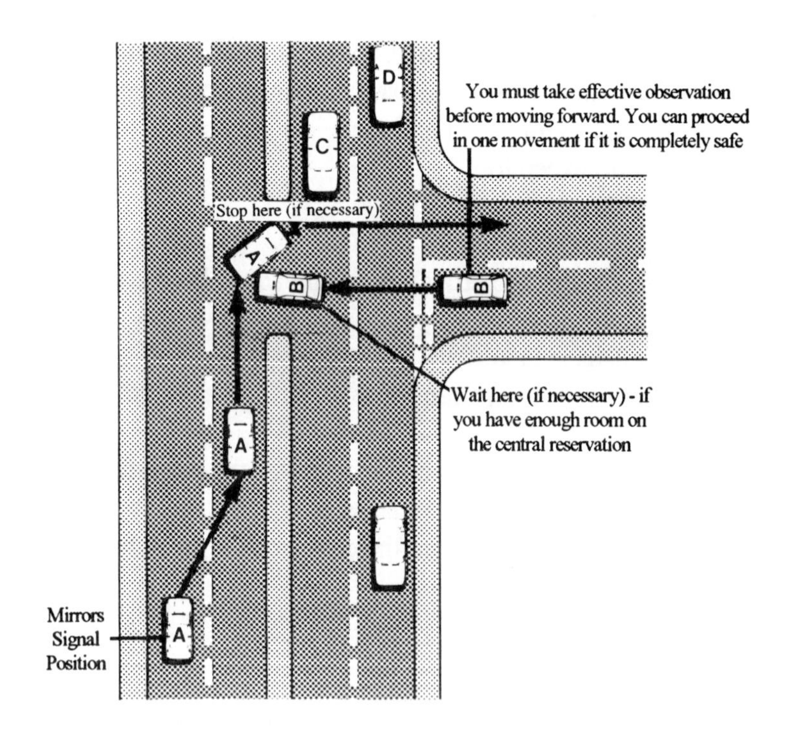

Figure 64. Dealing with dual carriageways.

KEEP LEFT

Do not hog or police the right-hand lane in case someone else wishes to overtake you. Although you may be driving to the maximum speed limit, other drivers may want to go faster and staying in the right-hand lane will only encourage them to either drive very close to your bumper, or overtake you on the left-hand side. If another driver wishes to exceed the speed limit that's their business and their problem if they get caught breaking the law! You should always drive in the left-hand lane of a dual carriageway unless you have very good reason for changing lanes (e.g. turning right, overtaking etc.). On the three-lane dual carriageway you may stay in the middle lane when there are slower vehicles in the left-hand lane, but you should return to the left-hand lane when you have passed them. The right-hand lane is for overtaking (or for right-hand turning traffic). If you use it for overtaking move back into the middle lane and then into the left-hand lane as soon as you can without cutting in.

TURNING RIGHT OFF A DUAL CARRIAGEWAY

Assume that you are driving down the left-hand lane of a dual carriageway when the driving examiner gives you the instruction to turn right at the next road. Apply the Mirrors (Look, Assess, Decide), Signal, Manoeuvre routine as soon as possible and when it is safe, position your car in the right-hand lane. Try to avoid slowing down because traffic in the right-hand lane may be going very fast and you may find it difficult to move across safely. As soon as your position is established, gently brake and change down gears (if necessary), just as you would for a right turn. When you reach the gap in the central reservation watching out for traffic crossing in front of you, stop at point X until the other road is clear for you to turn into. Remember you do not need to stop at point X if the other road is clear and there are no pedestrians to whom you need give way. The secret is to look well ahead and plan your driving to avoid stopping unnecessarily.

TURNING RIGHT ONTO A DUAL CARRIAGEWAY

Dual carriageways are treated as two separate roads. In the first road, traffic will be moving one way from your right, and in the second road beyond the central reservation, traffic will be moving one way from your left. You must only move across to the central reservation if it is wide enough for you to wait safely. On the other hand if the central reservation is not wide enough for you to wait safely, you must remain in the side road until you can cross the dual carriageway in one movement. Other vehicles usually travel very quickly on dual carriageways so you must make sure that you build up an ability to make a prudent and safe judgement of when it is safe to join your new road. It is very important to be ready to move off, so stay in first gear and when a safe opportunity comes along you should take it, or you could end up sitting there forever.

TURNING LEFT ONTO A DUAL CARRIAGEWAY

This is exactly the same as turning from a side road into a main road, but it is imperative to remember to take effective observation before emerging. That means looking right, left and right again. Don't just make superficial head movements. Watch out for pedestrians who may be crossing the road into which you are turning. Finally you should even watch out for somebody reversing, or possibly driving down the wrong side of the carriageway. This may seem ridiculous, but I have seen it happen.

USING A SLIP ROAD

When you are turning left onto a dual carriageway where there is a slip road, you should consider increasing your speed so that you can drive into a safe gap in the traffic at the same speed as the vehicles on the main road. However, if it is not safe to enter the dual carriageway by this method, you must be prepared to give way.

DEALING WITH DUAL CARRIAGEWAYS

QUESTIONS (refer to figure 64) (See page 248 for answers).

Q1. When should you move across to the central reservation if you wish to turn right onto a dual carriageway?

A. If road signs or markings tell you.

B. If it is very wide.

C. If it is wide enough for you to wait safely.

D. If it is safe.

Q2. How do you turn left onto a dual carriageway?
A. The same way as turning from a side road into a main road.
B. The same way as turning from a main road into a side road.
C. At speed.
D. None of these.

Q3. Name two reasons why it is important to drive at the maximum speed (conditions permitting) on a dual carriageway?
1. To **p**□□□□□□ holding up other **d**□□□□□□.
2. It is **e**□□□□□□□□ for your **f**□□□□□ driving after **p**□□□□□□ the driving test.

Q4. What must you do if it's unsafe to wait in the central reservation?
A. Remain in the side road until you can cross the dual carriageway in one movement.
B. Squeeze into the central reservation as soon as it is safe.
C. Wait until the police arrive.
D. None of these.

Q5. Why should you make full use of your mirrors before moving over to the right-hand lane of a dual carriageway?
A. In case another driver flashes you.
B. So that you can clean them if they are dirty.
C. To watch out for emergency vehicles.
D. Traffic may be moving very quickly.

Chapter 6

Lesson 17 - The emergency stop

During your driving test, the driving examiner will stop you at the left-hand side of the road and ask you if you understand his instructions so far. The examiner will then say, *"Very shortly I shall ask you to stop as in an emergency; the signal will be like this."* (he will demonstrate).*"When I do that, stop immediately and under full control, as though a child had run off the pavement."* After the emergency stop the examiner will say, *"Thank you, I will not ask you to do that exercise again."*

Once the examiner has given the signal to stop (the examiner will check to see if it is safe) you should apply the footbrake straight away. Do not check the mirrors as there is no time (you should know what is behind you if you were checking your mirrors properly). The footbrake should be pressed firmly and progressively but under full control. The clutch should only be applied just before the car comes to a halt. This will avoid the engine stalling (cutting out). If the clutch is applied before the footbrake the car will not slow down as efficiently and if you are travelling down a hill it will actually speed up. Always remember the sequence, **brake before clutch** and keep both your hands on the steering wheel to keep full control.

The amount of pressure you apply on the footbrake will depend on the road conditions. If the road is good, firm and dry, you can afford to brake firmly. However, if the road surface is wet and loose you will have to brake less firmly. If the brake is applied too hard and the car begins to skid, you may be faulted. If you realise that the car is skidding, and you remove your foot from the brake, then quickly re-apply it more gently - you will not be faulted, providing that you do not take too long to stop.

Remember, in poor weather conditions, rain, sleet or snow you must allow more time to stop. Once your car has stopped, apply the parking brake and select neutral. If you apply the parking brake whilst the car is moving, you may lock your rear wheels and cause your car to skid. Before you move off again, check your mirrors and look over both shoulders. The reason you check over your left shoulder is because your car may be far from the kerb and there is danger that a bicycle or motorcycle could pass up the inside lane. Remember that if your brakes and tyres are not in first class condition, you will take much longer to stop.

THE MAIN CAUSES OF SKIDDING

There are three different types of skids that may occur if you are driving a motor car: a front-wheel skid, a rear-wheel skid and a four-wheel skid. There are four main causes of skidding: excessive speed, harsh braking, fierce acceleration and coarse steering. Coarse (erratic) steering basically means whip lashing the steering wheel. A good driver never gets caught in a skid. If you are looking well ahead and driving at a speed appropriate to the road and traffic conditions, a skid should never happen.

THE CORRECTION OF SKIDS

If your car gets involved in a skid, you must know what caused the skid and the most effective way to correct it. As soon as you apply harsh pressure to the footbrake the occupants and the full weight of your car are thrown forwards, making the rear of your car much lighter. When this happens the rear wheels could lose their grip on the road. If you apply too much pressure on the accelerator the occupants of your car are pressed back in their seats, making the weight of your car much lighter at the front, and the front wheels could lose their grip on the road. If your car is cornering too fast, the occupants of your car are thrown sideways and a skid could again occur (see figure 65).

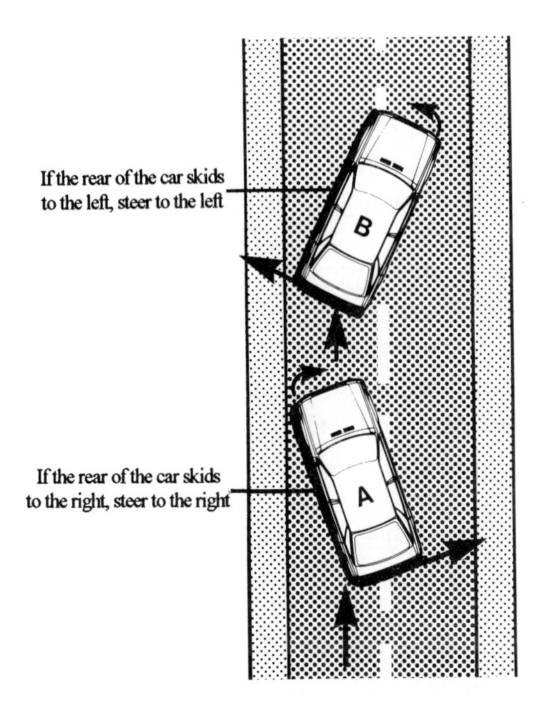

Figure 65. Controlling a skid.

The front-wheel skid

A front-wheel skid normally happens on a bend or corner when the front wheels of your car lose their grip on the road, and the car does not travel in the direction you intend. As soon as you realise this is happening, release the footbrake immediately and re-apply the footbrake more gently, straightening the steering to allow the front wheels to regain their grip on the road. Then steer to a safety line position.

The rear-wheel skid

If your rear wheels lose their grip on the road, and the rear of your car swings either to the right or to the left you are in a rear-wheel skid. It is normally caused by harsh braking or excessive speed for the road conditions. As soon as you realise this is happening you must take your foot off the brake pedal, and turn the steering wheel in the direction of the skid.

If the rear wheels slide to the right, turn the steering wheel to the right. If the rear wheels slide to the left, turn the steering wheel to the left. When you have gained full control, you can then steer your car to a safety line position.

The four-wheel skid

Finally, if all four wheels of your car lose their grip on the road, you are in a four-wheel skid. This occurs if you apply the footbrake too suddenly and you will feel the car sliding helplessly out of control in any direction. To correct this type of skid you should relax the pressure on the footbrake. This will allow the wheels to re-grip the road and then pump the brake pedal on and off (rhythmic or cadence braking) until your car regains control.

Anti-locking braking systems (ABS)

If your vehicle is fitted with anti-lock brakes, they can be extremely useful in an emergency. When the wheels are about to lock, a sensor control releases the brake and applies it again, which is really automatic rhythmic braking. In other words, you can keep the pressure on and steer at the same time.

TO SUM UP

Remember, a skid should never occur if you are driving properly. When some people get involved in a skid they usually blame the weather or road conditions. It is neither the weather nor ice on the road that causes a skid but the driver.

Good forward road observations and planning will prevent you skidding on black ice or wet and slippery road surfaces. If the roads are so bad, it would be much safer to keep off them unless your journey is so important that it cannot be avoided (see figure 66).

Figure 66. When stopping in an emergency, brake firmly and progressively.

THE EMERGENCY STOP

QUESTIONS (refer to figures 65 and 66) (See page 248 for answers).

Q1. Why is it important to apply the footbrake **before** the clutch?

A. You may stall the car.

B. You should brake and clutch at the same time.

C. You should apply the clutch before the footbrake to stop your car stalling.

D. If you clutch first you may gain speed and your braking will not be so effective.

Q2. What should you do as soon as your car has stopped?

A. Select neutral and apply the parking brake.

B. Apply the parking brake and select neutral.

C. Check your mirrors and move off if it is safe to do so.

D. Get out and check the tyres.

Q3. What does coarse steering mean?
A. Steering with one hand.
B. Steering with both hands.
C. Steering with one hand and resting your elbow on the door.
D. Erratic steering.

Q4. What type of braking should you apply to the footbrake before stopping when instructed to stop by the examiner?
A. Soft braking.
B. Very hard and sudden braking.
C. Firm and progressive braking.
D. Only brake when it is safe, not when your examiner tells you.

Q5. What will happen if you have to carry out an emergency stop and your brakes and tyres are not in first-class condition?
A. You will take much longer to stop.
B. You will skid.
C. You will take an extra three seconds to stop.
D. You will take an extra ten seconds to stop.

Q6. Name three different types of skids that may occur if you are driving a motor car? Fill in the missing words.
1. The **f**□□□□ wheel skid.
2. The **r**□□□ wheel skid.
3. The **f**□□□ wheel skid.

Q7. Name the four main causes of skidding? Fill in the missing words.
1. **E**□□□□□□□□ speed for the conditions.
2. **H**□□□□ braking.
3. **F**□□□□□ acceleration.
4. **C**□□□□□ steering.

Q8. Is this statement true or false?
A good driver never gets caught in a skid.

Q9. Why might your car skid if you apply harsh pressure to the footbrake?
A. The occupants and the weight of your car are thrown forwards thus making the rear of your car much lighter.
B. The occupants and the weight of your car are thrown backwards thus making the front of your car much lighter.
C. Your car will not be able to grip the road.
D. None of these.

Q10. How do you correct a rear-wheel skid?
A. Depress the clutch.
B. Take your foot off the brake pedal and turn the steering wheel in the opposite direction of the skid.
C. Pump the brake pedal on and off.
D. Take your foot off the brake pedal and turn the steering wheel in the direction of the skid.

Q11. How do you correct a four-wheel skid?
A. Apply the parking brake and turn the steering wheel quickly to the left.
B. Relax the pressure on the footbrake and turn the steering wheel in the direction of the skid.
C. Relax the pressure on the footbrake and then pump the brake pedal on and off (rhythmically) until your car gains full control.
D. Depress the clutch.

Q13. Why is it important to keep both hands on the steering wheel whilst carrying out an emergency stop?
A. So that you don't put the parking brake on too early.
B. So that you to keep full control of your car.
C. In case another vehicle hits the side of your vehicle.
D. In case the steering wheel spins erratically.

SOME COMMON FAULTS COMMITTED BY LEARNERS: EMERGENCY STOP

- Not stopping quickly enough.
- Not reacting quickly enough.
- Not braking firmly and progressively.
- Not reacting when given the command to stop.
- Slow reaction when given the command to stop.
- Locking the wheels causing the car to skid.
- Turning the steering wheel the wrong way when the car skids.
- Applying or reaching for the parking brake before stopping.
- Removing one hand from the steering wheel before stopping.
- Applying the clutch before the footbrake.
- Applying the footbrake and the clutch at the same time.
- Not observing properly after the emergency stop.
- Moving off when unsafe to do so after the emergency stop.
- Not applying the parking brake or selecting neutral after stopping.
- Failing to release the parking brake before moving off.

Lesson 18 - The driving test, the Highway Code, other motoring matters and some myths

THE DRIVING TEST - FOOD FOR THOUGHT

Most learners fail their driving test because of insufficient instruction and practice. A good driving instructor has the knowledge and experience to judge when you are ready. Attempting to sit your driving test too soon is both a waste of your money and the examiner's time. You should spend your money at learning **how to drive** and not how to pass the driving test. You will be ready to sit your driving test as soon as you can drive and manoeuvre your car consistently and with confidence without any supervision or guidance from your instructor, and when you have achieved plenty of road sense and gained experience of different types of road and traffic conditions.

APPLYING FOR THE TEST

You can obtain a test application form from your driving instructor. Send your completed form with the correct fee to the appropriate Driving Standards Agency office. Once you receive your driving test appointment card, inform the Driving Standards Agency office immediately if it is not possible for you to keep your appointment.

THE DAY OF THE TEST

Ensure that you arrive at the test centre early, allowing sufficient time to park your car close to the centre. You should park in a legal, safe and convenient place. Make sure your car displays "L" plates at the front and rear of your car - avoid putting them on the windows. The car you use must be properly licensed, registered and insured. The seat belts must be clean, untangled and they must work properly. It is important that all the windows, lights and indicators are clean and you should remove all stickers and mascots (e.g. fluffy dice) that may impair your vision. Sit in the waiting room at least ten minutes before the scheduled time of your test. Do not worry about anyone else talking - I've heard more rubbish coming from the test centre waiting room than a psychiatrist's treatment surgery. Have your provisional driving licence and appointment card.

ENTER THE EXAMINER

When the driving examiner calls your name, greet him with a smile to show that you are confident. The examiner will ask you to sign your name on a form, and then request that you lead the way to your vehicle. If you do not understand English very well, or you are deaf and unable to speak, you may take an interpreter with you but ask the examiner for permission. The interpreter must not be your driving instructor and must not interfere with the conduct of the test in any way. Sometimes two examiners will be present at the test. The Supervising Examiner is testing the first examiner and he will sit in the back seat to ensure your examiner is testing you within the Driving Standard Agency's guidelines. The Supervising Examiner will not interfere with the conduct of the test, and does not have the authority to overrule the examiner's decision.

THE EYESIGHT TEST

The examiner will then ask you to read a number plate of a stationary vehicle over the prescribed distance. If you are unsuccessful he will bring you closer to the vehicle and give you another chance. Should you fail this test, the examiner will use a measuring tape to determine the precise distance using another vehicle. If you are unsuccessful on this occasion, you will fail the test and the examiner will issue a Failure Certificate. Once you have passed the eyesight test, the examiner will ask you to get into your vehicle and make yourself comfortable.

When the examiner has checked your car he will then say, *"Follow the road ahead unless the traffic signs or road markings direct you otherwise, or unless I ask you to turn, which I'll do in good time. Move off when you are ready please."* The examiner will not use the words corner, crossroads, junctions or traffic lights. It is your responsibility to recognise that they are coming up and you must deal with them accordingly.

SAFETY CHECKS BEFORE STARTING THE ENGINE

When you get into your vehicle you should check the following:

- All the doors are properly closed.
- Adjust your seat (if necessary).
- Fasten your seatbelt.
- Make sure your mirrors are properly adjusted.
- That the parking brake is on.
- That the gear is in the neutral position.

Do not waste time by taking a long time over these checks. The seat and the mirrors should already be in the correct position if you drove the car to the test centre. Start the engine and carry out the Preparation, Observation and Move routine before moving off.

TIPS FOR THE TEST

During the test, make sure that you use the accelerator, clutch, gears, footbrake, parking brake and steering properly and smoothly and that you move away safely and under control. Always depress the clutch just before stopping. If you stall your engine, remain calm and simply apply the parking brake and select neutral. Use the correct gear for your speed and the road conditions. Change gear at the correct time before any hazard or bends on the road. Never coast by letting your car run with the gear lever in neutral. You should neither watch the examiner nor look down at the foot and hand controls whilst driving. Avoid late or harsh braking. In most situations, only firm pressure is needed to brake safely. Avoid overuse of the parking brake, but apply it where necessary. The examiner will expect you to drive with the traditional "push and pull" method whilst turning and do not steer too early or too late. Steer in a controlled and safe manner. Make sure you carry out the Mirrors (Look, Assess, Decide), Signal, Manoeuvre routine before making any driving decision.

MOVING AWAY

The examiner will expect you to move off safely and under control on level ground, from behind a parked vehicle and on an uphill gradient. Make sure you release your parking brake and always check your Mirrors, Look, Assess, Decide and give a signal if any road users would benefit. Remember to check your blind spot by looking round for traffic and pedestrians. Never move off if you would make another driver or cyclist slow down or alter their course. Follow the road ahead as the examiner told you. Don't worry, the examiner will know you are nervous and he will give you directions in good time, in a clear and unmistakable manner. The examiner will not try to trick you because he is there to ensure that you are a safe and competent driver and he will not expect you to drive perfectly. The examiner will be polite and you will drive on routes specially selected for the driving test which will include all types of roads and traffic conditions.

MAKING NORMAL PROGRESS

Drive normally, make normal progress and try to keep up with the flow of traffic - conditions permitting. You must build up speed before changing into a higher gear and avoid selecting first gear for every turn. You will probably come across some give way junctions or crossroads. Make sure you regulate your speed on the approach. Drive straight ahead unless you are told otherwise. Don't take too long to prepare for moving off, and avoid hanging around junctions waiting for something to happen. Many learners desperately try to please the examiner by being overcautious but they usually end up becoming a nuisance, and fail their test for undue hesitancy.

THE EMERGENCY STOP

Try to stop as soon as possible and under full control as soon as your examiner gives you the signal. Once you have completed the emergency stop, the examiner will say, *"Thank you. I shall not ask you to carry out that exercise again. Drive on when you are ready, please"*. This is to avoid you thinking that another emergency stop instruction has been given if the examiner makes any movement with his hand. Make sure that you check over both shoulders before moving off again. If a real emergency stop arises during your test, you may not be asked to carry out this exercise.

MANOEUVRING EXERCISES

Soon after you have moved off, the examiner may ask you to stop and to reverse your car into a side road, either to the right or the left or reverse park. He may then ask you to turn your car round in the road, using forward to reverse gears so that it is facing the opposite direction. Always proceed under low-speed control making proper use of the clutch, accelerator, brakes and steering to achieve reasonable accuracy. Avoid striking the kerb and keep a look out, giving way to other vehicles and pedestrians during the manoeuvring exercises.

CARE IN THE USE OF SPEED

Once you have completed all your manoeuvres, the examiner will then ask you to move off and you should be prepared to deal with any hazards you may come across. Watch your speed does not break the speed limit and do not drive too fast for the road and traffic conditions. Ensure that you can stop safely in the distance you can see to be clear. Always keep a safe distance from the vehicle in front. Remember that if your vehicle is travelling at 30 mph, it will travel approximately 14 metres (45 feet) every second. There's an old saying, ***"When skating over thin ice, be wise with speed".***

GENERAL ROAD POSITIONING

Keep to the left during normal driving unless you have a legitimate reason for not doing so. When approaching roundabouts, make sure that you take the correct lane on the approach to and through the roundabout. Where lanes are marked, keep to the middle of the lane if possible: do not hug the middle of the road or drive in the gutter. Keep looking well ahead to avoid weaving in and out between parked vehicles. If you have to overtake another vehicle, always move back into the left-hand side of the road (conditions permitting), as soon as you can see the vehicle you have overtaken appear in your interior mirror.

DEALING WITH ROAD JUNCTIONS

Keep a good look out for give way junctions and any unmarked crossroads and be prepared to stop if necessary. If you do stop, avoid allowing your car to cross the markings painted on the road or past the kerbline of the junction. Regulate your speed on the approach and take effective observation before moving into any junction. If you are turning right, position your car just left to the centre of the road. However, keep well left if you are turning right out of a narrow road and avoid cutting the corner. If you are turning left keep over to the left and do not swing out. Always give way to pedestrians who are crossing the road.

ACTING ON SIGNS AND SIGNALS

Act properly if you come across any stop signs, red traffic lights or markings on the road. Never proceed through a green traffic light unless the way is clear. Obey all signals given by police officers, traffic wardens and school crossing patrols.

OVERTAKING, MEETING AND CROSSING THE PATH OF OTHER VEHICLES SAFELY

If you have to either overtake, meet or cross the path of other vehicles, make sure that you do it safely. Allow enough room when you are overtaking another vehicle or cyclist and do not cut in too sharply after overtaking. If the road narrows and you are in any doubt whether there is enough room for two vehicles, hold back and let the approaching vehicle through. Remember, ***"Never be the meat in the sandwich".***

DEALING WITH PEDESTRIAN CROSSINGS

Keep looking well ahead and if you see a pedestrian crossing ahead, exercise care and be prepared to give a slowing down arm signal if it would help other road users. Stop at the crossing and drive on only when it is legal and safe.

ALERTNESS AND ANTICIPATION

Always look well ahead and think before you make any driving decision. Try to anticipate what other road users will do, including pedestrians, and act accordingly. If you are good enough as a driver, the examiner will pass you. An examiner is a professional and recognises mistakes caused by nerves as opposed to a learner not being properly trained for the test.

PASS OR FAIL

The examiner will pass you providing that you have not committed any serious or dangerous faults. If you pass, the examiner will ask you for your licence and require you to sign the pass certificate. However, if you pass or fail, the examiner will hand you the driving test report form, on which will be marked the points which caused your failure.

Figure 67. "Have I passed?"

THE HIGHWAY CODE AND SOME MYTHS

In this chapter, typical Highway Code questions and other motoring matters are listed, together with the correct answers. It is essential to learn the Highway Code properly as this will help you to pass the theory test and to drive safely and competently, whether as a learner or a qualified driver.

HIGHWAY CODE AND OTHER MOTORING MATTERS

QUESTIONS (See page 248-249 for answers).

Q1. What are the last two observation checks you should make before moving off from the side of the road?

A. You should check the blind spot over your shoulder but then signal before moving off.

B. You should check the interior and outside mirrors.

C. You should check the blind spot over your shoulder but then make sure you look forward before the car moves.

D. You should check your interior mirror and left shoulder.

Q2. Where should you always check before turning left? Fill in the missing words.

Always check your **m**□□□□□□ for **c**□□□□□□□ who may have come up on the **l**□□□-**h**□□□ side. Also check the **r**□□□ into which you are **t**□□□□□□.

Q3. What are the three main factors which cause skidding? Fill in the missing words.

Fierce **a**□□□□□□□□□□□, **h**□□□□ braking and erratic **s**□□□□□□□.

Q4. How would you treat a crossroad where the traffic lights had failed?

A. Follow the same procedure as for an unmarked crossroad.

B. Follow the same procedure as for a major crossroad.

A. Follow the same procedure as for a minor crossroad.

D. Follow the same procedure as for a pedestrian crossing.

ROAD TRAFFIC SIGNS

The three basic types of traffic signs, are those which give orders (circles), warnings (triangles) and information (rectangles). There follows 96 different road traffic signs. Each sign has a possible four answers - only one answer is correct. Answers are given on page 249.

1.
A. Proceed straight ahead only.
B. Give way to the left and right.
C. Crossroads.
D. Wait here.

2.
A. Give way to the left.
B. Give way to the right.
C. Turn left only.
D. T-junction.

3.
A. Proceed straight ahead only.
B. Side road.
C. Give way to the right.
D. Major road approaching.

4.
A. Staggered junction.
B. Give way to the left and right.
C. Crossroads.
D. Your right of way only.

5.
A. Double bend first to the left.
B. Double bend first to the right.
C. Slippery road.
D. Staggered junction.

6.
A. Keep moving to the left.
B. Keep moving to the right.
C. Tunnel approaching.
D. Roundabout.

7.
A. Dual carriageway finishes.
B. Road narrows on both sides.
C. Bottleneck ahead.
D. None of these.

8.
A. Road narrows on the left.
B. Motorway ahead.
C. Road narrows on the right.
D. Road narrows.

9.
A. Tunnel ahead.
B. Dual carriageway starts.
C. Dual carriageway ends.
D. Two main roads merge.

10.
A. Two-way traffic.
B. Fast moving traffic in both directions.
C. Beware of oncoming traffic.
D. None of these.

11.
A. Your right of way, both left and right.
B. Give way to the left and right.
C. Crossroads.
D. Two-way traffic on route crossing ahead.

12.
A. Steep hill upwards.
B. Only partial parking restrictions.
C. Steep hill downwards.
D. Limited access.

13.
A. Speed restrictions in force.
B. Beware of speeding traffic.
C. Ice on the road.
D. Slippery road.

14.
A. Road humps.
B. Ramp ahead.
C. Uneven surface.
D. Tunnel with limited vision ahead.

15.
A. Other danger - a plate will indicate the nature of the danger.
B. Beware of oncoming traffic.
C. Beware of crossroads.
D. Beware of speeding restrictions.

16.
A. Limited vision ahead.
B. Building works ahead.
C. Uneven surface.
D. Tunnel.

17.
A. Uneven surface.
B. Checkpoint ahead.
C. Opening or swing bridge.
D. Fast flowing water ahead.

18.
A. Hump bridge.
B. Tunnel.
C. Speed ramps.
D. None of these.

19.
A. Steep hill ahead.
B. Road chippings.
C. Risk of falling or fallen rocks.
D. Road with no
road surface ahead.

20.
A. Opening or swing bridge.
B. Quayside or riverbank.
C. Fast flowing water ahead.
D. Beware quayside only.

21.
A. Children going to or from school.
B. Children going to a play area.
C. Children running.
D. Children playing outside school.

22.
A. Icey surface.
B. Uneven pavement.
C. Beware pedestrians.
D. Pedestrian crossing.

23.
A. Elderly pedestrians likely to cross.
B. Old peoples home.
C. Blind pedestrians likely to cross.
D. Blind or deaf pedestrians
likely to cross.

24.
A. Toddler and playgroup.
B. School.
C. Pedestrians.
D. Pedestrians in road.

25.
A. Warning of buses
crossing the road ahead.
B. Give way to trams only.
C. Give way to buses only.
D. Warning of trams
crossing the road ahead.

26.
A. The maximum safe headroom
under a bridge or other overhead
obstruction.
B. The minimum safe headroom
under a bridge or other overhead
obstruction.
C. Beware of other vehicles
over the height shown.
D. Beware of highsided vehicles.

27.
A. Level crossing.
B. Steam trains ahead.
C. Railway museum ahead.
D. Level crossing without
a gate or barrier.

28.
A. Electricity substation ahead.
B. Staggered junction.
C. Give way to the left and right.
D. Electrified overhead cable.

29.
A. Pedal cycle route ahead.
B. No bicycles.
C. Bicycles only.
D. None of these.

30.
A. Snow on the road.
B. Loose chippings on the road.
C. Water on the road.
D. Mud on the road.

Red rings or circles tell you what you must not do.

31.
A. No through road.
B. Wait here.
C. No entry for lorries only.
D. No entry for vehicular traffic.

32.
A. No motor vehicles.
B. Motor vehicles only.
C. No overtaking.
D. No right of way for motorcycles.

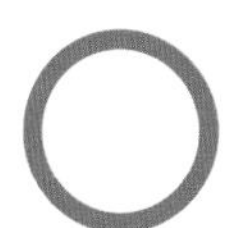

33.
A. No vehicles except bicycles being pushed by hand.
B. No vehicles.
C. No entry for vehicular traffic.
D. No waiting.

34.
A. No motor vehicles.
B. No motor vehicles except motorcycles without sidecars.
C. Motor vehicles only.
D. No right of way.

35.
A. No vehicles over maximum width shown.
B. Road narrows to width shown.
C. Bridge approaching of width shown.
D. None of these.

36.
A. No vehicles over maximum gross weight shown in tonnes.
B. Goods vehicles over maximum gross weight shown in tonnes.
C. Loading area for goods vehicles.
D. No goods vehicles over maximum gross weight shown in tonnes.

37.
A. No U turn.
B. Motorway ends here.
C. Motorway starts here.
D. Sharp bend approaching.

38.
A. No left turn.
B. No U turn.
C. Sharp bend to the right.
D. No right turn.

39.
A. No overtaking.
B. Narrow road.
C. No motor vehicles.
D. No motor vehicles except motorcycles without sidecars.

40.
A. You have priority.
B. One way street.
C. Road narrows.
D. Priority must be given to vehicles from the other direction.

41.
A. School.
B. Toddler and playgroup.
C. Vehicles must not go beyond the sign where displayed by a School Crossing Patrol.
D. Pedestrians in road.

42.
A. The maximum speed at which traffic may travel, if it is safe to do so.
B. The minimum speed at which traffic may travel.
C. The maximum speed at which traffic may travel.
D. None of these.

43.
A. No vehicles over the height shown may pass the sign.
B. No vehicles over the width shown may pass the sign.
C. Only vehicles over the height shown may pass the sign.
D. Only vehicles over the width shown may pass the sign.

44. *(to apply from 1.1.97)*
A. No buses.
B. No vehicles with over 6 seats (excluding driver) or local buses.
C. No vehicles with over 10 seats (excluding driver) or local buses.
D. No vehicles with over 8 seats (excluding driver) or local buses.

45.
A. Route for pedal cycles only.
B. Riding of pedal cycles prohibited.
C. Route recommended for pedal cycles.
D. Pedal cycle route ahead.

46. Complete the following. No stopping on the main carriageway....
A. Except at a layby, at any time - not even to set down passengers.
B. Except at a layby at any time.
C. Except at a layby.
D. None of these.

Blue circles tell you what you must do.

47.
A. Proceed in direction indicated by the arrow.
B. Do not proceed in direction indicated by the arrow.
C. Priority for vehicles travelling in direction indicated by the arrow.
D. One way traffic.

48.
A. Roundabout.
B. One way traffic.
C. Mini-roundabout (give way to traffic from the immediate left).
D. Mini-roundabout (give way to traffic from the immediate right).

49.
A. Two roads converge.
B. Vehicles may pass either side to reach the same destination.
C. Vehicles may not pass either side.
D. None of these.

50. At what speed does this sign indicate that traffic must travel?
A. Less than the maximum shown.
B. Less than the minimum shown unless it is unsafe or impracticable to do so.
C. Less than the minimum shown unless you see an ambulance.
D. More than the maximum shown.

51.
A. The end of a minimum speed requirement.
B. The start of a minimum speed requirement.
C. The end of a maximum speed requirement.
D. The start of a maximum speed requirement.

52.
A. Route for trams only.
B. Route for buses only.
C. No access for trams.
D. No access for buses.

53.
A. Route for trams and pedal cycles only.
B. No access for buses and pedal cycles.
C. No access for trams and pedal cycles.
D. Route for buses and pedal cycles only.

54.
A. No access for pedal cycles and pedestrians.
B. Shared route for pedal cycles and pedestrians only.
C. Beware no pavements.
D. Separated track and path for pedal cycles and pedestrians.

55.
A. Separated track and path for pedal cycles and pedestrians.
B. Beware no pavements.
C. Shared route for pedal cycles and pedestrians only.
D. No access for pedal cycles and pedestrians.

Blue rectangles are used for information signs, except on motorways where blue is used for direction signs.

56.

A. One way traffic.

B. No access straight ahead.

C. Proceed in direction indicated by the arrow.

D. Priority must be given to vehicles from the other direction.

57. What does this sign indicate that vehicles may do?

A. Not park partially on the verge or footway.

B. Not park partially on the verge.

C. Park partially on the footway or at someone's driveway.

D. Park partially on the verge or footway.

58.

A. Vehicles may park partially on the footway.

B. Vehicles may park partially on the verge except at night.

C. Vehicles may park partially on the verge or footway.

D. End of area where vehicles may park wholly on the verge or footway.

59.

A. A mandatory width restriction ahead.

B. A mandatory height restriction ahead.

C. A mandatory length restriction ahead.

D. A mandatory weight restriction ahead.

60.

A. With-flow bus lane ahead which pedal cycles and taxis may not use.

B. With-flow bus lane ahead which no other vehicle may use.

C. With-flow bus lane ahead which pedal cycles and taxis may also use.

D. Contra-flow bus lane ahead which pedal cycles and taxis may also use.

61.

A. With-flow bus lane.

B. With-flow bus lane ahead which no other vehicle may use.

C. Bus lane ahead.

D. Contra-flow bus lane.

62.

A. With-flow pedal cycle lane ahead.

B. End of pedal cycle lane.

C. Route recommended for pedal cycles.

D. Contra-flow pedal cycle lane ahead.

Waiting restrictions.

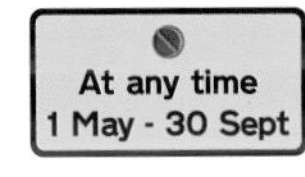

63.

A. Waiting only between the dates shown.

B. Residents parking only between the dates shown.

C. No waiting between the dates shown.

D. None of these.

Loading restrictions.

64.

A. Loading for residents only.

B. Loading prohibited between 9.00 hours and 17.00 hours.

C. End of loading area.

D. Loading prohibited for a shorter period.

Motorway signs and signals.

65.
A. No motorcycles allowed on the motorway.
B. Motorway regulations start to apply to the road.
C. Motorway regulations end.
D. No parking on the motorway.

66.
A. Junction 25 of the motorway approaching in half a mile.
B. Junction 25 of the motorway is closed.
C. No turning off the motorway.
D. None of these.

67. Countdown markers indicate the distance to the start of the deceleration lane. How far does each bar represent?
A. 200 yards.
B. 300 yards.
C. 400 yards.
D. 100 yards.

68.
A. Use the second junction off the motorway.
B. No turning off the motorway for two junctions.
C. Two junctions follow in quick succession.
D. Use the first junction off the motorway.

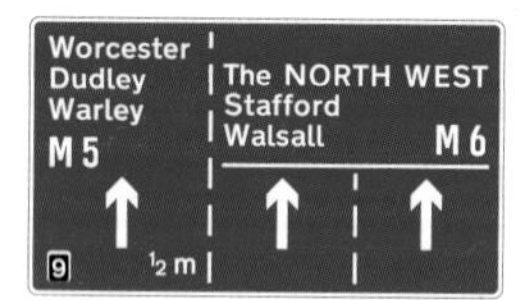

69.
A. The junction of the motorway has limited access.
B. The junction of the motorway is closed.
C. No turning off the motorway.
D. The left hand lane of a motorway leads only to another motorway or route at the junction ahead in the distance shown.

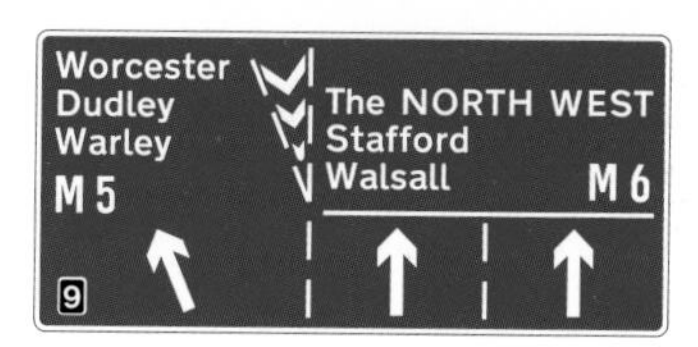

70.
A. Where two routes diverge. Countdown markers are used at this type of junction.
B. Where two routes converge. Countdown markers are not used at this type of junction.
C. Where two routes converge. Countdown markers are used at this type of junction.
D. Where two routes diverge. Countdown markers are not used at this type of junction.

Police patrol vehicles only

71.
A. To be used only by the Police.
B. Not to be used by the Police.
C. No picnicking.
D. None of these.

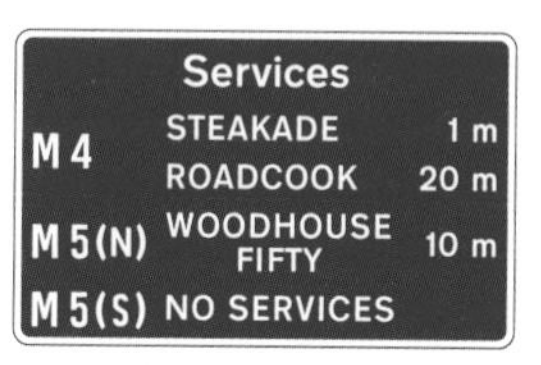

72.
A. This sign will appear at about a mile in advance of a motorway service area.
B. No services available.
C. Services available at the next exit.
D. Availability of services ahead.

73. At what intervals are marker posts located at the back of the hard shoulder to show the direction to the nearest emergency telephone.
A. 200 yard.
B. 300 yard.
C. 100 yard.
D. 150 yard.

74.
A. The end of the motorway.
B. Motorway closed.
C. The start of the motorway.
D. Only two lanes of the motorway are open.

75.
A. Stop, all lanes ahead closed.
B. Change lane.
C. End of restriction.
D. Do not proceed any further in this lane.

Primary route direction signs.

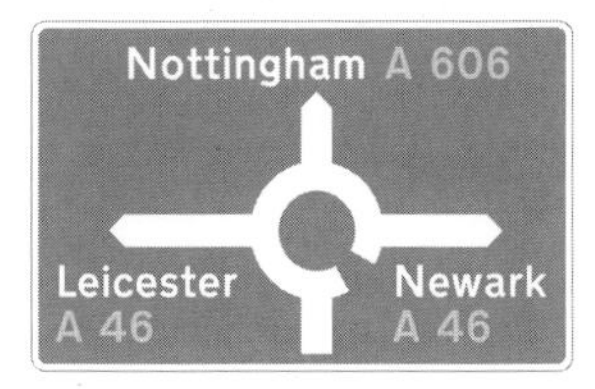

76. What are the colours on a primary routes sign?
A. Green background, yellow route number and white lettering and border.
B. Yellow background, green route number and white lettering and border.
C. White background, yellow route number and green lettering and border.
D. Blue background, yellow route number and white lettering and border.

77. Countdown markers indicate the distance to the start of the deceleration lane. How far does each bar represent?
A. 150 yards.
B. 200 yards.
C. 250 yards.
D. 100 yards.

78.
A. Non-primary route ring road.
B. No right of way.
C. Primary route ring road.
D. No reversing.

79.
A. No reversing.
B. No right of way.
C. Primary route ring road.
D. Non-primary route ring road.

80. On which roads does this sign indicate where additional lanes join the road, the number of lanes, the direction from which they are joining and which traffic lanes take priority?
A. Dual carriageway.
B. Slip road.
C. Main carriageway.
D. Motorway.

81. As above.
A. Slip road.
B. Motorway.
C. Main carriageway.
D. Dual carriageway.

Tourist signs

82.
A. Elephants on the loose.
B. Safari park.
C. Nature reserve.
D. Zoo.

83.
A. Motor museum.
B. English Heritage.
C. Agricultural museum.
D. Theme park.

84.
A. National Trust.
B. English Heritage.
C. Castle.
D. Site of Roman remains.

Service signs

85. Where does this sign indicate to?
A. An Automobile Association telephone.
B. A telephone.
C. A Royal Automobile Club telephone.
D. A Green Flag telephone.

86. Where does this sign indicate to?

A. Public toilets.
B. Hospital.
C. Telephone.
D. Public toilets which have facilities for disabled people.

87.

A. Forestry Commission land - keep out.
B. No picnicking.
C. Picnic area.
D. Christmas trees for sale.

88.

A. Camping site.
B. Camping and caravan site.
C. Caravan site.
D. No camping.

89.

A. Cycle parking place.
B. No parking.
C. Cycles only.
D. No cycling.

90.

A. Large Goods Vehicles parking only, telephone and toilets.
B. No Large Goods Vehicles.
C. No facilities available.
D. Parking facilities open to all.

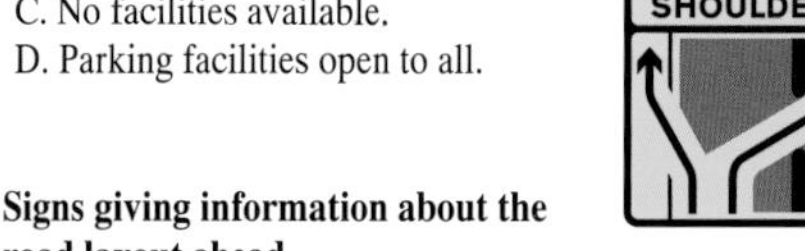

Signs giving information about the road layout ahead.

91.

A. Cul-de-sac.
B. No through route for vehicular traffic ahead.
C. Wait here until further notice.
D. Motorway starts.

92.

A. Traffic travelling in the direction of the white arrow have priority.
B. Traffic travelling in the direction of the red arrow have priority.
C. No through road.
D. One way street.

93. What does this sign indicate will happen in 800 yards?

A. All lanes are closed.
B. The two right-hand lanes of a motorway are closed. The two left-hand lanes remain open.
C. The two left-hand lanes of a four lane dual carriageway are closed. The two right-hand lanes remain open.
D. The two right-hand lanes of a four lane dual carriageway are closed. The two left-hand lanes remain open.

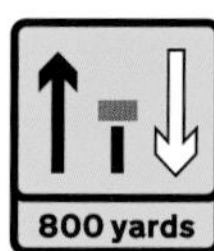

94. What does this sign indicate will happen in 800 yards?

A. No through road.
B. The left-hand lane of a three lane single carriageway road is closed.
C. The middle lane of a three lane single carriageway road is closed.
D. The right-hand lane of a three lane single carriageway road is closed.

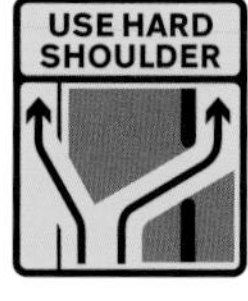

95.

A. Traffic using the right-hand lane should move to the hard shoulder, traffic using the left-hand lane should move to the other carriageway.
B. Traffic using the left-hand lane should move to the hard shoulder, traffic using the right-hand lane should move to the other carriageway.
C. No through road.
D. None of these.

96.

A. Sharp bend ahead.
B. Uneven road surface.
C. Use all three lanes.
D. Sharp bend ahead where traffic is diverted on to a temporary road for a short distance.

Q5. What would it indicate if you see a pedestrian carrying a white stick with two reflectorised bands?
A. That a pedestrian has difficulty in walking.
B. That a pedestrian is blind.
C. That a pedestrian has difficulty in hearing.
D. That a pedestrian is both deaf and blind.

Q6. What is an unmarked crossroad?
A. Where two roads cross and there are no road markings.
B. Where two roads cross and there are no traffic lights.
C. Where two roads cross and there are no stop signs.
D. Where two roads cross and there is no pedestrian crossing.

Q7. What is the first thing you should do if you are involved in an accident?
A. Switch off the engine.
B. Stop.
C. Extinguish any cigarettes.
D. Exchange insurance details.

Q8. What is the "two-second rule"?
A. You have two seconds to cross in front of another vehicle.
B. You have two seconds to clear a box junction.
C. You should never get closer than two seconds in time to the vehicle in front.
D. You have two seconds to negotiate a roundabout.

Q9. What should you do at a level crossing with neither gates nor barriers?
A. Wait until the traffic lights change to green.
B. Cross as quickly as possible.
C. Ring the police.
D. Look both ways, listen and make sure no trains are coming.

Q10. Why should you be careful when driving near parked ice-cream vans? Fill in the missing words.
Be **c**□□□□□□, **c**□□□□□□□ are more interested in **i**□□-**c**□□□□ than traffic.

Q11. Which are the age categories that two out of three pedestrians fall into who are killed or seriously injured on the road?
A. Under 15 or over 60.
B. Under 12 or over 50.
C. Under 8 or over 40.
D. Under 10 or over 80.

Q12. What is the correct position before turning right out of a narrow road?
A. Well over to the right.
B. Well over to the left.
C. Well over to the middle of the road.
D. Whichever is the most convenient.

Q13. What is a motorway?
A. Motorways are roads longer than one mile.
B. Motorways are where you can travel as fast as you like.
C. Motorways are roads with more than 2 lanes.
D. Motorways are main roads with 2 or more lanes and have limited access.

Q14. What would you do if you drive past your intended exit from a motorway?
A. Continue on to the next exit.
B. Stop on the hard shoulder and reverse back when it is safe.
C. Cross over the central reservation when it is safe.
D. Do an emergency stop and reverse at speed.

Q15. What should you do if a tram stops at a platform, either in the middle or at the side of the road?

A. Wait behind the tram until it moves off.
B. Continue driving on the tram lines.
C. Follow the route shown by the road signs and markings.
D. Overtake the tram.

Q16. What should you do if something falls from your car whilst travelling on a motorway?
A. Drive on.
B. Stop in the hard shoulder and retrieve the item when it is safe.
C. Carry on to the next exit and stop at the first petrol station.
D. Stop on the hard shoulder at the earliest emergency telephone and call the police.

Q17. On motorways, there are coloured reflective studs called "cats eyes" in the road to help drivers. Match the colour of studs to their function by placing the appropriate colour in the brackets.
A□□□□ - on the right-hand edge of the carriageway.
R□□ - between the hard shoulder and carriageway.
G□□□□ - separates the slip-road from the motorway.
W□□□□ - at lane lines.
B□□□□□ G□□□□ - at contraflow systems and road works.

Q18. What is the third lane on the motorway for?
A. The fast lane.
B. Overtaking.
C. The priority lane for the traffic police.
D. Avoiding Large Goods Vehicles.

Q19. Why is it important that you pay particular attention to your mirrors on the motorway?
A. In case another driver is travelling too close behind you.
B. To look out for any aggressive drivers.
C. So that you will know when to activate the heated rear window.
D. Because of the higher speeds of other traffic.

Q20. Is it an offence to pick up a hitch-hiker on any part of a motorway?
A. Yes.
B. No.
C. Only during daylight.
D. No. Unless they look in danger.

Q21. What 4 main items should be in perfect order on your car?
A. Tyres, fog lights, heated rear window, horn.
B. Brakes, indicators, mirrors, seatbelt.
C. Brakes, lights, steering and tyres.
D. Tyres, steering, cigarette lighter, brakes.

Q22. What two colours of traffic lights show together?
A. Red and green.
B. Green and amber.
C. Amber and green.
D. Red and amber.

Q23. What does it mean when you see a traffic light depicting red and amber together?
A. Carry on if the way is clear.
B. Stop. Do not pass through or start until GREEN shows.
C. Give way to pedestrians.
D. Give way to all traffic.

Q24. What traffic light comes on after amber alone?
A. Amber.
B. Green.
C. Red.
D. A green filter light.

Q25. What two things should you **not** do when being overtaken? Fill in the missing words.

1. **I**□□□□□□□ **s**□□□□.
2. **C**□□ **o**□□ into the **p**□□□ of the **o**□□□□□□□□□ vehicle.

Q26. Are you permitted to reverse your car in a one way street to park your car between two stationary vehicles?
A. No. But you may reverse in a quiet street.
B. Yes. For no more than ten metres.
C. No. One way means one way.
D. Yes. For no more than fifteen metres.

Q27. Is a driver at a road junction required to give way to pedestrians? Which of the following statements is true.
A. You must give way to pedestrians at all times.
B. You must give way to pedestrians who are crossing the road into which you are turning.
C. You must give way to pedestrians if they are under the influence of alcohol.
D. You should only give way to blind pedestrians.

Q28. Which two things should you ensure you do before leaving your car?
A. The parking brake is on and the door is locked.
B. The parking brake is on and the gear lever is in neutral.
C. The parking brake is on and the lights are switched off.
D. The parking brake is on and the engine is switched off.

Q29. What should you do if you become tired on a journey?
A. Stop and rest at a suitable parking place.
B. Turn the radio up and open the window.
C. Open the window and pop your head out for some fresh air.
D. Drive faster to ensure you reach your destination more quickly.

Q30. When may you overtake in the inside lane? Which of the following statements are true.

A. In slow moving congested traffic, when the vehicles on the outside lane are moving more slowly than you are.
B. When you are filtering straight on or to the left.
C. When the vehicle ahead has signalled right and has taken up the correct position for turning.
D. When drivers are cruising in the middle lane.

Q31. What should you do when a bus signals its intention to pull out from a bus stop? Fill in the missing words.
Give way to **b**□□□□ indicating to move out from **b**□□ stops if you can do so **s**□□□□□. **L**□□□ out for **p**□□□□□ leaving the bus and **c**□□□□□□□ the road.

Q32. Can alcohol seriously affect your driving ability?
A. Yes. Even the smallest amount of alcohol can affect your driving.
B. No. As long as you have drunk less than two pints of lager.
C. No. As long as you have drunk less than one pint of lager with a large meal.
D. No. Only after five pints of strong lager.

Q33. What must you do at a stop sign?
A. You do not have to stop providing you are travelling very slowly and take effective observation before emerging.
B. You must stop. Apply the parking brake and select neutral.
C. Your car must come to a complete stop at the stop line.
D. Change into second gear.

Q34. What must you do when you hear the siren of a police, ambulance or other emergency vehicle?
A. Drive on at speed.
B. Jump a red light if you hear the siren of an emergency vehicle.
C. Leave your car and direct the traffic to help the emergency vehicle.
D. Take whatever action is possible (with safety) to allow that vehicle clear passage.

Q35. What should you do when you arrive at a box junction with the intention of turning right and there is a steady stream of traffic coming towards you?
A. You are not permitted to enter a box junction if there is any oncoming traffic.
B. If your exit road is clear, you are permitted to enter the box junction and wait for a safe gap in the traffic.
C. You have priority over other traffic and can turn right in front of closely approaching vehicles if you enter the box junction first.
D. Wait for slow moving vehicles.

Q36. What should you do if you are dazzled by an approaching vehicle's headlights?
A. You should dazzle the other driver back.
B. You should slow down or stop.
C. You should carry out an emergency stop.
D. Close your eyes.

Q37. Which of these statements about driving in freezing conditions are true?
A. Always drive closely behind the vehicle in front.
B. Always apply the parking brake at the same time as the footbrake whilst stopping.
C. Always drive in the right-hand lane of a dual carriageway in freezing conditions.
D. Always drive with great care even if the roads have been gritted.

Q38. Complete the following sentence. A vehicle seen in a convex mirror could be....?
A. Closer than you think.
B. Further away than you think.
C. Two seconds closer than you think.
D. Five seconds closer than you think.

Q39. Who is responsible for ensuring that the **child** wears her seatbelt when you are driving with a child, her mother and father in your car?
A. The child's mother.
B. The child's father.
C. You are.
D. The child.

Q40. What is indicated by your vehicle continuing to bounce when you press down on the front wings when testing your car's suspension?
A. Worn shock absorbers.
B. Worn tyres.
C. Worn brakes.
D. Worn bodywork.

Q41. What is your **maximum** speed limit when you are towing a trailer on the motorway?
A. 40 mph.
B. 50 mph.
C. 70 mph.
D. 60 mph.

Q42. What is the National **maximum** speed limit when you are driving along a single carriageway outside the built-up area?
A. 50 mph.
B. 40 mph.
C. 60 mph.
D. 30 mph.

Q43. What is your **maximum** speed limit when you are driving along a dual carriageway or motorway?
A. 60 mph.
B. 70 mph.
C. 50 mph.

D. 40 mph.

Q44. What is your **maximum** speed limit when you are towing a caravan on a single carriageway?
A. 40 mph.
B. 70 mph.
C. 60 mph.
D. 50 mph.

Q45. What is the **minimum** level of insurance cover required before you can drive a motor vehicle on the road?
A. Third party.
B. Fully comprehensive.
C. Third party, fire and theft.
D. Third party and theft.

Q46. What must you do if you are driving along a busy road in a built-up area, and your hand-held telephone rings?
A. Answer it immediately in case it is an emergency.
B. Find a safe place to stop and then answer it.
C. Grip the steering wheel firmly then answer it.
D. None of these.

Q47. What do the letters **FPN** stand for?
A. Fireman parking nearby.
B. Fine pay now.
C. Fixed penalty notice.
D. Free parking now.

Q48. What must you do if your vehicle is **not** displaying a current vehicle excise licence (tax disc)?
A. Produce a valid tax disc from the glove box.
B. Your tax disc is not out of date for more than 14 days.
C. Do not use your vehicle on the road.

D. None of these.

Q49. What **could** it mean if your ignition warning light comes on?
A. The brakes have failed.
B. The alternator has failed.
C. The battery is flat.
D. The oil is running low.

Q50. Which way should your front wheels be facing, if you park your car facing downhill on the left-hand side of the road close to the kerb?
A. Slightly to the right.
B. Straight ahead.
C. To the right.
D. To the left.

Q51. What **could** it mean if your ignition warning light comes on?
A. The engine has overheated.
B. The engine timing needs adjusting.
C. The fan belt has snapped.
D. The alternator has failed.

Q52. When may a driver flash the headlights of the vehicle?
A. Acknowledge another vehicle's presence.
B. Warn of his presence.
C. Warn other drivers that a speed trap lies ahead.
D. To indicate to other drivers to come out from a junction.

Q53. A driver of a slow moving vehicle should telephone the signal man before crossing a level crossing with automatic half barriers. How fast is 'slow moving' in this case?
A. 8 mph.
B. 15 mph.
C. 10 mph.
D. 5 mph.

Q54. What is 'kick-down' used for in a car fitted with automatic transmission?
A. Aid rapid acceleration.
B. Decrease acceleration.
C. Aid braking power.
D. None of these.

Q55. Which way should you leave your front wheels facing if your car is parked facing **uphill** on the left-hand side of the road close to the kerb?
A. To the right.
B. To the left.
C. Straight ahead.
D. Slightly to the right.

Q56. What should you do if you are being overtaken by another vehicle?
A. Decrease your speed.
B. Increase your speed.
C. Remain at the same speed.
D. Beep your horn to acknowledge the other driver.

Q57. Who is legally responsible for ensuring that an **adult** passenger wears a seat belt?
A. Passengers don't have to wear seat belts.
B. The driver.
C. Both the driver and the passenger.
D. The passenger.

Q58. What does aquaplaning a vehicle mean?
A. Applying the parking brake on a wet road to skid round a corner.
B. The failure of the brakes after driving through a flood.
C. The effect of a sheet of surface water causing the tyres to make no contact with the road.

D. None of these.

Q59. What will be the closing gap between two vehicles approaching each other at 60 mph?
A. 120 mph.
B. 50 mph.
C. 100 mph.
D. 90 mph.

Q60. Which way should you leave your wheels turned if your car is parked facing **uphill** on the left-hand side of the road without a kerb?
A. To the right.
B. To the left.
C. Straight on.
D. Slightly to the right.

Q61. When does a place where other vehicles may be hidden from a driver's view (called a 'dead ground') occur?
A. A bridge.
B. A bend in the road.
C. A road that has collapsed.
D. A dip in the road.

Q62. Cross ply and radial tyres may be fitted to a vehicle in the following arrangement?
A. Cross ply on the front - radials on the rear.
B. Radials on the front - cross ply on the rear.
C. Radials on the nearside - cross ply on the offside.
D. Cross ply on the nearside - radials on the offside.

Q63. Which side do the forces acting upon your car when you are driving round a left-hand bend, cause the extra weight to be thrown?
A. The rear wheels.
B. The nearside wheels.

C. The offside wheels.
D. The front wheels.

Q64. What should you do if you see the oil warning light come on?
A. Change the oil filter as soon as practical.
B. Reduce your speed to under 20 mph.
C. Speed up.
D. Stop as soon as it is safe to do so.

Q65. Which gear should you use when moving off on packed snow?
A. First gear.
B. The highest gear possible for the conditions.
C. Reverse gear.
D. Third gear.

Q66. What is likely to occur if you allow the tyres of your vehicle to run at **below** their recommended pressures?
A. They will burst.
B. They will overheat.
C. They will cause excessive fuel consumption.
D. They will cause uneven road handling.

Q67. To which fault is coasting related?
A. The footbrake.
B. The indicators.
C. The gears.
D. The accelerator.

Q68. What should you do as well as select first gear, if you drive through a flood?
A. Slip the clutch, keep the engine speed up and move the car slowly.
B. Under no circumstances slip the clutch.
C. Keep the speed of the car up and drive through as quickly as possible.

D. Try and splash any pedestrians.

Q69. How long is a driver allowed if required by the police to produce his vehicle documents at a police station of his choice?
A. Two weeks.
B. Six days.
C. Five days.
D. Seven days.

Q70. What is the name of the part of the ignition system of a car which transforms the voltage from 12V to about 25000V?
A. The battery.
B. The coil.
C. The distributor.
D. The alternator.

Q71. What enables the outside wheel to travel further, and hence faster, than the inner wheel when a car is travelling around a corner?
A. Differential.
B. The gear box.
C. The clutch.
D. The accelerator.

Q72. Exhaust gas contains carbon monoxide which is poisonous. To whom is carbon monoxide in the atmosphere particularly harmful?
A. Diabetics.
B. Asthmatics.
C. Heart disease sufferers.
D. Cancer sufferers.

Q73. What is the minimum **legal** tread depth across the whole width of the tread of a car tyre?
A. 2.6 mm.
B. 1.3 mm.

C. 1.6 mm.
D. 2.9 mm.

Q74. Where must you not overtake when within the zig-zag lines on the approach to a pedestrian crossing?
A. A police vehicle.
B. None of these.
C. A cyclist.
D. The vehicle nearest the crossing whether moving or stopping.

Q75. From what is it necessary to disconnect the drive from the engine to when changing gear?
A. The gearbox.
B. The clutch.
C. The diaphragm spring.
D. The accelerator.

Q76. What does a car battery contain?
A. Citric acid.
B. Carbolic acid.
C. Acetic acid.
D. Diluted sulphuric acid.

Q77. What are most circuits protected by in the electrical system?
A. Earth wires.
B. Electrodes.
C. Fuses.
D. Batteries.

Q78. What must you ensure if you carry a spare fuel can?
A. It is made of hard plastic or metal.
B. It has a handle.
C. It has a special pouring cap.
D. It is an approved type for carrying fuel.

Q79. Why should you avoid letting your fuel tank run too low?
A. You may cause a build-up of residue in the engine.
B. It could cause a fire in the engine compartment.
C. You could run out of fuel on the motorway.
D. It is bad for your engine.

Q80. What can happen if you use the wrong type of fuel for your car?
A. Your car may stall.
B. You may damage the fuel gauge.
C. You may damage the valves and cylinder head.
D. You may damage the alternator.

Q81. Which type of fuel must not be used in a vehicle fitted with a catalytic converter?
A. Unleaded fuel.
B. Any type of petrol.
C. Lawn mower fuel.
D. Leaded fuel.

Q82. Why can diesel fuel be environmentally-friendly?
A. If the engine has had new oil.
B. If the engine is tuned correctly.
C. If the car has passed an MOT.
D. If the engine is hot.

Q83. What must you ensure before you can check the amount of oil in the engine?
A. That the vehicle is on an incline.
B. That the vehicle's engine is warm.
C. That the vehicle is on level ground.
D. That the vehicle's engine is running.

Q84. What might happen if you run the engine of a car with the oil level below the minimum mark?

A. You may run out of oil.
B. You may damage the clutch.
C. You may damage the alternator.
D. You may damage the engine.

Q85. What may happen if you add too much oil well above the maximum mark?
A. You may damage the engine seals and gaskets.
B. You may damage the oil gauge.
C. You may damage the gear box and clutch.
D. You may damage the alternator.

Q86. When should you remove the radiator cap?
A. When the engine is hot.
B. When the engine is cold.
C. During the daytime.
D. When the engine is no warmer than 50 degrees Celsius.

Q87. What should you do if you are in any doubt about your vehicle's ability to brake safely?
A. Inform the police.
B. Contact your insurers.
C. Have it checked when your car is due for its next service.
D. Have it checked immediately.

Q88. Why must the headlights of your car be properly adjusted?
A. To blind other drivers who have just blinded you.
B. To see better on country lanes late at night.
C. To avoid dazzling other road users.
D. So that you can flash other drivers.

Q89. How many times must the indicators flash per second?
A. 1 - 3.
B. 1 - 2.

C. 3 - 4.
D. 2 - 3.

Q90. What must you do if you suspect there is any wear in the steering mechanism?
A. Hit the steering wheel with a hammer.
B. Get it checked out when your car is due for a service.
C. Seek qualified advice immediately.
D. Wait for the MOT.

Q91. What must you do if you have any doubts about the road-worthiness of your vehicle?
A. Continue to drive but book in your car for a service.
B. Sell it immediately.
C. Listen out for any unusual noises or banging sounds whilst driving and then report it to a qualified mechanic.
D. Get your car checked over by a qualified and reputable mechanic.

Q92. What should every car carry?
A. A warning triangle.
B. A first aid kit.
C. A fire extinguisher.
D. A box of tissues.

Q93. What does a catalytic converter help to reduce?
A. Hot air from an exhaust pipe.
B. The exhaust gases containing carbon monoxide.
C. Risk of fire in the engine compartment of a car.
D. Cold air from an exhaust pipe.

Q94. Where will a roof rack with a heavy load affect your cars handling?
A. On bends.
B. The reverse parking exercise.

C. The turn in the road manoeuvre.
D. On hills.

Q95. What will you need before towing a caravan?
A. A fifth gear.
B. Heavy duty brake pads.
C. A licence.
D. An exterior towing mirror.

Q96. On what will the overall stability of both the caravan and towing vehicle depend?
A. The correct weight distribution.
B. The correct engine power.
C. The correct caravan and car.
D. The correct tyre pressure.

Q97. What must you have if your vehicle is more than 3 years old?
A. A current service book.
B. A current MOT certificate.
C. A current vehicle transport licence no. 177/200.
D. Insurance.

Q98. How many mgs of alcohol in 100 ml of blood is the current legal limit for driving?
A. 100.
B. 90.
C. 80.
D. 75.

Q99. What may be affected if water sprays up under the bonnet?
A. The alternator.
B. The exhaust pipe.
C. The clutch cable.
D. The electronic control units.

SOME MYTHS AND POPULAR MISCONCEPTIONS

QUESTIONS

Q. Do examiners have a quota of learners to pass each day?
A. No. This is absolute nonsense. If you are good enough to pass on the day, the examiner will pass you.

Q. Will I fail if I cross my hands on the steering wheel?
A. If you cross your hands and you lose control of your steering the examiner may fail you so use the "pull and push" method.

Q. Will the examiner fail me immediately and tell me to drive back to the test centre if I commit a serious fault at the start of my test?
A. No. The examiner will carry on until the end of the test. However, if a pattern of dangerous driving is displayed, the examiner will terminate the test in the interests of public safety and fail the candidate.

Q. Will the examiner ask me to turn at a junction at the last moment?
A. The examiner will give you instructions in good time, in a clear and unmistakable manner.

Q. Is the examiner trying to trick me if the asks me to take the next road on the right and the entrance is marked "**NO ENTRY**"?
A. No! When you are asked to turn and the road is marked "**NO ENTRY**" you should take the next available road.

Q. Can I restart the engine in gear if I stall?
A. Yes. With experience you will have the confidence to restart the engine in first gear, with the clutch pedal down on level ground.

Q. What happens if my car breaks down during my driving test?
A. The examiner will give you a couple of minutes to try and rectify the fault. If you fail to do this, the test will be terminated and the

examiner will return to the test centre. Your test fee will be forfeited and you will have to re-apply for another test.

Q. Am I permitted to cut corners in my driving test?
A. You should avoid cutting corners unless it is completely safe and absolutely necessary.

Q. Do I have to turn my car round in three distinct movements when carrying out the turn in the road exercise?
A. Not necessarily. The amount of turns you take will be dictated by the width of the road and the length of your car.

Q. Can I change gear and turn at the same time?
A. Yes, providing the steering is set on a curved course. Do not attempt to turn and change gear at the same time.

Q. What would the driving examiner do if a learner drove in a dangerous manner during in the driving test?
A. He may abandon the candidate's test in the interest of public safety.

Q. My father said I will fail my driving test if I change from fourth gear straight into second gear. Is this true?
A. No. Any gear changing method is correct if executed properly and safely.

MORE FROM OTTER PUBLICATIONS.......

PILLARS OF JUSTICE, the homeowner's guide to the law (1 899053 03 4, 192 pp, £6.95) guides the layman through the many legal aspects of purchasing, owning and running a home. The easy to understand language makes the book very accessible and a helpful glossary of terms explains the legal jargon. The key areas covered include:

- The legal aspects of property ownership
- Buying and selling a house and the associated pitfalls
- Insurance
- Building, improving and extending your property
- Dealing with the utility companies
- Renting out your home
- Dealing with the neighbours
- Dealing with tradesmen/consumer law generally
- Home security
- The legal aspects of debt

WORKING FOR JUSTICE: the employee's guide to the law (1 899053 06 9, 224 pp, £7.95), aimed at all employees, is a guide through the many legal aspects of working for somebody else. Now that employment can no longer be taken for granted, a well-informed knowledge of the law as it affects us is critical. The key areas covered include:

- Employment status
- Pay
- Unfair dismissal
- Wrongful dismissal
- Redundancy
- Disciplinary matters
- Discrimination
- Trade Union membership
- Maternity
- Health and safety
- Transfer of undertakings
- Employment law in Northern Ireland

How to order:-
Through your local bookshop or in case of difficulty, please send a cheque made payable to Otter Publications, 5. Mosse Gardens, Fishbourne, Chichester, West Sussex, PO19 3PQ, ☎ 01243 539106.

Chapter 7

Lesson 19 - Automatic transmission, motorway driving and trams

DRIVING WITH AUTOMATIC TRANSMISSION

It is easier and safer to drive an automatic car than a manual car because your hands are in more contact with the steering wheel, there is less gear changing to worry about, and it is less tiring and frustrating whilst driving in traffic. Learning to drive in an automatic car is very useful for older and disabled people. Since it is easier to drive an automatic car it can be dangerous if you become too confident. However, exactly the same standard of driving is required with an automatic car in your driving test. Like a manual car, an automatic car does have gears but an automatic car can change itself to a higher gear as your road speed increases and to a lower gear when it decreases. In other words, the gears are changed for you, depending upon your road speed, car load and the position of the accelerator pedal.

Most automatics are fitted with a selector lever with positions usually marked P-R-N-D-2-1. P (Park) and R (Reverse) are usually safe-guarded by notches, so that they are not selected in error. They can be selected when the driver operates a release catch to clear the notch. If you select position "D" (drive), the automatic transmission changes through the gears, both up and down for you. However you will under certain circumstances have to select D.1 and D.2 by manually moving the selector lever. The following are the selector positions in detail.

P. ***(Parking)***

This position should be used when parking. It mechanically locks the transmission and it should only be selected when your car is stationary with the engine switched off.

R. ***(Reverse)***

This position allows you to move backwards and should only be selected when the car is stationary otherwise you may cause damage to your car.

N. ***(Neutral)***

This position means no gear has been selected and the car cannot be driven forwards or backwards.

D. ***(Drive)***

This position allows you to drive forward and by simply pressing the accelerator pedal the gears will change up or down automatically depending on the road speed, vehicle load and the position of the accelerator.

D. ***2***

Many automatic transmissions have three forward gears. Position D2 may be used instead of "D" (Drive), allowing you to lock the automatic transmission in second gear. A useful gear for moving off on a slippery road surface or when negotiating a roundabout to stop your car running away from you.

D. ***1***

This position allows you to lock the automatic transmission in the first gear position. Useful for driving in slow moving traffic or driving down a very long steep hill because unnecessary gear changes will not take place and you will keep full control of your car. These are the five main selector positions found on most automatic cars but there are many variations between different models and you should consult the appropriate vehicle handbook.

STARTING AND MOVING OFF

Before starting the engine you should check that the parking brake is on and the selector lever is at the N (neutral) position. Some automatic cars allow you to start with the selector lever in P (Park). Once you have started the engine and you wish to move off, simply apply the footbrake with the right foot*, select "D" (Drive), release the parking brake and carry out all your normal observation checks. If it is safe, gently press the accelerator down and you will move forward. As previously stated, the automatic transmission will change gears as necessary, depending on your road speed, vehicle load and the position of the accelerator pedal.

*One legged drivers are permitted to drive automatic cars whether right or left footed.

KICK-DOWN

Whilst driving you can use the accelerator pedal by fully depressing it to the floor quickly. By doing this you will override the gear and the next lower gear will be selected. This is very useful for quick acceleration, particularly before overtaking. This is commonly known as "Kick-Down". To return to the higher gear again simply ease the pressure on the accelerator pedal.

STOPPING SMOOTHLY

Stopping smoothly is relatively simple. All you have to do is look well ahead, pick your spot and make sure you choose a legal, safe and convenient place. Check your mirrors, then look and assess the road situation behind and to the sides of your car. Decide if a signal is necessary, then position your car close and parallel to the kerb. As soon as your car comes to a complete stop, apply the parking brake and select the neutral position.

THE PARKING BRAKE

The purpose of the parking brake is to secure the car for safety reasons when it is stationary or parked. For example, assume that you have stopped your car at a pedestrian crossing, the selector lever is in the D (Drive) position and you accidentally press the accelerator pedal. If the parking brake is not applied, your car will move forward onto the crossing with potentially dangerous consequences. You should also use the parking brake if your car has a tendency to "creep" forward. This may happen if the tick-over of the engine gives enough drive to move the car. Many drivers rely on creep to hold the car on an uphill gradient which could be dangerous as the car may roll back without warning if the engine stops for any reason.

AUTOMATIC TRANSMISSION

QUESTIONS (See page 249 for answers).

Q1. Which of the following statements are true.

A. It's less tiring and your hands are in more contact with the steering wheel.

B. You never have to operate the selector level.

C. You don't have to depress the footbrake to stop your car.

D. It makes driving easier.

Q2. Name the six selector positions normally fitted to automatic cars? Fill in the missing words.

1. P. **P**□□□□□□.
2. R. **R**□□□□□□.
3. N. **N**□□□□□□.
4. D. **D**□□□□.
5. D□.
6. D□.

Q3. What must you do before selecting the (D) Drive position?

A. Depress the accelerator.

B. Depress the footbrake.

C. Select reverse gear.
D. Look in your mirrors.

Q4. What should you remember to do before starting your car?
A. Check the parking brake is on and the lever is in (D) Drive.
B. Move the lever to (P) Parking, check the parking brake is on.
C. Check the parking brake is on and the lever is in (N) Neutral.
D. Move the lever to (P) Parking, check the parking brake is off.

Q5. When would you normally use the (P) Parking position?
A. To park when the car is stationary and the engine stopped.
B. To park when your car's parking brake has failed.
C. For parking instead of the parking brake.
D. At night.

Q6. Name two types of people who would benefit from learning in an automatic? Fill in the missing words.
1. The o--.
2. The d-------.

Q7. Is it possible to restart the engine with the selector lever in the (P) Parking position?
A. Yes. Providing you release the parking brake first.
B. No. Unless you are parked on lower ground.
C. No.
D. Yes.

MOTORWAY DRIVING

Once you have passed your driving test and gained your full licence, you will be permitted to drive on the motorways without a qualified driver accompanying you. However, on motorways you will be driving at very high speeds, especially if you are driving abroad. High speed motoring is safe if it is carried out with skill and responsibility.

A motorway is a main road for fast moving traffic with limited access. During this lesson we will cover many aspects of motorway driving so you will have the right skills and disciplines that will enable you to become an even better and safer driver. It is imperative that you check the general condition of your car before you decide to drive on the motorway because you will probably be driving at high speeds. You should always check that your tyres are in good condition, the tyre depth is within the legal limit and that your tyre pressures are set correctly. Make sure you that have enough fuel, oil and adequate water levels. Ensure your windows, headlights, indicators and mirrors are clean. If you are drawing a trailer, check and secure the load before commencing your journey. If you feel tired or unwell do not under any circumstances drive on the motorway. You may fall asleep and possibly kill yourself or someone else.

In a detailed survey carried out in the United Kingdom and the USA, researcher found that many motorway accidents were caused by drivers falling asleep at the wheel. Most accidents happened between 4 a.m. and 6 a.m. The investigators also found that sleep-related accidents were three times more likely to result in serious injury or death than any other road accident. This was because sleepy drivers failed to brake to prevent the accident - so the impact was worse. Their study also revealed that many drivers found long-distance motorway driving very monotonous. This caused them to daydream whilst driving, often going into "trances". In fact, the survey also revealed that many long-distance drivers had absolutely no recollection of large parts of their journey. **Remember,** ***"Stay awake, stay alive"***.

Joining and leaving the motorway

When you join the motorway, you will approach from a road called a slip road. As you come off the slip road you will enter the acceleration lane. The acceleration lane will allow you to adjust your speed so that it matches the speed of the traffic already on the motorway. Make sure you stay in the acceleration lane (do not drive on the hard shoulder) until it is safe to enter the motorway in the first lane. Do not force your way onto the motorway - stop if necessary.

Judging the speed of the motorway traffic before you emerge requires skill and patience, because traffic will be moving very fast. Stay in the first lane until you have become accustomed to the speeds of other vehicles using the motorway. If you wish to leave the motorway you will also leave by a slip road. Keep a good look out for the countdown markers as they will tell you how far away your exit road is. When you leave the motorway make sure you adjust your speed to suit the new conditions. If you miss your exit road you must carry on until you reach the next exit.

Driving on the motorway

Always drive in the first lane of the motorway unless you are overtaking or road signs and markings direct you otherwise. Some Large Goods Vehicles, coaches or any vehicle drawing a trailer must not use the third lane of a carriageway with three or more lanes unless there are exceptional circumstances. In normal circumstances, the second lane is the only one they may use for overtaking. You should therefore move into the first lane as soon as it is practicable to do so. Finally, if you see a Large Goods Vehicle emerging onto the motorway (an especially difficult manoeuvre due to their weight), it is courteous to adjust your speed or change lane to allow them access.

Watch out for any motorway speed restrictions or flashing light signals which will warn you of any hazards ahead. You will usually see them on overhead gantries or at the side of the carriageway. If you ever see any flashing amber lights, check your mirrors and if it is safe, use progressive braking to slow down (especially in poor weather conditions) until you are satisfied that it is safe to go faster again. If you break down or something falls off your car whilst driving on the motorway, move over to the hard shoulder as soon as it is safe. Many pedestrians are killed or seriously injured whilst standing or walking on the hard shoulder. Try to position your car as far over to the left-hand side of the hard shoulder as possible.

Warn any passengers of the dangers of passing vehicles, and place a warning triangle approximately 150 metres (160 yards) to the rear of your car. This will prevent you from being struck by another vehicle who may be positioned badly in the first lane. Look out for a telephone symbol with an arrow to tell you where to find the nearest emergency telephone (these are directly connected to a police control room). Do not under any circumstances cross the central reservation to use an emergency telephone. If you ever feel tired whilst driving on the motorway, wind your window down for ventilation and leave the motorway at the next exit or the nearest service station. When rejoining the first lane, build up your speed on the hard shoulder and wait for a safe gap in the traffic before emerging.

Lane discipline

On carriageways with three or more lanes the normal rule of, ***"Keep to the left"*** still applies. You may, however, stay in the second lane when there are slower vehicles in the first lane but you should return to the first lane when you have passed them. The third lane is for overtaking only. If you use it, move back to the second lane and then into the first lane as soon as you can without cutting in. The following are not permitted on the motorway:

- Learner drivers except LGV/PSV learners.
- Slow-moving vehicles (unless permission has been granted).
- Cyclists and riders of small motorcycles.
- Agricultural vehicles.
- Some carriages used by invalids.
- Pedestrians.

If you are driving on the motorway you must not stop except:

- In an emergency (for example, to prevent an accident).
- When you break down.

- When you are signalled to do so by the police, by an emergency traffic sign or flashing red light signals.

You may park only at a service area. You must not park on:

- The carriageway itself.
- The slip roads.
- The hard shoulders (except in an emergency).
- The central reservation.

You must not walk on the carriageway. In an emergency be particularly careful to keep children and animals off the carriageway and the hard shoulders.

Overtaking

Many **fatal** traffic accidents are caused by motorway overtaking. Overtaking is a safe manoeuvre providing it is done correctly with due regard for other road users. If you wish to overtake always use the Mirrors (Look, Assess, Decide), Signal, Manoeuvre routine. Keep well back from the vehicle in front and make sure you look in your mirrors early so that you can judge the speed and distance of the vehicles behind and decide the best time to overtake. Some drivers break the law and travel at speeds in excess of 100 mph. Be careful and only overtake if you are sure that it is completely safe. Once you have decided it is safe, overtake with determination and check your mirrors again to see if it is safe before you move back in. Never cut back in or overtake if it would force another vehicle to alter its speed or change direction. Remember, you may only overtake on the left if traffic is moving slowly in queues. Finally, always flash your headlights instead of using the horn (other drivers won't hear you) if you ever wish to warn other road users of your presence.

Look, assess, decide

After you have checked your mirrors, you can **quickly** glance over your shoulder to check for other road users in the blind spot -

especially motorcyclists, before you decide to change direction to the right or left. However, if you find it necessary to check your blind spot, you must be careful because a vehicle in front may make a quick lane change or brake sharply when you are looking over your shoulder and not at the road in front. When driving on the motorway always concentrate and look well ahead as far as possible. The earlier you see any danger, the more time you will have to take evasive action.

Driving at night

When driving on a motorway at night, you will sometimes see different types of coloured reflective studs. They are a guide to warn and inform you whilst driving. There are amber-coloured studs marking the right-hand edge of the carriageway, red studs between the hard shoulder and carriageway, green studs which separate the acceleration and deceleration lanes from the through carriageway and bright green studs which are found at contraflow systems and roadworks. If you ever have to overtake another vehicle or obstruction on a motorway at night keep your indicator on longer and signal sooner to warn other traffic.

Motorway fog

Fog is one of the most dangerous weather conditions in which to drive. Driving in fog can cause eye strain and your ability to anticipate the actions of other road users will be severely restricted. Therefore:

- Drive in the first lane of motorways and dual carriageways as much as possible.
- Don't hang on to the tail lights of the vehicle in front because it gives a false sense of security. In thick fog, if you can see the vehicle in front you are probably too close unless you are travelling too slowly.

- See and be seen. If you cannot see clearly use dipped headlights or front fog lights. Only use rear fog lamps when visibility is severely reduced.
- Use front and rear fog lights if visibility is seriously reduced, generally when you cannot see for more than 100 metres (328 feet). You must not use fog lights at other times. Remember to switch them off when visibility improves.
- Use your windscreen wipers and demisters. Check your mirrors and slow down. Keep a safe distance behind the vehicle in front of you. You should always be able to pull up within the distance you can see clearly.
- Be aware of your speed because you may be going much faster than you think. Do not accelerate to get away from a vehicle which is too close behind you.
- Open your window(s) so that you can hear any approaching traffic and keep your foot on the brake pedal (an extra warning for drivers behind) if you are waiting to turn at a road junction. Consider using your horn to warn other road users of your presence.
- When the word `fog' is shown on a roadside signal, but the road appears to be clear, be prepared for a bank of fog or drifting smoke ahead. Fog can drift rapidly and is often patchy. Even if it seems to be clearing, you can suddenly find yourself back in thick fog. If you must drive in fog, allow more time for your journey.

MOTORWAY DRIVING

QUESTIONS *(See page 249 for answers).*

Q1. Which routine should you use before making any driving decision when travelling on a motorway? Fill in the missing words.
The **M□□□□□□ (L□□□, A□□□□□, D□□□□□), S□□□□□, M□□□□□□□□** routine.

Q2. What is the absolute maximum speed at which you are permitted to drive on motorways?

A. 50 mph.
B. 60 mph.
C. 80 mph.
D. 70 mph.

Q3. Why must you observe slip roads when on the motorway?
A. They are reserved for road maintenance vehicles only.
B. To enable you to stop on them in the event of an emergency.
C. Other vehicles could be emerging onto the motorway.
D. To ensure that any vehicles cannot get in front of you.

Q4. What would indicate the nearest emergency telephone box if you breakdown on the motorway?
A. A police patrol box with an arrow.
B. A telephone symbol with an arrow.
C. A blue rectangular road sign at the edge of the hard shoulder.
D. A green rectangular road sign at the edge of the hard shoulder.

Q5. What is the third lane on a motorway for?
A. The restricted lane.
B. The fast lane.
C. Avoiding Large Goods Vehicles.
D. Overtaking only.

Q6. Name 4 safety checks you should carry out on your car before attempting to drive on the motorway? Fill in the missing words.
1. **T**□□□□.
2. **I**□□□□□□□□□.
3. **F**□□□.
4. **W**□□□□□□□□□ **w**□□□□□.

Q7. Why regulate your speed before entering the motorway?
A. You will never hold up any traffic behind you.
B. You should enter the motorway quickly to avoid an accident.

C. Traffic may be moving very quickly.
D. So that you can get in front of any oncoming traffic.

Q8 Why must you make effective use of your mirrors before changing direction on the motorway?
A. To watch out for motorbikes travelling in the third lane.
B. Other drivers may be travelling very fast.
C. To watch out for Large Goods Vehicles.
D. To watch out for motorbikes travelling in the first lane.

TRAMS

Trams are being reintroduced into cities throughout the UK to both provide a more efficient public transport system and a more environmentally friendly form of transport. Trams have been found to encourage tourism and commerce as a result of their convenience and safety. Here is a check list of do's and don'ts that will both help you to keep safe and maintain the smooth running of the tram system:

Do:

- Exercise care until you and other drivers are familiar with a different traffic system.
- Treat crossing points the same way as railway crossings.
- Be careful when turning or braking on the steel rails as they may be slippery even when they are dry.
- Obey all signals. Diamond shaped signs give instructions to tram drivers only. When there are no signals, always give way to trams.
- Watch out for trams that run close to the kerb or where the lines move from one side of the road to the other.
- Stop for additional pedestrian crossings where passengers will be embarking and disembarking from the trams.
- Be particularly mindful of cyclists and motorcyclists. Their narrow tyres may put them in danger when in contact with the rails.

Don't:

- Try to race trams. If you need to overtake, remember that the trams may be as long as 60 metres (200 feet). Try and overtake at stops if it is safe to do so.
- Drive between platforms at tramway stations. Follow any direction signs.
- Park where your vehicle will obstruct trams or other road users.
- Enter reserved areas for the tramway which are marked either with white line markings or a different type of surface, or both. These are often 'one way', but occasionally 'two way'.
- Be caught out by the speed and silence of the trams.

Lesson 20 - Defensive driving and dealing with emergencies

When driving, you often have to cope with unpredictable, irrational, offensive and, quite often, dangerous behaviour. To survive these conditions, it is imperative that you learn a defensive strategy. Driving instructors call this "defensive driving". This lesson aims to teach you defensive and evasive driving skills so that you can drive safely and survive on the road whilst driving. It is important to remember that you must never become complacent and you should be constantly vigilant against danger at all times when behind the wheel. This means expecting the unexpected and never being taken by surprise. You should question the actions of other road users and treat everyone as being potentially hostile until they prove otherwise. Always give yourself time and space so that you can anticipate the actions of other road users.

AVOIDING HOSTILITY

Never drive in a way which provokes reaction from other drivers. For example, do not hog the third lane, for someone may wish to overtake you. Although you may be driving to the maximum speed limit, other drivers may want to go faster and staying the third lane may result in open hostility, threats, physical violence or worse!

VEHICLE COMBAT

You should, at all cost, avoid getting into a situation where you may come across a driver who will try to antagonize you into "vehicle combat" or competitive driving. This type of driving can create a dangerous situation; for example, the other driver may prevent you overtaking by cutting in front of your vehicle or he may slam the brakes on suddenly. Alternatively, he may try to goad you into racing against him when you are stopped at traffic lights. Such a driver often undergoes a severe personality switch, changing from a person of quite normal disposition to an irrational psychopath! If you come across such a driver, you should restrain yourself from any involvement, for obvious reasons.

PLANNED DRIVING

There will be occasions when time spent on planning your route will prevent you from getting lost and will put you in a better position to deal with any hazards which may lie ahead. When your car is in motion, always keep an eye on what other drivers are doing and be aware of the general road and traffic conditions. Make full use of peripheral vision to avoid eye contact, as this may attract attention. However, you must avoid "information overload", in other words you must not become overwhelmed with so much information that you fail to observe any real danger at all. A poorly organised visual search system will be inefficient in collecting relevant information in sufficient time for you to react safely if you are attacked. It may also cause you to over-react to an incident where there is no real danger.

KEEPING SAFE

If you are setting out on a long journey, let other people know the route you are going to take and expected time of your arrival. Here are some other measures you can take to keep safe:

- Ensure that the car is maintained in good condition. Check the tyres, brakes and steering at the start of every journey.
- Always carry a personal alarm (obtainable from DIY shops) whilst driving and keep it where you can get access to it easily. Don't leave it at the bottom of your handbag. However, never leave your handbag on the passenger seat from where it can be snatched.
- Keep a map in the car, to avoid getting lost or having to ask directions, or else use an in-car or hand-held route finder. When you program your destination into the route finder it will provide you with quietest route, it will re-route you round any traffic jam and it will also calculate the estimated time of your arrival. This is

a very useful in-car navigation aid; it enables motorists to reach their destination safely and with the minimum amount of fuss.

- Keep the rear parcel shelf free from loose objects. This will prevent any chance of injury to passengers during any enforced emergency stop.
- Ensure that the windscreen is free from smears, the windscreen wipers are in good condition and that the windscreen wash is topped up. All these measures will prevent accidents.
- Make sure that the headlights are properly adjusted. This will maximise your own vision and minimise dazzle to others.
- Never leave children alone in your vehicle. A child can easily release the parking brake or open a door.
- Always have a torch in your car.
- If you stop for petrol or for a break, take your keys with you and check the rear seat when returning to your car (someone may have climbed into the back).
- When you return to your car, study it first to see if it has been tampered with. If it has, and you sense danger, leave your car alone and inform the police immediately.
- Make sure you have your car keys ready so that you can enter your vehicle quickly. When you get into your car, lock your doors immediately even when carrying a baby or holding an object.
- Remember that if your car has central locking it will unlock all the doors. Look around for any dubious-looking characters near you car before you use it.
- Avoid parking where there are hedges and walls.
- At night, always park your car in a well-lit street.
- If you have to leave your car in a tiered car park, try to position your car in a well-lit area, as near as possible to the ground floor, near a ramp and attendant's booth or as close to the entrance as possible.

- If it is within your means, purchase a mobile phone. Some companies now do a very low-price connection and rental for the infrequent user.
- If you see an emergency or an accident, drive on and inform the police as soon as possible.
- Make sure that your fuel tank is full. If you run out of fuel, change into neutral and use the momentum of the car to move to the side of the road in order to stop.
- Always carry spare fuel and make sure that you are a member of a well-known motoring organisation, in case your car breaks down.
- During wintry weather conditions, check the weather forecast.
- Carry an advance warning triangle. It is simple to fold and easy to stow away.
- Carry jump leads in case you have to recharge your battery.
- In winter carry a flask containing a hot drink.
- Carry a de-icer and a window scraper.
- Never, under any circumstances, pick up a hitch-hiker - even if they appear to be in distress. This could simply be a ploy. Some attackers use a good-looking girl as bait to stop drivers. As soon as the driver stops his vehicle, muggers emerge from cover and storm the vehicle.
- Carry a tow rope in case you break down.

If your car does break down and you have to walk to get help, carry out the following procedures:

- Before you leave your car, take a note of its location.
- Place your warning triangle, on a straight road, about 50 metres (55 yards), behind your car, on the road. If your car breaks down on a hilly or winding road, place the warning triangle where other drivers will see it in god time.
- Try to walk facing oncoming traffic so that no one can pull up behind you.

- If it is dark wear bright, preferably fluorescent, clothing or carry a torch so that a vehicle doesn't accidentally hit you. When there is no pavement and you have to walk on the road make sure that you keep as close to the verge as possible.
- Keep your distance from strangers (reaction space), as this will give you more time to react if you are attacked.
- Do not hitch-hike or take lifts from strangers.
- Avoid strangers by crossing the road.
- Cover up expensive-looking jewellery.
- Carry your handbag close to you in case someone grabs it.
- Keep your house keys and credit cards separate from your handbag.
- Don't take short cuts through dark alleys or across waste ground.
- If a car stops and you think someone is following you, cross the street to see if he is still tailing you. If the threat continues, don't be embarrassed to flag down a passing motorist. If you are attacked pick up any solid object or take off your shoe so you can smash a window and then scream for help. This will surprise your attacker and may frighten him away.
- Carry your screech alarm or a powerful whistle.
- Keep change and a phone card in case you have to call a garage or friend for help.
- Avoid standing near lonely bus stops, especially after dark.
- If you are mugged and your attacker is carrying a weapon, give the robber what he wants by emptying your handbag out on the ground and run away as quickly as possible.
- If you telephone for a taxi, be careful!

PREVENTING CAR THEFT

Some car thefts are carried out by determined professionals but the majority of cars stolen are committed by casual thieves who take advantage of an easy opportunity. A large proportion of car crimes are committed as a direct result of someone leaving a window open or a door unlocked. Do not hesitate in telephoning the police of any suspicious person tampering with your car. Give the police a description of the villain and **do not** attempt to challenge him ('have a go hero') as he may be carrying an offensive weapon or may be accompanied by someone else, possibly acting as a 'look out'.

You can get a series of electronic sensors built into either a door, the boot or even the bonnet; they trigger an alarm if any of them are forced open. Some cars are protected by an engine immobilisation device. The car cannot start until the driver "punches" his personal code into a key pad. To de-activate the entire security system the driver simply presses a remote control button on a key fob. A stolen car can mean having to walk home late at night. Here are some precautions you can take to prevent your car from being stolen, and some advice on how to quickly recover your vehicle if someone takes it without your consent.

- Always lock your car, even when leaving your vehicle unattended for a few seconds.
- Never leave children alone in your car as someone may abduct them.
- Never place items of value in your car then leave your vehicle unattended. You never know who is watching you. If it is essential to leave something of value in the vehicle, ensure it is well hidden from view.
- If your locks are worn, replace them.
- It would be a wise investment to fit a good-quality car alarm (use it at all times), or an immobiliser for extra security. A hidden cut-out switch can be cheaply fitted. You can also purchase an alarm which will activate when you press a button, either from inside or outside the car, as soon as someone attempts to steal it.
- You can get deadlocks fitted to the car doors so that they cannot be opened, even if a window has been broken.

- When leaving your car always ensure that the steering lock has been engaged and all the windows and doors are securely shut.
- To prevent your petrol tank from being siphoned, invest in a locking petrol cap. Locking wheel nuts will prevent expensive wheels and tyres from being stolen.
- You can purchase a car radio with a security code or one which can be removed every time you park.
- You can mark the car registration number of your vehicle on your car stereo or CD player with an ultraviolet (UV) pen that will show up only under ultraviolet light. This will help the police to trace the owner if they recover your goods.
- Never leave your driving licence, MOT certificate, registration document or insurance certificate in your car. These documents can help a thief to sell you car.
- Fit the best parking brake, gear lever or steering wheel clamp.
- Have your windscreen, wing mirrors, lights and windows etched with your registration number.
- Always remove the ignition key, even if you car is in you garage. Some cars are fitted with a warning alarm to let you know if you leave your key in the ignition.
- When you park, watch out for strangers showing interest in your car; they may be planning to steal it rather than admiring it.
- Avoid parking in residential side streets or in unauthorised car parks.
- If you do not own a garage, park as close to your home as possible, preferably where you can see your car.
- If you vehicle is towing a caravan there are many security items on the market you can purchase to help you protect your caravan. Crooks have been known to drive alongside an unprotected caravan, switch the van to their vehicle and then drive off.

CAR PHONES

Do not use a mobile telephone whilst your vehicle is moving, unless in an emergency or if you are speaking into a hands-free unit. Many accidents are caused by drivers losing control of their vehicle because they are steering with only one hand on the wheel. There is another danger associated with mobile phones: under certain conditions it is possible for a mobile phone to cause a spark which could ignite petrol vapour, causing a fire or explosion, if it was being used in a petrol-filling station, for instance. Furthermore, safety researchers have discovered that hand-held phone sets could activate airbags if the car has them fitted.

JOY RIDERS

The media is full of stories of the modern-day menace on the roads: joy riders. Joy riders are usually young men high on drugs or alcohol who steal cars for kicks, destroying and dumping them later. They drive erratically and at great speed, without regard for their own safety or the safety of others. Should you come across joy riders whilst travelling on the road, you should avoid them at all costs and not confront them. You should, however, record the registration number, a description of the vehicle and occupants and the direction in which the vehicle is travelling and then inform the police as soon as possible. The police nowadays have very sophisticated means of tracking joy riders, such as helicopters armed with infra-red cameras.

UNMARKED POLICE VEHICLES

If another driver indicates that he wants you to stop your vehicle at the side of the road, you should avoid doing so unless you are positively sure that it is a police officer in an unmarked police car. The signs to look for are as follows:

1. Blue flashing lights
2. Horns blaring.

After you have stopped, ensure that you are shown official identification. The police officer must also state his name, his police station and the reason he has stopped you. Often, undercover police can deliberately be dubious-looking characters, without the standard short-back-and-sides haircut, etc.

CAR-JACKING

Car-jacking is a modern term which originated in the United States of America. Women are the prime targets for the highwaymen who often work in gangs and surprise their victims when they are travelling alone. Attacks usually happen when the car has stopped at traffic lights. They approach their victims from a "blindspot" and sometimes target specific models of cars. The thugs force their victims out of their vehicles (sometimes using extreme violence) and then steal them. The robbers have calculated that, because of recent technological developments, modern cars are so well protected by sophisticated alarms and immobilisers that it is easier to try to steal them when they are on the move. You can get an anti-hijack device fitted in your car; then if you are ever car-jacked, switch the engine off, abandon your vehicle (run away from the intruder) and permit the car-jacker to take your car. However, if the car-jacker does not key a code into the system he will be extremely disappointed when the anti-hijack device disables your vehicle shortly after he has driven away, and he may also be locked in the car.

TAILGATING

Assume you are driving along and you see a vehicle behind driving too close to your bumper. If this happens to you, simply ease off the accelerator very gradually to ensure that he overtakes. If this subterfuge fails and you feel you may be in danger, stop your car as soon as possible at a safe place (for example, a petrol station, shop or pub). Put on your lights and continuously sound your horn very loudly and draw as much attention to yourself as possible.

SOUNDING YOUR HORN

You can use your horn as a signal to attract the attention of others. Always sound your horn if you have reasonable cause to do so. For example, suppose you are parked at the side of the road between two vehicles and vehicle in front starts reversing towards you. If you believe it is not going to stop, then in these circumstances it is in fact permissible, on account of the danger, to sound the horn to warn the other driver.

FLASHING YOUR HEADLIGHTS

Headlights can also be used as a signal to warn other road users of your presence; for example, during the hours of darkness, flashing your headlights can be a useful warning before overtaking another driver or, during daylight hours, you may flash headlights in lieu of a horn warning on motorways or any other fast road (where, due to the speed of the vehicles, other drivers may not hear the horn).

Flashing your headlights means exactly the same as sounding your horn, i.e. it lets other road users know you are there. Don't flash headlights at another driver or pedestrian for any other reason. It's dangerous, for example, to "flash" other drivers to emerge from a side road - they must be allowed to use their own judgement on when it is safe.

DAZZLED BY HEADLIGHTS

If an oncoming driver dazzles you with his vehicle headlights you should slow down and, if necessary, stop. Don't retaliate and avoid looking directly at oncoming headlights, in case another driver dazzles you again.

DEALING WITH TRAFFIC LIGHTS

Far too many road accidents are caused by drivers ignoring a red light and wrongly crossing your path. It is important that you observe traffic lights early and treat them with caution. Don't forget to regulate your speed correctly on the approach, and always take effective observation before emerging, in case you have to stop. Furthermore, if the traffic lights fail, proceed with extreme caution.

DEALING WITH LEVEL CROSSINGS

Many drivers and their passengers have been killed at railway level crossings. Always approach and drive over a level crossing with vigilance and caution. A driver should never enter a crossing until the road is clear. It is vital to avoid driving too close to another vehicle over the level crossing. It is also important that the driver should never stop on or just after the crossing, or park near the level crossing. If your vehicle breaks down, or if you have an accident on a railway crossing, you **must** carry out the following procedure:

- Get everyone out of your vehicle and tell them to stand a safe distance from the crossing.
- Look out for a railway telephone and use it immediately to tell the signal operator your predicament and follow his instructions.
- If it is practical before a train arrives, move your vehicle clear of the crossing.
- If you hear an alarm or see an amber light, abandon your vehicle and move quickly away from the crossing.

EMERGENCY VEHICLES

If you see blue flashing lights or hear the siren of any emergency vehicle, you must take whatever action is possible, with safety, to allow that vehicle clear passage. However, if you come across the incident the emergency vehicle is attending, you must concentrate on what is happening ahead or you could cause another accident.

DEALING WITH A TRAFFIC ACCIDENT

Many people panic or freeze when they are involved in a traffic accident. If you are involved in a traffic accident, always keep calm and carry out the following procedures:

1. **Stop** at the scene, and remain there for a reasonable period if any person has been injured or if there is damage to any other vehicle, property or licensed animals.

2. Switch your engine off; ask other drivers involved to the same.
3. Extinguish cigarettes - there may be petrol leakage.
4. Tell your passengers to leave your vehicle and get them to a place of safety. If any of your passengers are seriously injured, it would be wise to leave them in the vehicle and administer first aid.
5. Warn other traffic.
6. Call the ambulance service and the police.
7. At night make sure that no one stands at the rear of your vehicle as they may obscure the lights.
8. Try and move any vehicle if it is causing danger to other traffic, ask an independent person to note the original positions of vehicles.
9. Exchange your registration number, insurance and address details, and if different, that of the vehicle owner, to anyone who has reasonable grounds to ask for those details.
10. You must, if injury is caused to another person, produce your certificate of insurance either to any other person who has reasonable grounds or to a police officer.

If for any reason you do not comply with the above, you must report the accident at a police station or to a police officer as soon as reasonably practicable or within 24 hours. You must also report if another person was injured and you did not produce your certificate of insurance at the time. If the certificate is not available you must still report the accident, but can produce the certificate to the police within seven days. If there is an allegation or possibility that your vehicle's presence on the road was a factor you must also comply with the above. Your insurance details can be requested if someone else holds you responsible for the accident. This can be made at a later stage and does not have to be at the scene of the accident.

You can purchase a special hammer with a chromium-plated head a razor-sharp blade so that you can shatter the side window of your car and cut the seat belt if you are trapped during a crash. The hammer comes with a plastic holder which is easily attached inside the car. It also has a fluorescent knob so you can locate it more easily in the dark.

DRINKING AND DRIVING

In a survey carried out in the United Kingdom, one in five deaths on the road were caused by drivers who had been drinking. Many drivers mistakenly believe that they are safe to drive because they have only consumed a very small amount of alcohol.

In fact, event he smallest amount of alcohol can increase a driver's reaction time and cause him to misjudge distance and the speed of oncoming vehicles. Various circumstances can account for the variation in time it takes to metabolise alcohol. Some people have more effective livers than others, but the combination of height, weight and body water content is an acknowledged factor. It has been medically proved that alcohol is quickly absorbed into the bloodstream, which affects the brain and impairs driving ability. Drivers also have a greater tendency to take risks particularly in dangerous manoeuvres such as overtaking.

Drinking and driving is irresponsible and extremely dangerous. Remember someone may be driving with their alcohol level at nearly zero and driving perfectly legally, but their performance is still less than it would be if they had not been drinking at all. The only way to stay alive is *not* to drink and drive.

DRUNKEN PEDESTRIANS

We are all aware of the dangers and consequences of drinking and driving. However, another menace on the road is the drunken pedestrian. In a survey of traffic accidents involving pedestrians, in the United Kingdom, a quarter of these pedestrians were found to be under the influence of alcohol. They wander or stagger off the pavement onto the road, into the path of vehicles, causing them to swerve. Swerving suddenly to avoid a pedestrian can be highly dangerous, as you may hit or be struck by another vehicle overtaking you, or you may even collide with oncoming traffic.

You should therefore apply good forward planning whilst driving and be particularly mindful of drunken pedestrians who may step out from behind parked vehicles without warning. When you are approaching parked vehicles, always look underneath them so you can see if there are feet moving beyond them. Watch the behaviour of drunken pedestrians at all times so that you can anticipate their actions and stop safely. Take extra care at night especially when passing places where people socialise and drink.

HOW TO AVOID ACCIDENTS WITH PEDESTRIANS

Take account of pedestrians and animals, and be prepared to slow down or perhaps stop if they run out in front of you without any warning. Elderly people, who are less alert, need more time to cross the road. Never put them under pressure to cross the road quickly or leave them stranded in the middle of the road. Children are unpredictable and they rely on you for their safety. Many children die in road accidents every year. The vast majority of these happen in built-up areas where the speed limit is 40 mph or less. Look out for people with white walking sticks or guide dogs. Remember that some people who are deaf or hard of hearing will not hear your car approaching.

ANIMALS IN THE STREET

If you are driving at speed, do not brake or swerve to avoid a dog or cat darting out in front of you if other vehicles are travelling closely behind you. The driver behind could run into your rear or you may even collide with oncoming traffic. It may seem cruel, but it is far safer to hit the animal, even though this is the last thing you want to do. Many people have been seriously injured or killed when drivers have swerved suddenly to avoid a dog or cat.

Remember that if you are involved in an accident which causes injury or death to an animal (horse, cattle, ass, mule, sheep, pig, goat or dog) you must:

1. Stop.
2. Give details to anyone having reasonable grounds for requiring them, and,
3. If you do not do so at the time, report the accident to the Police within 24 hours.

DRIVING ABROAD

More people drive abroad nowadays, but his can be unsafe if you are not properly prepared. It would be prudent to contact any of the major motoring organisations so that you can plan your trip. They provide invaluable information and advice on computerised routes, motoring regulations, correct documentation and emergency telephone numbers. The can also provide cover for roadside assistance or emergency garage repairs; vehicle recovery or collection; legal protection; car hire, fares and hotel accommodation; and emergency credit for motoring abroad. It is also important to remember that in some Islamic countries there are different laws regarding women driving. You can be at your most vulnerable to muggers when you are driving in known tourist areas. Attacks usually happen when driving a rented car because the attackers can then easily identify you as a tourist.

If you are hiring a car at your vacation destination, avoid collecting it at night but instead hire a taxi to take you to your hotel or apartment. When you collect the car the following morning plan the safest route back and take time to familiarise yourself with the location and function of the car's minor and auxiliary controls before leaving the rental company's premises. Moreover, try not to dress like a tourist. Hide your wallet or purse in concealed, zipped or button packets. Try not to dress conspicuously - that means no Hawaiian shirts shorts or sandals, especially when it is raining.

The Channel Tunnel

The Channel Tunnel is a remarkable feat of engineering. Journey time between platforms is 35 minutes, 27 minutes being underground.

There is a 24 hour service, loading and unloading time can take 8 minutes and at peak times there is a 'ferry service' every 15 minutes.

The tunnel is buried 150 feet beneath the seabed for most of its route and is bored through a thick, watertight layer of chalk. Drivers sit in their cars, although you may leave your car if you wish. An aerial built along the length of the tunnel allows people to listen to their car radio and a ventilation system has been designed to extract car fumes rapidly.

In the event of fire, foam-injection systems and fire extinguishers are activated. Even if these fail, passengers are able to pass through a fire barrier to another carriage. The carriages are designed to withstand the worst blaze for at least 30 minutes allowing the train to reach one of the terminals. Each carriage has two emergency doors wide enough for wheel-chairs. If the fire was so bad that the train could not be moved, passengers would be able to walk safely through cross-passages leading into the service tunnel. Security measure include the routine use of electronic devices capable of detecting plastic and other types of military explosives, and x-ray machines located at each terminal will screen vehicles.

DEALING WITH FIRE

Many serious and sometimes fatal accidents can be prevented by taking correct and prompt action should fire break out in the engine compartment of your vehicle. Fire can spread through a vehicle in seconds. It is therefore essential that you always carry a fire extinguisher in your vehicle. If you smell burning or suspect that there is a fire in the engine compartment, you must stop your vehicle at a safe place as quickly as possible and switch off the engine. The first priority is for the safety of any passengers who may be travelling in the vehicle with you.

Make sure that they all exit as quickly as possible by selecting the safest route and keep them well away from the car. Contact the fire brigade immediately. Under no circumstances open the bonnet wide as you will create a draught of air which will fan the fire and you may cause a mini-fireball. As soon as you open the bonnet slightly, direct your fire extinguisher through the small gap and fully extinguish the fire. If you do not have a fire extinguisher in the car, avoid opening the bonnet and call the fire brigade instead.

SEAT BELTS

Wearing a seat belt is not just a legal requirement - it makes good sense. Research shows that a person not wearing a seat belt can be seriously injured or killed in a crash when a vehicle is travelling at speeds as low as 12 mph. If a baby is travelling in the car with you, make sure that you use an approved baby carrier suitable for the child's weight. Failing to wear a seat belt may also affect your claim for compensation if you are involved in an accident.

TYRE BLOWOUT

If one of your tyres blows out, the car may pull to one side. The risk is increased if the brakes are applied. You should grip the steering wheel firmly, take your foot off the accelerator and roll the car to a stop by the side of the road at a safe and convenient place. Remember, if you use hard braking, this will only make things worse. Before you attempt to change the wheel, always move your vehicle to a safe and convenient place first. This is a sensible precaution to take as you may expose yourself to danger from other vehicles. Always carry a legal spare tyre and proper equipment to change a wheel.

LOOSE WHEELS

If 'clanking' noises are heard, this may be due to loose wheel nuts. Slow down gently, stop and retighten the nuts. As a precaution, drive to a convenient garage where a mechanic can check the wheel, its nuts and bolts and wheel bearings. If the wheel comes off, the car will drop at the affected corner, resulting in a strong pull to one side. Counter this by firm steering and gentle, progressive braking to bring the car to a halt. One important point; refrain from overtightening the wheel nuts as they may become impossible to loosen in an emergency.

SHATTERED WINDSCREEN

If your windscreen shatters when you are driving, you should punch a hole in the windscreen from the inside of the car, wide enough for you to see through. This will enable you to carry on driving until you decide it is safe to stop. If loose chippings are being thrown up at your windscreen from the road surface or from a passing lorry, the best protection to stop you windscreen from shattering is to place the fingertips of one of your hands hard against the glass. This absorbs the impact.

LIGHTS FAILING

If both headlights suddenly cut out, slow down quickly. Use any other source of illumination you have, e.g. fog lights, spot lights or emergency four-way flashers. They can all help you to drive at a slow speed to safety.

WINDSCREEN WIPERS FAILING

If your windscreen wipers suddenly stop during heavy rain, keep driving straight ahead. Crouch over the wheel and place your face close to the windscreen so that you can see where you are going and pull into the side of the road as soon as possible.

BRAKES FAILING

Should your brakes suddenly fail, pump the brake pedal on and off and apply the parking brake quickly but progressively. Do not yank it. Start selecting lower gears to act as a brake on the engine. Run the edges of your wheels against the kerb. If you have time, switch on the lights to warn other road users of your presence.

ENGINE FAILING

If the engine seizes up, this may be due to overheating caused by a broken fan belt or lack of coolant. Complete seizure results in the driving wheels locking. De-clutch immediately and move the gear stick into neutral. Check the mirrors, signal and move the side of the road, making sure not to cut in front of other vehicles.

ACCELERATOR STICKING DOWN

In many cases, this is due to a broken throttle return spring. Do not try to lift the pedal with your foot. Simply check the mirrors, change into neutral, switch off the ignition (but do not remove the ignition key as this will cause the steering wheel to lock), coast to the side of the road without crossing in front of any other vehicles, and stop.

TRAPPED INSECT

If you are driving and you notice an insect such as a bee, wasp or hornet trapped inside your vehicle, do not lash out with your hand. This will only antagonise the insect. Open a window so that it can fly out - if this fails, pull into the side of the road and open the door.

BONNET FLYING UP

Do not panic. Steer on the same course, braking progressively, signal and move carefully to the side of the road, again ensuring not to cut across any other vehicles. Winding down the driver's side window may assist forward vision.

COLLISION COURSE

If another driver falls asleep or loses control and his vehicle is heading straight towards you, you should sound your horn and flash your lights. Avoid driving onto the other side of the road, even if you think it is clear. The oncoming driver may wake up or gain control and pull left at the last moment. If you have to run off the road to avoid a collision, earth banks and ditches are far safer to hit than poles or trees. If it is impossible to run off the road, turn your vehicle at an angle to avoid a head-on collision.

AIRBAGS

Airbags are designed to protect you and your passengers in the event of a collision. Airbags are most commonly installed on the driver's side only. The airbag is fitted in the centre of the steering wheel and it is designed to operate in the event of a significant frontal or front corner impact (about 18 mph), where the driver's head would otherwise hit the steering wheel, with the risk of serious injury. In the event of a crash the airbag will fully inflate in less than a second and it will make contact to protect the driver, then deflate to absorb the impact, again in less than a second after it has been activated.

FLOODED STREETS

On the approach to flooded areas, always drive through water at a very slow speed in a low gear. It would be prudent to leave your car and check the depth of the water and also for any hidden obstruction or subsidence. If the water is deep, slip the clutch and apply the accelerator to keep the engine running fast. Check your brakes afterwards to ensure that the brake linings are dry.

DRIVING INTO DEEP WATER

If your car should happen to crash into deep water and become totally submerged, it is highly important to remain calm. You should allow your car to fill with water until the level is almost at the top. You should then take one last gulp of air before opening the door or window and swimming to safety. You will be unable to open the door prior to this because of the pressure difference, and if you open the window too early, too much water would gush in at once.

STRANDED IN SNOW

Weather conditions can alter rapidly during winter months. If your car gets bogged down in heavy snow and you cannot break free, it is crucial that you know how to survive until help reaches you. It is best to prepare for the worst as you may have to wait for some time. The will to survive varies considerably in human beings, but evidence shows that some individuals have been able to survive extreme winter conditions for very long periods of time. The most fatal mistake is to leave your engine running continuously, as you may fall asleep and then, because of the sudden cold, die without recovering consciousness if the engine cuts out or runs out of fuel. It is safer to switch the engine off and on periodically in order to conserve petrol. To survive severe winter conditions remember the following points:

- Have and maintain a positive mental attitude.
- Push negative thoughts out of your mind.
- Conserve energy.
- Exercise to prevent painful stiffness and to maintain body warmth. This must be carried out slowly and frequently to conserve energy and should not be overdone.
- Protect the body from cold and damp.
- Guard against boredom and depression. Keep yourself and any passengers occupied.
- Unless you know for a fact that help is at hand, do not wander off in search of food. You may get frostbite or hypothermia.
- Ration any food that may be carried in the car.
- Light a fire as soon as possible. Ideally, light three fires in a triangle shape (this is an international distress signal). Consider using your car's cigarette lighter if you have no matches.
- Write the word "HELP" on the snow in very large letters to it can be easily seen from the air.
- Cover your vehicle and the aerial with brightly coloured items so that you can be seen from the air by any rescue team. Remember to brush off any snow covering frequently.
- Never eat snow or ice as it will reduce body temperature and cause sore lips, gums and tongue. Always use melted snow or ice.

Remember, in cold areas exposure causes death before lack of fluids or food. Many deaths in the middle-aged and elderly are caused by strokes and heart attacks brought on by exposure to the cold. Research shows that within half an hour of considerable cooling of the body, blood becomes more liable to clot. Anyone suffering from exposure should be provided with heat as soon as possible.

Before setting off on your journey during severe weather conditions always ask yourself is your journey absolutely essential?

You should carry the following equipment in your car if you believe there is any possibility of blizzard conditions:

- Emergency food and water.
- Spare fuel.
- Shovel.
- Snow chains.
- First aid kit to include water purification tablets and lip balm.
- Knife and torch.
- Sleeping bag(s) or blanket(s).
- Metal container for heating food and water.

MOVING OFF IN DEEP SNOW

If you are starting off in deep snow and you encounter wheel spin, do not race the engine because your wheels will dig in further. To overcome this problem you should move your car slightly backwards and then forwards until you break free. Use the highest gear possible. In these conditions, it is a good idea to carry a spade and place old sacks or car mats under your wheels so that your tyres can grip more easily, to stop your car being embedded in the snow. Always remove any heavy snow lying on top of your vehicle before moving off. When you brake, weight is transferred to the front of your car; any snow that has not been cleared from your vehicle's roof may suddenly fall onto the windscreen and your vision will be severely restricted. Many serious accidents have occurred in this way.

The bitterness of poor driving instruction remains long after the sweetness of a low price has been forgotten.

ANSWER SECTION

Lesson 1 - The safety checks - Q1. 1. Doors, 2. Seat, 3. Steering Wheel, 4. Seatbelt, 5. Mirrors, **Q2**. D, **Q3**. A, **Q4**. C, **Q5**. C, **Q6**. A.

Lesson 1 - The foot controls - Q1. 1. Accelerator, 2. Footbrake, 3. Clutch, **Q2**. B, **Q3**. D, **Q4**. A, **Q5**. C, **Q6**. B, **Q7**. 1. Right, 2. Right, 3. Left, **Q8**. Gas.

Lesson 1 - The hand controls - Q1. C, **Q2**. B, **Q3**. A, **Q4**. C, **Q5**. B, **Q6**. 1st - 10, 2nd - 20, 3rd - 30, 4th - 30, 5th - 50. **Q7**. 4th - 3rd - 20, 3rd - 2nd - 10, 2nd - 1st - 5. **Q8**. D, **Q9**. C, **Q10**. 1. Gradient, 2. Traffic lights, 3. Pedestrian crossing, 4. Queuing, vehicles, **Q11**. A, **Q12**. B, **Q13**. A, **Q14**. B.

Lesson 2 - Moving off - Q1. Parking brake, gear lever, neutral, **Q2**. Preparation, Observation, Move, **Q3**. A, **Q4**. C, **Q5**. B, **Q6**. B, **Q7**. 1. Holding, Parking brake, 2. Letting, clutch, 3. Gas, pedal, down, **Q8**. A, **Q9**. C, **Q10**. A, **Q11**. B.

Lesson 2 - Changing gear - Q1. C, **Q2**. D.

Lesson 2 - Stopping - Q1. C, **Q2**. B, **Q3**. D.

Lesson 3 - Mirrors - Q1. A, **Q2**. D, **Q3**. A, **Q4**. B, **Q5**. C, **Q6**. C.

Lesson 3 - Signals - Q1. A, **Q2**. C, **Q3**. D, **Q4**. C.

Lesson 4 - Approaching and turning corners - Q1. Mirrors, Signal, Manoeuvre, **Q2**. C, **Q3**. D, **Q4**. A, **Q5**. D, **Q6**. B, **Q7**. A, **Q8**. B, **Q9**. C, **Q10**. C, **Q11**. A, **Q12**. C, **Q13**. 1. Wrong, side, road, 2. Vision, road, restricted, 3. Conflicting, traffic.

Lesson 5 - Dealing with road junctions - Q1. A, **Q2**. C, **Q3**. C, **Q4**. A, **Q5**. Gear, speed, speed, visibility, **Q6**. D, **Q7**. 1. Check, emerge, danger, road, 2. Vehicle, mistakenly, emerge, **Q8**. B, **Q9**. A. **Q10**. D, **Q11**. C, **Q12**. A, **Q13**. B.

Lesson 6 - Dealing with crossroads - Q1. C, **Q2**. A, **Q3**. 1. Minor, 2. Major, 3. Uncontrolled, **Q4**. C, **Q5**. B, **Q6**. C, **Q7**. 1. Regulate, speed, 2. Power, accelerate, **Q8**. C, **Q9**. A, **Q10**. D, **Q11**. B, **Q12**. B, **Q13**. C, **Q14**. Gear, match, speed, speed, match, visibility.

Lesson 7 - Reversing in a straight line - Q1. D, **Q2**. B, **Q3**. A, **Q4**. Preparation, Observation, Move, **Q5**. D, **Q6**. C.

Lesson 8 - Turning round using forward and reverse gears - Q1. C, **Q2**. A, **Q3**. 1. Static, 2. Moving, **Q4**. D, **Q5**. A, **Q6**. Preparation, Observation, Move, **Q7**. D.

Lesson 9 - Reversing to the left - Q1. 1. Type, 2. Forward, clear, obstruction, 3. Position, reverse, **Q2**. Control, observation, accuracy, **Q3**. 1. Static, 2. Moving, **Q4**. Preparation, Observation, Move, **Q5**. D, **Q6**. D, **Q7**. B, **Q8**. C, **Q9**. A, **Q10**. C, **Q11**. D, **Q12**. 1. Seatbelt, 2. Mirrors, right, blind, spot, **Q13**. B.

Lesson 10 - Reversing to the right - Q1. A, **Q2**. 1. One, way, street, 2. Side, main, road, 3. Crossroads, **Q3**. D, **Q4**. C, **Q5**. D, **Q6**. A, **Q7**. B.

Lesson 11 - Reverse parking between two vehicles - Q1. D, **Q2**. A, **Q3**. B, **Q4**. Preparation, Observation, Move, **Q5**. C, **Q6**. B, **Q7**. D.

Lesson 12 - Judging speed - Q1. D, **Q2**. C, **Q3**. 1. Legal, requirement, 2. Speed, limit, regulating, safe, **Q4**. 1. Passing, children,

2. Driving, weather, road, 3. Passing, school, **Q5**. D, **Q6**. A, **Q7**. 1. 23, 75, 2. 53, 175, 3. 96, 315.

Lesson 12 - Making normal progress - Q1. D, **Q2**. B, **Q3**. 1. Make, progress, 2. Avoid, holding, **Q4**. B, **Q5**. A, **Q6**. 1. Show, examiner, looking, 2. Avoid, confusing.

Lesson 12 - General road positioning - Q1. 1. Turning, right, 2. Avoid, filter, lane, 3. Road, markings, signs, 4. Form, danger, **Q2**. C.

Lesson 13 - Overtaking other vehicles safely - Q1. C, **Q2**. 1. Breaking, law, overtake, 2. Overtake, safely, 3. Enough, speed, power, 4. Safely, time, 5. Safe, gap, 6. Necessary, **Q3**. D, **Q4**. Approach, rear, safe, distance, Position, Speed, Mirrors, Signal, Manoeuvre, safe, **Q5**. D, **Q6**. 1. Step, parked, cars, 2. Door, open, warning, **Q7**. 1. Gauge, length, vehicle, 2. Both, firmly, steering, wheel, knocked, draught, **Q8**. A, **Q9**. 1. Allow, overtaking, pull, in, 2. Cause, slow, down, change, direction, **Q10**. D, **Q11**. B.

Lesson 13 - Meeting other vehicles safely - Q1. D, **Q2**. Mirrors, Look, Assess, Decide, Signal, Manoeuvre, stop, **Q3**. B, **Q4**. D, **Q5**. C, **Q6**. A.

Lesson 13 - Crossing the path of other vehicles - Q1. A, **Q2**. C, **Q3**. B, **Q4**. B, **Q5**, A, **Q6**. 1. Possibility, overtaking, slow, down, alter, 2. Pedestrian, pavement, walk, time, slow, alter.

Lesson 14 - Dealing with traffic lights - Q1. A, **Q2**. C, **Q3**. 1. Turning, right, traffic, lights, 2. Avoid, filter, lane, 3. Signs, markings, 4. Parked, obstruction, blocking, lane, 5. Convenient, **Q4**. D, **Q5**. A, **Q6**. B.

Lesson 14 - Dealing with pedestrian crossings - Q1. C, **Q2**. D, **Q3**. Pedestrian, light, controlled, **Q4**. B, **Q5**. Mirrors, Signal, Manoeuvre,

Q6. A, **Q7**. 1. Pelican, 2. Zebra, 3. Puffin, 4. Toucan, **Q8**. C, **Q9**. D, **Q10**. C, **Q11**. A, **Q12**. D, **Q13**. 1. Following, intention, slow, 2. Pedestrians, confidence, preparing, stop, **Q14**. B, **Q15**. 1. Legal, 2. Turn, back, 3. Someone, stepping, crossing.

Lesson 15 - Dealing with roundabouts - Q1. A, **Q2**. C, **Q3**. D, **Q4**. B, **Q5**. B, **Q6**. C, **Q7**. A, **Q8**. C, **Q9**. D.

Lesson 16 - Dealing with box junctions - Q1. D, **Q2**. A, **Q3**. B.

Lesson 16 - Dealing with dual carriageways - Q1. C, **Q2**. A, **Q3**. 1. Prevent, drivers, 2. Essential, future, passing, **Q4**. A, **Q5**. D.

Lesson 17 - The emergency stop - Q1. D, **Q2**. B, **Q3**. D, **Q4**. C, **Q5**. A, **Q6**. 1. Front, 2. Rear, 3. Four, **Q7**. 1. Excessive, 2. Harsh, 3. Fierce, 4. Coarse, **Q8**. True, **Q9**. A, **Q10**. D, **Q11**. C, **Q12**. B.

Lesson 18 - Highway Code and other motoring matters - Q1. C, **Q2**. Mirrors, cyclists, left, hand, road, turning, **Q3**. Acceleration, harsh, steering, **Q4**. A, **Q5**. D, **Q6**. A, **Q7**. B, **Q8**. C, **Q9**. D, **Q10**. Careful, children, ice, cream, **Q11**. A, **Q12**. B, **Q13**. D, **Q14**. A, **Q15**. C, **Q16**. D, **Q17**. Amber, red, green, white, bright green, **Q18**. B, **Q19**. D, **Q20**. A, **Q21**. C, **Q22**. D, **Q23**. B, **Q24**. C, **Q25**. 1. Increase, speed, 2. Cut, out, path, overtaking, **Q26**. C, **Q27**. B, **Q28**. D, **Q29**. A, **Q30**. A, B, C, **Q31**. Buses, bus, safely, look, people, crossing, **Q32**. A, **Q33**. C, **Q34**. D, **Q35**. B, **Q36**. B, **Q.37**. D. **Q38**. A, **Q39**. C, **Q40**. A, **Q41**. D, **Q42**. C, **Q43**. B, **Q44**. D, **Q45**. C, **Q46**. B, **Q47**. C, **Q48**. C, **Q49**. B, **Q50**. D, **Q51**. C, **Q52**. B, **Q53**. D, **Q54**. A, **Q55**. A, **Q56**. C, **Q57**. D, **Q58**. C, **Q59**. A, **Q60**. B, **Q61**. D, **Q62**. A, **Q63**. C, **Q64**. D, **Q65**. B, **Q66**. A, **Q67**. C, **Q68**. A, **Q69**. D, **Q70**. B, **Q71**. A, **Q72**. B, **Q73**. C, **Q74**. D, **Q75**. A, **Q76**. D, **Q77**. C, **Q78**. D, **Q79**. A, **Q80**. C, **Q81**. D, **Q82**. B, **Q83**. C, **Q84**. D, **Q85**. A, **Q86**. B, **Q87**. D, **Q88**. C, **Q89**. B, **Q90**. C, **Q91**.

D, **Q92**. A, B & C, **Q93**. B, **Q94**. A, **Q95**. D, **Q96**. A, **Q97**. B, **Q98**. C, **Q99**. D.

Lesson 19 - Automatic transmission - Q1. A, **Q2**. 1. Parking, 2. Reverse, 3. Neutral, 4. Drive, 5. 1, 6. 2. **Q3**. B, **Q4**. C, **Q5**. A, **Q6**. 1. Old, 2. Disabled, **Q7**. D.

Lesson 19 - Motorway driving - Q1. Mirrors, Look, Assess, Decide, Signal, Manoeuvre, **Q2**. D, **Q3**. C, **Q4**. B, **Q5**. D, **Q6**. 1. Tyres, 2. Indicators, 3. Fuel, 4. Windscreen, wipers, **Q7**. C, **Q8**. B.

Road traffic signs - 1. C, **2**. D, **3**. B, **4**. A, **5**. A, **6**. D, 7. B, **8**. C, **9**. C, **10**. A, **11**. D, **12**. C, **13**. D, **14**. A, **15**. A, **16**. D, **17**. C, **18**. A, **19**. C, **20**. B, **21**. A, **22**. D, **23**. A, **24**. D, **25**. D, **26**. A, **27**. D, **28**. D, **29**. A, **30**. B, **31**. D, **32**. A, **33**. A, **34**. B, **35**. A, **36**. D, **37**. A, **38**. D, **39**. A, **40**. D, **41**. C, **42**. A, **43**. A, **44**. D, **45**. B, **46**. A, **47**. A, **48**. D, **49**. B, **50**. B, **51**. A, **52**. A, **53**. D, **54**. B, **55**. A, **56**. A, **57**. D, **58**. D, **59**. B, **60**. C, **61**. D, **62**. A, **63**. C, **64**. C, **65**. B, **66**. A, **67**. D, **68**. C, **69**. D, **70**. D, **71**. A, **72**. D, **73**. C, **74**. A, **75**. D, **76**. A, **77**. D, **78**. C, **79**. D, **80**. C, **81**. A, **82**. D, **83**. C, **84**. B, **85**. A, **86**. D, **87**. C, **88**. B, **89**. A, 90. A, 91. B, 92. A, 93. D, 94. C, 95. B, 96. D.

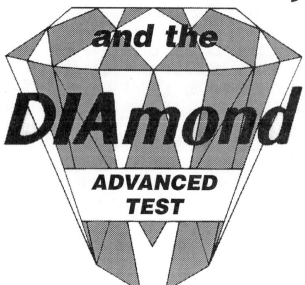